THE RELUCTANT SUPERPOWER

The Reluctant Superpower

United States' Policy in Bosnia, 1991–95

Wayne Bert

St. Martin's Press
New York

St. Martin's Press, Scholarly and Reference Division,
175 Fifth Avenue, New York, N.Y. 10010

First published in the United States of America in 1997

This book is printed on paper suitable for recycling and
made from fully managed and sustained forest sources.

Printed in Great Britain

ISBN 0–312–17252–4

Library of Congress Cataloging-in-Publication Data
Bert, Wayne, 1939–
The reluctant superpower : United States' policy in Bosnia,
1991–95 / Wayne Bert.
p.   cm.
Includes bibliographical references and index.
ISBN 0–312–17252–4
1. Yugoslav War, 1991–   2. Balkan Peninsula—Foreign relations–
–United States.   3. United States—Foreign relations—Balkan
Peninsula.   4. Security, International.   5. United States—Foreign
relations—1989–   6. Bosnia and Hercegovina—History—1992–
I. Title.
DR1313.B46   1997
949.703—dc21   96–46168
                                                                        CIP

For the victims

History is replete with examples of decision-makers who were too cautious, who underestimated the probability that a decisive stand could lead to a highly desired goal.

Robert Jervis

Contents

List of Tables and Maps

Tables

Maps

Preface

Watching, and becoming increasingly frustrated by a war that pricked the consciences of America, Europe and the world, but to which the US seemed unwilling to respond, goaded me into writing this book. Previous wars in which the US was involved, starting with Vietnam, seldom seemed to generate books that gave an overview of the conflict, what was at stake for the US, and the shape of US policy. This information could be found, but had to be pieced together from many sources. This effort to survey the problem of the war in the former Yugoslavia and provide a sort of primer on the war, that would appeal to specialists as well as concerned general readers, is the result.

Such a comprehensive approach, obviously, risks superficiality. I am not a Balkan expert, this brief survey of US policy and decisions on Bosnia ignores many nuances and details, and some chapters of this book could themselves be expanded into a book. Nonetheless, I believe this attempt serves a purpose by giving an outline definition of US policy, and evaluating that policy in the context both of what was happening in the former Yugoslavia and the significance of the war from the American perspective and the state of American public opinion.

The Bosnian War generated intense emotion, both among participants and observers. Not surprisingly, citizens, observers, analysts, and officials in the West developed and held strong opinions on the war and what US and NATO policy should be. The divide between American and European views often appeared as a yawning chasm. I lean toward one version of the American view, although there was and is plenty of oversimplification on both sides. I have tried to understand and be fair to other perspectives. The reader can judge whether I have succeeded.

Numerous people have assisted in the completion of this book. I particularly want to thank Willard Elsbree, William Messmer, Dean Curry and an anonymous reviewer for critiquing earlier versions of the manuscript. Roger Kanet assisted in finding a publisher, and Jack Wiedemer, Randall Guynes, Ricardo Morin and George Weitzenfeld also contributed encouragement, criticism, or advice. Kerstin Jagerbo read the book in draft, as well as encouraging, criticizing, and advising. The responsibility for the final text, however, is solely mine.

Reston, VA   WAYNE BERT

Chronological Highlights of the Wars of Yugoslavia's Dissolution

1987

December: Slobodan Milosevic engineers the ouster of his former patron, Ivan Stambolic, from the presidency of Serbia, using the claim that Stambolic was too indulgent toward the Albanian population of Kosovo.

1989

March: At Milosevic's instance, legal changes in Yugoslavia vitiate the autonomous status of Kosovo and Vojvodina.

June: At a mass rally of Serbs in Kosovo, Milosevic threatens inter-communal violence.

1990

April: Pro-independence forces win free election in Slovenia. Led by Franjo Tudjman, nationalists win first free election in Croatia.

July: The Croatian Assembly adopts a variety of nationalist measures. Croatian Serbs declare autonomy from Croatia.

November: In first free elections in Bosnia and Herzegovina, vote splits along ethnic lines.

December: Serb voters elect Milosevic president.

1991

March: Serbian leader Milosevic and Croatian leader Franjo Tudjman meet and reportedly agree to divide Bosnia and Herzegovina between them.

May: Serbia blocks the scheduled rotation of offices that would have made the Croat, Stipe Mesic, head of Yugoslav presidency. Croatia and Slovenia threaten to secede.

June: Secretary of State James Baker travels to Belgrade for meetings with leaders of all the Yugoslav republics, urging them to remain united. Nonetheless Croatia and Slovenia soon declare independence while signaling their willingness to negotiate. Yugoslav forces attack Slovenia prompting the EC to dispatch a mediating mission. Its leader, Jacques Poos of Luxembourg, declares: 'This is the hour of Europe, not the Americans.'

July: Fighting end in Slovenia, but conflicts increase in Croatia.

August: Fighting further intensifies in Croatia with the Yugoslav army taking on a more active role on the side of the Serbs.

September: The UN Security Council votes to embargo all arms deliveries to Yugoslavia

December: The EC announces that it will recognize Slovenia and Croatia in one month and will do the same for any other republic of the former Yugoslavia that meets constitutional and human rights criteria set by its Badinter Commission. Macedonia and Bosnia and Herzegovina apply for recognition. The Badinter Commission requires that Bosnia and Herzegovina hold a referendum. Germany decides not to wait for its fellow EC members and proceeds to recognize Croatia and Slovenia. Serbs in Croatia declare themselves the Republic of Serbian Krajina.

1992

January: Cease-fire takes hold in Croatia. UN observers arrive, to be followed (two months later) by peacekeeping forces.

February: Referendum in Bosnia and Herzegovina yields overwhelming vote for independence, but Serbian population mostly boycotts the vote.

March: Irregular Bosnian Serb forces begin attacks against non-Serb civilians and the Bosnian government.

April: The United States recognizes Bosnia and Herzegovina and also Croatia and Slovenia. The EC, which had already recognized the latter two, recognizes Bosnia and Herzegovina as well.

May: The United States and the EC withdraw their ambassadors from Belgrade. The United Nations adopts economic sanctions against Yugoslavia. Croatia, Slovenia, and Bosnia and Herzegovina are admitted into the United Nations. The UN Security Council imposes economic sanctions on Yugoslavia.

July: President Bush, dismissing appeals for American action in Bosnia, likens the conflict there to a 'hiccup.'

August: US and UN officials raise alarms about reports of atrocities by Serbs and the existence of concentration camps. The United Nations and the Conference on Security and Cooperation in Europe appoint special officers to investigate human rights abuses. The Security Council authorizes the use of 'all necessary measures' to ensure delivery of humanitarian aid in Bosnia.

October: The UN Security Council votes to impose a 'no-fly' zone over Bosnia but does not authorize any means of enforcement.

November: UN Human Rights Commission Special Rapporteur Tadeusz Mazowiecki issues a report saying that Serbian 'ethnic cleansing' in defiance of Security Council resolutions is undermining the authority of the United Nations.

December: Secretary of State Lawrence Eagleburger proposes exempting Bosnia from the UN arms embargo, but no action follows. Also, at an international conference, Eagleburger calls for war crimes prosecutions and names a list of suspects starting with Serbian president Milosevic and Bosnian Serb leader Radovan Karadzic.

1993

January: Hakija Turajlic, deputy prime minister of Bosnia, is executed by Serbian fighters while the French UN forces under whose 'protection' he was traveling look on passively. UN representative Cyrus Vance and EC representative David Owen propose a settlement (that they had adumbrated in

October) based on dividing Bosnia into ten provinces and giving each major ethnic group dominance in three.

February: Secretary of State Warren Christopher announces the Bosnia policy of the new administration. It avoids any forceful action, brushes aside the Vance–Owen plan to divide Bosnia and Herzegovina into ethnic cantons, but embraces the 'Vance–Owen negotiations' and pledges to support them with 'the weight of American diplomacy'. The UN Security Council authorizes the creation of a tribunal to prosecute war crimes.

March: The UN Security Council authorizes the use of force to enforce no-fly zone. The United States initiates airlifts of humanitarian supplies to Bosnian civilians.

April: The 'parliament' of the Bosnian Serbs rejects the Vance–Owen plan, which had been accepted readily by the Bosnian Croats and grudgingly by the Bosnian government under US pressure. Full-scale fighting breaks out between Bosnian government forces and Bosnian Croats, creating a triangular war.

May: The Clinton administration announces its decision to embark on a policy of 'lift and strike', moving to lift the arms embargo on Bosnia and to undertake airstrikes against the Serbs. Christopher travels to Europe to seek the concurrence of allies, but Britain and France reject this policy, and Washington backs down. Instead, it embraces the Joint Action Program proposed by Russians and West Europeans to create 'safe areas' for Muslims and Bosnia. These are declared by the UN Security Council.

August: As the siege of Sarajevo tightens, America says it will not tolerate the city's strangulation, and NATO threatens airstrikes. The Serbs pull back slightly from two peaks overlooking the city, and the threat is withdrawn.

1994

February: A shell lands in an outdoor market in Sarajevo, killing sixty-eight and wounding hundreds. NATO demands that Serbian heavy weapons be withdrawn from within 20 kilometers of the city and announces a ten-day deadline. The United Nations succeeds in diluting this ultimatum so that all Serbian weapons need not be withdrawn but merely placed under UN observation.

March: Through American mediation, Muslims and Croats in Bosnia agree to stop fighting each other, to join their territories, and to affiliate in some way with Bosnia.

April: Serbian forces turn their attention to another 'safe area,' Gorazde, shelling it and violating its perimeter. Defense Secretary William Perry declares that America will do nothing to stop Gorazde from being overrun but is quickly contradicted by National Security Adviser Anthony Lake. NATO delivers a new ultimatum to the Serb forces, demanding relaxation of the siege of Gorazde. This ultimatum, too, is diluted, but it succeeds in staying the Serbs from conquering the city.

June: In a reversal of policy, America joins with Europeans in endorsing a settlement based on territorial division, granting Serbs de facto sovereignty over 49 percent of Bosnia and Herzegovina while reserving 51 percent for the coalition of Muslims and Croats. This becomes known as the 'contact group' plan, and all Bosnian parties are told they have until the end of July to 'take it or leave it'. The Croats and the Muslims accede, but the Serbs refuse.

August: Yugoslavia announces severance of ties with Bosnian Serbs. The next month it agrees to international monitoring of its border with Bosnia to ensure that war material does not continue to flow to the Bosnian Serbs. But officials of the United Nations and Western governments and journalists continue to report frequent violations of this putative embargo.

1995

May: In response to increasing Serbian attacks on Sarajevo and on UN peacekeepers, NATO bombs some Bosnian Serb ammunition dumps. The Serbs retaliate by taking hostage nearly 400 UN peacekeepers, and the bombardment is halted. Croatian government forces, in a surface offensive, recapture western Slavonia, one of the sectors held by Croatian Serbs.

June: The Bosnian Serbs release UN hostages, receiving in exchange a secret pledge that no further NATO attacks will occur.

July: Bosnian forces overrun the 'safe areas' of Srebrenica and Zepa, while the United Nations and NATO refrain from any intervention to stop them. An estimated 5000–10 000 Muslim POWs are subjected to mass extermination. The Senate votes by more than two-thirds to lift the arms embargo on Bosnia.

August: In a lightning offensive, the army of Croatia rolls through most remaining areas held by the Croatian Serbs since 1991, recapturing all except eastern Slavonia along the border with Serbia. The Serb residents of the recaptured territories flee en masse to Serbia or Serb-held sections of Bosnia. In response to Serbian artillery attacks killing dozens in downtown Sarajevo, NATO undertakes its first significant airstrikes against the Serbs. These continue over a few weeks. The House votes by more than two-thirds to lift arms embargo on Bosnia.

September: In negotiations mediated by US Assistant Secretary of State Richard Holbrooke in Geneva, all three parties to the Bosnian struggle formally agree to framework for a settlement dividing Bosnia and Herzegovina along the 51–49 per cent formula. This formula now approximates the division of control on the ground, since in the preceding weeks a combined Muslim–Croat offensive has wrested significant swathes of territory from Serb control.

October: A cease-fire takes effect throughout Bosnia and Herzegovina. Although numerous previous cease-fires had been announced during the course of the war, this one is the first that is generally obeyed.

November: Meeting in Dayton, Ohio, the presidents of Serbia, Croatia, and Bosnia and Herzegovina agree to a settlement based on a territorial division. Bosnia and Herzegovina will retain its legal international personality, but in practice it will be divided into two 'entities', one Serbian and the other Croat and Muslim.

December: The Dayton agreements are formally signed in Paris. American and other members of a 60 000-person international peacekeeping force, under the auspices of NATO, begin to take up positions between the Serbian and the Muslim–Croat sections.

This chronology is reproduced by permission of the American Enterprise Institute for Public Files Research, Washington, DC and is reprinted from Joshua Muravchik, *The Imperative of American Leadership: A Challenge to Neo-Isolationism* (Washington, DC: AEI Press, 1996).

1. Countries comprising the former Yugoslavia as of 1994

Negotiations for an official name for the Former Yugoslav Republic of Macedonia (F.Y.R.O.M) still in progress.

Source: US Department of State.

Introduction

The abrupt turnabout in US (and European) Bosnia policy in late summer 1995 substantiated the critics' contention that the policy up to then had been a failure. After more than three years of attempting to promote negotiations without involving itself in significant military action, the West reversed itself and began serious air strikes, just as President Clinton had suggested in his 1992 campaign. Here I adopt the critics' premise that the early policy was a failure, and that some version of the more militant policy, which would have required a closer match between the military situation on the ground and the premises of negotiations, should have been adopted much earlier in the conflict.

Part I of this book looks at the international system in the post-Cold War era and assesses the changes that have occurred in the international system and how they affected the situation in Yugoslavia. It sets the stage for analysis of a conflict that takes place and a policy that is formulated in a very different setting than was the case during the Cold War period to which we had all become accustomed. Part I provides the context for future policy making, and it is to this issue that I return in the conclusion. General readers, who are mostly interested in the specific Yugoslav conflict, may want to skip this section and go directly to Part II from this Introduction.

Part II sketches a brief history of the Yugoslav situation, a brief chronology of the events that led to the disintegration of the nation, perspectives on the disintegration, and a discussion of the nature of the war that was waged there. This section is far too brief to do the situation justice, but the sources cited in these chapters provide abundant resources to inform any interested reader on these topics. The focus of this book necessitated only a brief look at the background developments in the former Yugoslavia.

Part III looks at the conflict from the perspective of US interests and perceptions. It examines the views of Americans on the nature of US interests there, the foreign policy mood and opinions in the US, and some of the concepts ('ancient ethnic hatred') and assumptions (civil or international war) that formed the images in the minds of Western policy makers. Finally, the role of the Vietnam conflict in shaping the Western debate on the war and the extreme reluctance to intervene is also examined.

Part IV deals with the content and formulation of the US policy in the former Yugoslavia. Chapter 9 focuses on the early US diplomacy and the policy of the Bush administration towards the former Yugoslavia after the conflicts in Croatia and Bosnia had broken out. Chapter 10 discusses the diplomatic and military options and the pressures and obstacles facing the Clinton administration. Chapter 11 discusses how and why the Clinton administration, which came to power promising to change the Bush policy, ended up supporting and continuing the policy of passivity and acquiescence in Serb and Croat dismantlement of Bosnia. Finally, Chapter 12 looks at the change in American policy in late summer 1995, assesses the magnitude and significance of the change, and attempts to explain the Clinton turnaround to a firmer and more activist policy.

The concluding part of the book assesses US policy in the light of the post-Cold War decision-making environment, suggests why US policy was so ineffective for three years, suggests how US policy could have been made more effective, given the domestic context in which it had to be made, and assesses the lessons that can be applied to future post-Cold War foreign-policy decisions.

While I dispute the premises of much of the Bosnia policy of the West, I do not believe that the choices were easy or the solutions obvious. On the contrary, I have the greatest sympathy for those political leaders who had decisions on Bosnian policy thrust upon them. This does not, however, relieve one of the obligation to provide criticism when appropriate. A half-dozen themes are developed in this book, some contributing to criticism of US policy, others suggesting the difficulties of making policy choices. I hope I have struck a balance between legitimate criticism on the one hand, and appreciation of the difficulties inherent in formulating sound policy on the other.

One key theme is that the conflict in Yugoslavia, while multifaceted and complex, was precipitated by the rise of Slobodan

Milosevic and his authoritarian Serb nationalist movement. While many commentators and analysts have stressed the complexity of the Yugoslav situation and the events that took place there, there is no escaping the important role played by Milosevic's movement, which was unique among the post-Yugoslav nationalisms. On this point, US official analysis was correct; it was only in formulating a policy to match the perception of the Serbs' key role that we failed for so long.

A second theme is that there was a limited US security interest in Yugoslavia, but a substantial humanitarian one. Since countries seldom make significant sacrifices for humanitarian interest, it is not surprising that American policy there was pacific for so long. These trends were accentuated by the strangeness of the post-Cold War international environment, in which old guidelines and policies could no longer be relied upon, and which encouraged a relaxed rather than urgent atmosphere with the passing of the decades-long superpower standoff. Politicians were not anxious to rush in on uncharted territory, especially when the territory has the reputation the Balkans does for foreign-policy mischief.

A third theme is the passive nature of the US and Western response to the conflict in the former Yugoslavia. The timidity of the response and the willingness of the West to endure humiliation at the hands of an insignificant power like Serbia was particularly striking, given the robust history of Western policy during the Cold War, and the frequent willingness to go to the brink of war to counter Soviet moves. Part of the contrast can be explained by the lack of a perceived security interest in Yugoslavia, but I also argue that the lingering ghost of the Vietnam trauma on American policy is critical in explaining the Western propensity for passivity in Bosnia. The need for American strategic leadership, in the absence of European initiatives, was particularly striking in Bosnia.

A fourth and related theme is the role of public opinion in shaping US policy in Bosnia. On the one hand, the public's perception that no vital US interests existed in post-Cold War Yugoslavia encouraged the political leadership to refrain from any kind of costly military involvement. On the other hand, however, the American public was concerned and shamed that many atrocities were being committed during the conflict with no appropriate response by the West. The half-in–half-out behavior of the American leadership in the Yugoslav theatre can thus be explained. While there was an unwillingness to get involved in a way that could cost American lives, at the same time public officials were concerned not to appear callous and unconcerned. For too long, the leadership of two administrations refused to take meaningful military action to resolve the situation, but also refused to allow (much less encourage) the Bosnians to arm and take the measures necessary for their defense, consistent with the American claim that we had no interest justifying intervention. Ironically, in seeking to escape the dilemma confronted in Vietnam, the US created another compromise 'down the middle' policy, now in Bosnia, with frustrating, but this time not fatal consequences for the US.

A fifth theme is the assumption that early in the war the West could have taken low-cost actions that would have had a substantial impact on the war. While bombing cannot accomplish miracles, it can accomplish a lot. The comparisons between the success of bombing in the Gulf War and the difficulties that the same strategy would encounter in the mountainous terrain and inhospitable weather of Yugoslavia were too facile by far. In any case, supplying the Bosnian troops with arms and training would have supplemented action from the air and slowed, if not stopped Serb advances. The serious bombing in 1995 showed that a modest bombing campaign could have a decisive impact on Bosnian Serb capabilities. The Bush administration must take the biggest share of the blame for failing to act when the war was young, no UN troops were in place in Bosnia, and the maximum element of surprise was available to the West. That decisive intervention would have deterred not only Serb, but Croatian aggression as well, is too often overlooked.

A closely related assumption is that even if such actions had been unsuccessful, the West had little to lose by trying. The concerns of many foreign-policy specialists about credibility and deterrence, and the assumptions that once action is begun it must be escalated until the political objectives are met (à la Vietnam model) were exaggerated even during the Cold War. They are of even less concern in a post-Cold War world where we do not have to worry about a superpower that is waiting to fill every power vacuum, no matter how minuscule. Equally suspect was the theme of the Europeans that prosecuting that war would only spread it to hitherto peaceful areas. The reverse was more likely the case.

Finally, the book begins and ends with assertions that the new post-Cold War world presents extremely difficult choices to foreign-policy makers, and that guidelines for those decisions are extremely difficult to develop. Under the new conditions, however, some new assumptions must be accepted and old ones abandoned. Foremost among these is the belief that foreign policy actions are nice and neat with well-defined goals, costs, strategies, and starting and ending points. The post-Cold War world is a much 'messier' world where limited conflicts will be fought for limited and often shifting objectives, and with strategies that are difficult to formulate, costs that are uncertain, and entrance and exit points that are not obvious. As an example of this, Bosnia has been a premier exhibit.

Part I

The International Setting

1 The United States and the Post-Cold War International System

CHANGES IN THE INTERNATIONAL SYSTEM

The international system underwent momentous changes with the end of the Cold War. The bipolar nature of the Cold War international system led to tense standoffs and crises between nuclear armed superpowers, whose influence and competition extended to virtually every corner of the globe. With the demise of this system, issues that had previously been of secondary significance and suppressed by superpower pressure, such as ethnic war and the breakup of a nation as in Yugoslavia, became both important and more likely. The end of the Cold War therefore transformed the international system and began a new era in international politics.

The Cold War international system had two superpowers of roughly equal power, locked in a struggle for power and spheres of influence. The 'tightness' of this relationship varied, tending to become more relaxed as the Cold War waned, but some generalities about superpower behavior that spanned the entire era can be suggested.[1] Both superpowers watched carefully the movements of the other, and each tended to intervene or increase its influence in any area where the other was not dominant. The tenser the Cold War, the more careful each superpower was to ensure the other did not advance its cause or increase its power. The best way to do that was for a superpower to increase its sphere of influence whenever possible, and to oppose the extension of the other superpower's influence whenever necessary. The result was an international system where, from the perspective of the small nations, there was a constant threat of intervention by a superpower. This was resisted as much as possible, as the two superpowers were played off against each other by small non-aligned countries to extract the best possible price for falling under a superpower's sphere of influence and giving up some sovereignty and influence. There were limits to a small country's ability to bargain, however, since too much resistance could result in a less advantageous deal than was otherwise attainable.

The result was a stable bipolar system in which major changes or shifting of power was unlikely, since both sides observed each other carefully, each side did its best to avoid an unexpected increase in influence by the other side, and even minor shifts of influence or movements of armaments could precipitate a significant crisis. The system tended to be stable and predictable, in spite of the fact that nuclear weapons made it possible that a miscalculation or an accident could have set off a nuclear holocaust.

Under those conditions, the bloc formed around each superpower tended to perform many of the traditional functions of the nation-state, especially that of keeping order.[2] Order and peace was kept both within the bloc (this was true much more of the Warsaw Pact than of NATO) and, through constant vigilance and pressure, between the blocs. The fact that this order and peace was often maintained at the expense of the smaller nations, which had their sovereignty abridged and their freedom of action limited, was of only secondary concern to the superpowers. The result, however, was a period of peace which approximately equaled in longevity the nineteenth century international systems of Metternich and Bismarck and 'now compares favorably ... with some of the longest periods of great power stability in all of modern history.'[3]

The post-Cold War period was to be quite different. The collapse of the Soviet Union removed the relative symmetry of power between the US and Russia, and security needs became less urgent. In the absence of tension between the superpowers, blocs became superfluous and alliances lost their purpose. Instead of constant competition and tension over superpower influence throughout the world, the collapse of the Soviet threat led to a kind of indifference to many global developments on the part of the United States. Diminished interest in Yugoslavia fits this pattern well.

Third-world conflicts were no longer given high priority, as they mattered much less to a United States that no longer had to fear Russian intervention and an expansion of Russian influence. At the same time, the atmosphere in the third world changed radically, from Cold War paranoia about neo-colonialist schemes against third-world countries, to frequent requests for US assistance in settling civil war or overthrowing tyrannical regimes. But the US was now much less enthusiastic about intervention. It did intervene in Somalia in a humanitarian role, and after much procrastination, intervened in Haiti, a very popular move among Haitians. The Somalia intervention, initially popular, turned sour after resistance from armed Somalia groups and a sizeable part of the population grew hostile to the US presence. In spite of a public backlash against the Somalia operation in the US, President Clinton still carried out an intervention in Haiti, a very controversial move. For those countries not on the US's doorstep, however, intervention was much less likely in the post-Cold War world. Bosnia was a prime recipient of this harsh lesson.

Yugoslavia, a member of neither bloc during the Cold War, was still affected by it. A bitter antagonism developed between the Soviet Union and the Yugoslavs after Tito's split with Stalin in 1948. Although its internal organization in many ways emulated Soviet organizational principles, Yugoslavia was regarded by the West as a key bargaining chip in its competition with the Soviets. While ostensibly on its own and setting its own foreign policy course, Yugoslavia received considerable aid from the West and any major deviation from its chosen course in foreign policy would have immediately had the attention of both superpowers. Major deviation from Yugoslavia's overall foreign-policy direction might have triggered aid cutoffs, sanctions or, in an extreme case, even intervention.

As the Cold War receded, however, intense superpower attention to events in the Balkans also receded, clearing the way for innovative policies and new directions in political economic organization, including elections and a more free press, the establishment of new political parties, inauguration of new relationships among the republics, and the development of demagogic political movements and leaders. The rash of free elections held in individual republics in Yugoslavia coincided with similar changes in the rest of Eastern Europe. Tito's death had been an important catalyst that, given the pressures on the Yugoslav federation, began the unraveling that accelerated once the Cold War faded away.[4]

A resurgence of nationalism, ethnic identity and ethnic politics, or in some cases, identity with a religion or historically important civilization, accentuated the new freedom of action in the post-Cold War era and encouraged extremists to promote their causes, often by violent means. Samuel P. Huntington argued that the fundamental source of conflict in this new international system is culture, and that the clash of civilizations will dominate world politics. Interestingly, the conflict in Yugoslavia seems to fit this pattern, if one equates empire and religion with culture. Bosnia was most under the control of the Ottoman (Islamic) Empire, Croatia more closely identified with the (Catholic) West, and Serbia often under Russian (Orthodox) influence.[5]

The impact of the transformation of the international system, in Yugoslavia as in Rwanda, Somalia, Liberia, Sudan and elsewhere, was an extensive round of bloodletting uninhibited by the dampening influences of superpower condominium. These kinds of conflicts did take place during the Cold War, and indeed some, such as Vietnam and Afghanistan, were encouraged by one or both superpowers and stimulated by the ideological fuel of the Cold War. What is different now is that the US and other powers have lost interest in promoting these conflicts but they also have less interest in controlling them. In many cases they deplore them, but they also are unprepared to pay the price necessary to prevent or stop them, and there is therefore little pressure for extremists to moderate their demands or programs.

Scholars are divided on the impact of nationalist movements and the desirability of accommodating or even encouraging it. It is argued that nationalism has survived one universalist assault after another and will continue to do so. Small states are viable and secessionist activities tend to come in waves and will not produce runaway disintegration. Furthermore, the problem is illiberalism and militarism, not nationalism.[6] In response it may be suggested that the most visible and troublesome nationalisms are precisely the ones that are not liberal. Further, the 'fragmenting effects of nationalism' lead to the kinds of insoluble situations one finds in Lebanon and Northern Ireland.[7] But probably the biggest problem with accommodating the forces of nationalism is that one frequently ends up engaging in an exercise similar to peeling an onion. Just as the removal of each layer of onion leads to another, each alteration of boundaries leads to another minority problem that must be solved. Bosnia is a perfect example. When Yugoslavia disintegrated, Bosnia became independent. But the Bosnian Serbs demanded their independence from Bosnia. But Bosnian Serb independence would threaten Muslims living in numerous cities of otherwise Serb dominated areas, not to mention those who identify as Yugoslavs and don't want to be in any ethnic state. Ultimately, the only answer is a liberal polity that protects the rights of the minorities who live there, as there is no practical (and certainly no moral) way to ensure ethnically homogeneous states. But whatever one's assessment of the impact of nationalist movements, the one thing all analysts agree on is that nationalist demands and fragmentation have been increasing.

These new conflicts have not matched the number of casualties and the systematic exterminations of the two world wars, or the Stalinist and Hitlerian tyrannies of the twentieth century – the 'politics of organized insanity' – but the killings in Rwanda and Bosnia, to take two examples, did recall the methods and brutality of the earlier period.[8] The numerous examples of brutality, the seeming indifference of the great powers and their inability to act, led some to speak of 'dilemmas of global disorder', and of a feeling of being 'cast adrift … losing the familiar signs and moorings of the cold war.'[9]

The new international situation in which the United States found itself in the early 1990s and in which the Bosnian War was to be set was, in some ways, a relief after the continual tension and threat of nuclear annihilation that accompanied the Cold War. But the US found itself without a clear mission for its armed forces, and with a realization that the military would see few crises jeopardizing its vital interests and requiring a quick response that would automatically be supported by the public. The new localized, brutal conflicts in the world appeal to citizens' humanitarian instincts and seem to call for intervention, especially when receiving high visibility through the electronic media, but there is also a realization that intervention might be costly, and without any kind of immediate payoff that would generate public support. This dilemma has led some to suggest the US must drastically revise its expectation of the role of the US and the role the military plays; we must adapt to the

> political perception that our military forces are not essential to our country's life or independence and that the function of our military will be to protect secondary interests, to discharge our responsibility to protect others, and to respond if the world changes or if it is more dangerous than we think.[10]

As the crisis in Bosnia would show, this prescription for US political/military policy and the changes it requires are not easy to implement.

THE US POSITION AND ROLE IN THE NEW SYSTEM

A debate that began before the extent of the Russian collapse was clear, but the continuation of which coincided with the end of the Cold War, concerned the alleged decline in American power. If Russian capabilities and will to wield world power has nearly collapsed (except for its still lethal nuclear arsenal), it is less clear how US capabilities should be evaluated. Noting the decreasing share of GNP the US held in the world economy, some questioned the ability of the US to maintain its current role and to maintain the level of military expenditure necessary to meet the nation's perceived defense requirements.[11] Others took the position either that things are not so bad as they seem, or that while there are problems they can be corrected.[12] The likely shape of America's role in the world may be best capsulized by saying that the US will remain a great power, but will no longer exercise hegemony.[13]

The whole argument over US capabilities became less intense with the end of the Cold War, since with that development even the most hawkish defense planner conceded that it was no longer necessary to maintain the previous level of defense expenditures. The whole debate over decline turns out to be less important than the argument that has superseded it, not over what the US can do, but what it wants to do and what proportion of its resources it is willing to divert from domestic needs to foreign policy and military resources. The current debate, in other words, discusses options which are well within America's capability to fund and carry out, but the end of the Cold War has scaled back considerably the potential extent of international involvement. President Bush at one point stated that the US had plenty of will to lead in international affairs, but had only a small wallet. The facts are the opposite; the US has the resources to do many things, but has only a very modest amount of will to do them.[14]

The interesting question, and the one that is relevant during the conflict in Bosnia, is not what US capabilities are, but rather what role it wants to play in international politics. Nowhere was that dilemma more acute than in the case of Yugoslavia, which epitomized the dilemma of defining a role and creating guidelines for US involvement and intervention in a new world in which such guidelines do not yet exist. This world is one in which, startlingly, 'the age-old motives for intervention are suddenly all but extinct'.[15] Internationalists continue to argue for free trade and maintenance of a significant military force and the willingness to use it to defend interests – even humanitarian interests – but they also advocate a much more limited level of intervention than the nation was prepared to undertake throughout the Cold War.

Arguing against involvement, a neo-isolationist group exists on both the right and left of the political spectrum. This position on the right is best represented by Pat Buchanan who challenged President Bush for the Republican nomination in 1992, and was a strong contender for the 1996 Republican nomination. He favors protectionist trade policies, and generally opposes any kind of foreign entanglement or limits on US 'sovereignty'.[16] While only a minority of the population identifies with his position, one survey found that foreign affairs now constitutes a much less important set of problems for the general populace than has been the case for many years, and for the leadership, the smallest ever since the survey was begun in 1974. The same survey found a precipitous decline from the 1990 levels of public support for defending the security of America's allies (61 to 41 per cent), protecting weaker nations against foreign aggression (57 to 24 per cent), support for the promotion of human rights (24 per cent decline), and support for efforts to improve living standards in underdeveloped countries (19 per cent decline).[17]

There continue to be strong advocates for involvement and even military intervention in the conflicts around the globe. One analyst complains about a group of 'new moralists' among the American leadership who want the US to embark on new post-Cold-War crusades to protect victims, spread democracy and promote economic development.[18] But while most internationalists continue to argue for free trade and maintenance of a significant military force and the willingness to use it to defend interests – even humanitarian interests – many of them also advocate a much more limited level of intervention than the nation was prepared to undertake throughout the Cold War. Somewhere in between the positions of Buchanan's 'America Firsters' and those favoring an active internationalist policy are those who have taken a more limited view of what the US role should be, and choose a stance on intervention depending on the merits of individual foreign-policy cases. After the Congressional elections of 1994, however, the isolationist influence on policy was strengthened, especially by the power of the newly elected freshmen Republicans in the House of Representatives. While the Republican Party itself is badly split on foreign-policy issues, and the isolationist faction did not gain enough strength to hinder Clinton ability to dispatch troops to Bosnia, their influence was an important factor in ensuring that a time limit of a year was put on troop deployment there.

Closely related to the question of how much involvement and intervention the US would undertake, is what the purposes of US policy should be. In justifying the 1991 Gulf War, President Bush invoked the image of a 'new world order,' to entail 'new ways of working with other nations ... peaceful settlement of disputes, solidarity against aggression, reduced and controlled arsenals and just treatment of all peoples.' But this grandiose version of a liberal international order was de-emphasized after the war as President Bush, no longer in need of inspired rhetoric to bolster support for the war, returned to a more limited conception of what could and should be required of American foreign policy. More at home with a realist approach to foreign policy, he stressed state-to-state relations and the pursuit of limited security interests, instead of the focus on universal human rights and democratic values, relations with people as well as states, and reliance on international laws and institutions, all implied by the concept of the new world order.[19] But his switch to a more realist approach fit well with his Bosnia policy, which was one of strict nonintervention based on the premise that no important US interest was as stake there. But the rhetoric on Bosnia, a stinging indictment of Serbian aggression and a promise it would not be tolerated, still continued to reflect the broader and more idealistic appeals he had used so well in the Gulf War. Bush used the rhetoric of Wilson and Carter, but thought and acted like Nixon.[20]

President Clinton, at home with the rhetoric of liberal internationalism, went one better than Bush and promised military intervention in Bosnia during the 1992 campaign. But once in office, the problem was more difficult and more complex than the President, inexperienced in foreign policy, had supposed. The decisive action he had promised was delayed as he and his staff searched for a policy that would have an acceptably low number of negative consequences. But Peter Tarnoff, Clinton's undersecretary of state for policy, in a controversial statement said early in Clinton's presidency that the US had neither the influence, the inclination or the money to use military force. Therefore, he suggested, the administration's deliberate inaction on Bosnia represented a new foreign policy based on 'setting limits on the amount of American engagement.'[21] Clinton made many statements about his intentions and purposes, many of them contradictory and inconsistent, but he reflected the dilemmas of a president attempting to make policy in a world where old guidelines had broken down, where action to prevent conflict could no longer be justified with the apocalyptic images of the Cold War, but where the urge to influence events such as Bosnia was still strong. On Bosnia, both Bush and Clinton mouthed the objectives of liberal internationalism, although Clinton promised military actions to match the rhetoric. In the old Cold War world, idealist rhetoric and realist actions could often be confused as congruent and consistent with each other, since the global vigilance against Soviet aggression could also be interpreted as opposition to dictatorship and support for human rights. In the new post-Cold War world, the confusion in both Presidents' policies reflected the new environment where leaders and at least some of the public still were sympathetic to the promotion of American ideals, but the military force to do so could not be justified by security concerns.

Another controversial issue is to what degree the US should go it alone, that is, make its own decisions on military action as opposed to working within a multi-national regional or international framework. This question was at the heart of much of the debate on whether the United States should take a more assertive role in Yugoslavia, whether or not the Europeans followed. The Clinton administration initially approved a document putting strict limits on US participation and the role of US troops in multilateral peace operations, led by the UN and regional organizations,[22] but the Republican-led Congress has promoted even more restrictive policies. Notwithstanding the discussion of these issues and the increased leeway for the use of meaningful multilateral and international forces now that the Russians do not routinely exercise a UN Security Council veto, there is less change in the US role than may at first appear. Unlike some smaller nations that routinely participate in UN operations, the US is still powerful enough that it will almost certainly act on its own, if necessary, to defend what is considered an important interest. It finally did take the lead by moving more aggressively in Yugoslavia and was able to persuade the Europeans to go along. It will prefer to operate under some kind of multi-national cover whenever possible to enhance the legitimacy of the action (as in the Gulf war). But the cause of the US timidity in Bosnia lay not in the reluctance of its allies to intervene, although that was a factor, but in the American lack of confidence that there was an interest at stake and the lack of an elite commitment to build public support for an operation that could have been politically costly.

The conflicting interests and confusion over chains of command and jurisdiction between NATO and the UN in military decisions in Bosnia were more symptoms of disagreement among allies than a cause of the military indecisiveness. Of course the involvement of both NATO and the UN and the need to secure the approval of both before taking significant action was a cumbersome and bureaucratic procedure which invited weak responses. But the main reason for the weak military response was the fundamental unwillingness of the *governments* involved to risk military action, the timidity of the Europeans and the reluctance of the US to provide leadership. The bureaucratic approach of the UN and its symbiotic relationship with the Serbs through most of the conflict is well documented,[23] but the policy differences on military actions between NATO and the UN reflected only small differences over the degrees of appeasement. Otherwise NATO would have taken action on its own. If the allies had agreed on a military solution and the need to implement it, the contradictions and discrepancies between NATO and the UN would have quickly been cleared up, not least because NATO had the planes. This is in fact exactly what happened once the will to take stronger action materialized in the summer of 1995. There has been a great deal of nonsense uttered about the counterproductive role of the UN in appeasing the Serbs in the former Yugoslavia, and by people who ought to know better. Such claims are useful to some because the UN provided a useful scapegoat on which to shift the blame for policy failures so as to protect the real culprits responsible for UN timidity, the leaders and citizens of the Western powers.

Criticism of the US willingness to lead in the Yugoslav crisis is legitimate. But the criticism should be of a lack of its own will and purpose, not of a propensity to give up its power to act to multilateral institutions, or subordination of its policy preferences to multilateral decisions which did not match its preferences. Richard N. Haass has it right that the US should provide leadership, while as much as possible acting as the head of formal alliances and informal coalitions. The leadership provides the opportunity to build consensus and a sense of legitimacy, and hence support for US principles and actions, while discouraging opposition. But it also allows the US to avoid bearing the entire financial and human burden of action.[24] How much leadership should be provided and how much consensus should be sought depends on the importance of the interests and principles, and the overall situation. For the most part, if the will to act is present, a way to act will be found. The European reluctance to provide leadership (and hence the susceptibility to following someone who will lead) was amply demonstrated in Bosnia. And the US failure to provide the leadership that both the allies and the UN required is also embarrassingly evident.

2 What Should Policy Be? Guidelines for Intervention

In his book on intervention, Richard N. Haass wisely suggests that no foreign policy doctrine or intellectual edifice is likely to emerge that will provide consensus on 'how specific local events are to be viewed and what the United States should do about them.'[1] Decisions such as those on Bosnia will continue to be made on a case-by-case basis, the kind of analysis that will allow consideration of the numerous variables, and the varying weight and priority that will have to be assigned to them depending on the circumstances of each unique case. As we have just seen, the end of the Cold War system complicates the equation for determining US interests in the former Yugoslavia and elsewhere.

The futility of trying to craft guidelines for intervention is confirmed by examining a few of the efforts to date to provide those guidelines. An early, much-discussed effort was that of former Secretary of Defense Caspar Weinberger. He listed six conditions that should be met before American forces were committed abroad:

1 Forces should only be committed to combat if a vital national interest or a vital interest of our allies is involved
2 If we put troops in, we should do so wholeheartedly and with the intention of winning
3 There should be clearly defined political and military objectives
4 The relationship between our objectives and the size, composition and disposition of the forces we have committed must be continually reassessed and, if necessary, adjusted
5 Before troops are committed, there must be reasonable assurance that Congress and the public will support the action
6 The commitment of troops should be a last resort.[2]

14

Granting the difficulty of his task, it is not hard to find flaws in Weinberger's six principles. The last guideline, recommending the commitment of troops as only a last resort, one hopes is a universally accepted principle. It is hard to imagine an instance where a counter-argument would carry the day, but one can imagine disagreements on when 'last resort' has been reached. Taking the rest in order, the first guideline, that troops should be committed only if a vital interest is at stake, only begs the question of what is a vital interest and opens up an eternal debate. If by vital interest he means a security interest, the definition is narrower and more precise. If he includes humanitarian issues, it can be more broadly defined. To exclude humanitarian concerns completely is difficult, because politicians almost always justify foreign policies by invoking humanitarian principles. Above all, this guideline forces the debate back to the context of the individual decision.

The second principle of putting in enough troops to win is also ambiguous. As Colin Powell points out, all wars are limited. A decision must still be made as to what exactly we want to accomplish and what size force will be required. Weinberger himself admits that sometimes very limited responses may be adequate. He uses the example of Germany's occupation of the Rhineland before World War II, where the use of a little force by the French might have prevented World War II. Some have argued that limited measures taken early in the Bosnian War would have stood a good chance of stopping the Serb advance and ending a problem that has dragged on for years. Colin Powell, normally a strong proponent of this principle, cites approvingly the US commitment of a pair of Phantom fighter jets in the Philippines in December 1989 to discourage a *coup d'état* then underway. Would Powell have supported committing whatever force was necessary to 'win' if this foray had failed?[3] Unfortunately, proclaiming the principle is the easiest part of formulating a policy; interpreting and implementing it to accomplish what needs to be done in a particular instance is where the difficulty lies (the devil is in the details). The *reductio ad absurdum* of this principle is that one must always be prepared to commit all your forces and be prepared for all-out war if the situation requires it. At best, the question of how much force is needed to 'win' must be left to subjective interpretation in specific circumstances.

Guideline three, having clearly defined political and military objectives, is undoubtedly a good idea. Still, it is sometimes difficult, in the complex post-Cold War situations in which we find ourselves, to start out with clear-cut objectives, and in some cases it will be necessary to change objectives as the situation develops. But on balance, this guideline provides a useful goal for the policy-maker.

Regarding Weinberger's number four, it is hard to imagine anyone arguing the contrary case. It is always good to reassess how well the strategy and the resources that have been committed are capable of doing the job and one hopes the commander-in-chief and those working for him do so frequently. Number five, ensuring public and Congressional support before committing to a conflict is also desirable if the conflict is expected to last at least a modest length of time and to be costly. In some cases, however, a president may be able to build support after the troops have been committed. At other times, even though the support was there for the initial commitment, the changing nature of the conflict may decrease support as casualties mount, as was the case in the Korean War and in Somalia.[4] It is doubtful that Weinberger would have argued that we should not have entered the Korean War, since he undoubtedly regarded the stakes for the US as high.

In fairness to Weinberger, his guidelines were formulated before the momentous changes that ended the Cold War were clear. It is not entirely fair to judge them against the world as we know it now. But they do illustrate the difficulty of constructing any useful foreign-policy roadmap for our time. The basic problem is avoiding, on the one hand, having principles so general as to be platitudinous, or on the other hand, principles that are so specific and restrictive as to be useless.

Later attempts by officials to construct guidelines have reflected the same problems. Former President Bush, in a speech in early 1994, suggested that military force should be used when the stakes warrant its use, where no other policies are likely to prove effective, where its application can be limited in time and scope, and where potential benefits outweigh the costs and sacrifices. He went on to state that the relative importance of an issue is not a suitable guide to the use of force, since in some cases using force would not be the best way to protect a vital interest, but force might be the best way to deal with a problem that does not represent a vital interest.[5] These principles all represent good advice, but they are for the most part truisms with which nobody is likely to quarrel. The former president does offer the insight that the inclination to use force should not necessarily be proportionate to the importance of the issue, and the emphasis on comparing the costs and benefits of a given policy reflects an emphasis seldom heard, and one that is particularly relevant in a post-Cold-War world where military intervention is likely to be limited and for less than vital interests. Guidelines used during the Cold War tended to look only at the value of the interest involved as a criteria for intervention, and to assume that if necessary, the US should intervene without too much attention to cost. When there are many opportunities for intervention, and most involve less than vital interests, a cost-benefit approach to decisions on intervention is necessary.

Secretary of state Warren Christopher has stated that there should be four strict tests for the use of force: (1) the goal must be stated clearly, (2) there must be a strong likelihood of success, (3) there must be an exit strategy, and (4) the action must win sustained public support. As the *New York Times* pointed out, Christopher offered the diplomatic equivalent of the cautious military advice offered by Colin Powell, the former Chairman of the Joint Chiefs of Staff.[6] General Powell has on several occasions laid out a doctrine that reflects a distrust of 'limited' wars and suggests considerable caution in choosing when to intervene.[7] Noting that he has seen the results of 'limited' wars in Vietnam and Lebanon, where there was the establishment of a US 'presence' without a defined mission, he attributes the military successes in the Bush administration to matching the use of military force to the political objectives. 'As soon as they tell me it's limited, it means they do not care whether you achieve a result or not,' he notes. 'As soon as they tell me "surgical," I head for the bunker'. General Powell favors an approach that explicitly and clearly defines the objective of the military action, plans for and uses the amount of force necessary to achieve the objective, and then withdraws when the job is completed. When the military has a clear set of objectives, as in Panama, the Philippine coup and Desert Storm, the result has been success. When the policy is murky or nonexistent, the Bay of

Pigs, Vietnam and Lebanon, the result has been disaster. When we do a little surgical bombing or make a limited attack and the desired result is not obtained, 'a new set of experts then comes forward with talk of a little escalation'.

In a later debate over guidelines for intervention related to Weinberger's second principle, former Secretary of Defense Les Aspin distinguished between the 'all or nothing' school, which he identified with Colin Powell, and the 'limited object-ives' school, which he identified with former British Prime Minister Margaret Thatcher. The Powell group would limit the activities of the military to clearly military objectives, that is, they would not engage in humanitarian work, but more im-portantly they believe that once involvement commences, it must be seen through to victory. As Aspin puts it, if you aren't willing to put the pedal to the floor, don't start the engine. The overwhelming force necessary to do the job should be put in immediately and the job done quickly. This all-out assault on the problem at hand, quickly finishing off the job, gets around two problems that have dogged the US fighting limited wars in the past, especially in Vietnam. The first is the problem of gradual escalation, where if the first low-level use of force does not do the job, then more must be introduced. This gradual escalation leads to an endless quagmire, resulting neither in an end to the war, nor a decisive victory. The ass-umption of this school is that quick and decisive intervention with the level of force already at a maximum level will be enough of a shock to the enemy that the job will be success-fully accomplished. Gradual escalation, on the other hand, allows an acculturation to the increasing level of violence and does not force the enemy to surrender.

A related argument bolstering this approach is that it lessens the problem of attaining public support. A decisive action that is quickly successful is more likely to be supported by Congress and the public than one that drags on with gradually escalating casualties. In any case, it will be over quickly, avoiding the pro-longed period during which public opposition could continue to build.

The limited objectives school has several counter arguments to the assumptions of the all-or-nothing school. On the most general level, they simply argue that increasingly the kinds of crises and trouble spots we confront in today's world are not the kind susceptible to the traditional solutions of all-out war. Rather, they are situations which call for a limited response, a specific solution aimed at a specific problem, not necessarily committing the US to the defeat of the enemy or complete control of the situation. In the Bosnian situation, people who believed that airpower would have a limiting and dampening effect on Serb activities favored using bombing, but not necessarily following it up with ground action if air power did not attain the desired objectives. The argument made here is that if this kind of military action is not undertaken, if we become involved only in situations where we can go all out, we will seldom intervene. We may have the finest military in the world, but it will seldom be used because the ideal situations demanded by these traditional guidelines will never obtain.[8]

In defense of the limited-objectives school, one can also argue that the end of the Cold War – the collapse of the Soviet Union – makes the limited objective form of warfare more feasible. Lacking the concern with always having to follow a failed action with escalation in order to show resolve and reassure allies – a requirement probably exaggerated even during the Cold War – we now have the luxury of picking and choosing our place and time for offensives, and equally important, picking and choosing when to discontinue them. Credibility in achieving the desired ends is not directly related to winning every engagement.

Related to this is the possibility of doing more cost-benefit analysis. If military activity can be broken into smaller slices, with more freedom to try to influence certain aspects of the conflict without having to worry about overall credibility, then a specific action can be attempted if it appears that achieving the objectives will warrant the cost. If the objectives are not achieved, then a government can withdraw from the conflict without suffering a fatal blow to its prestige. These issues will be explored more fully in Chapter 8.

Rejection of the assumptions of the 'all-or-nothing' school therefore provides the flexibility that will allow more intervention in a post-Cold-War situation such as Yugoslavia than would be possible under Weinberger's guidelines. This adaptation in no way solves the problem of whether to intervene, when to intervene, or how to intervene. But it does give more freedom to make decisions to intervene in ways that will not necessarily compromise American credibility, as the old assumptions would suggest. Partial or limited interventions, when they seem advisable in a particular instance, may be evaluated on a case-by-case basis, and undertaken without necessarily requiring follow-up and escalation. While such decisions run the risk of undertaking actions that will not accomplish the desired goals, were it possible to intervene only on an all-or-nothing basis, in many cases no military action at all could be taken. Such was the case in Bosnia until August of 1995.

This discussion has validated the earlier suggestion that few guidelines exist for deciding when to intervene and that most decisions will have to be made on a case-by-case basis.

At best we can compile a list of questions to ask, a set of baselines from which to start discussion. Richard Haass suggests four tests which any proposed military intervention should pass: (1) that it be worth doing, (2) that it be doable, (3) that likely benefits exceed likely costs, and (4) that the ratio of benefits to costs be better than that provided by another policy.[9] The first two are truisms, although in any given decision on intervention there may be considerable disagreement on whether these two tests are met. The last two tests on cost–benefit analysis, extend President Bush's suggestion and they are useful, as suggested before, since in the past when we were not used to dealing with 'limited' wars, we have tended to make decisions solely on the basis of whether something needed to be done. An explicit comparison of costs and benefits is essential in the more limited confrontations which we now face, which often do not involve vital interests, but often involve something worth doing, provided the cost is not too high.

However scrupulously a leader considers the important factors, in the end he must live with the reality that decisions are neither easy nor guaranteed to succeed. President Kennedy's musings on making decisions are telling, and in no place more applicable than to the decisions on intervention in Bosnia. Regarding the plan of choice for responding to the Cuban missile crisis he said. 'There aren't any good solutions … whichever plan I choose, the ones whose plans we're not taking are the lucky ones – they'll be able to say "I told you so" in a week or two. But this one seems the least objectionable.'[10]

Part II

The Yugoslav Setting

3 The Development of the War in Yugoslavia

THE BALKAN SETTING

The splitting of the Roman Empire between East and West by the Emperor Constantine in the fourth century AD may be seen as an harbinger of the fate of Yugoslavia. Since then, the 'tectonic plates' of imperial, religious, and racial interests have ground together in the Balkans. Rome and Constantinople, Catholicism and Orthodoxy, Christianity and Islam, and in later years, Germans and Slavs, Russia and the West, 'all have clashed along a shifting fault line running down the middle of the former Yugoslavia (or, more precisely, through the territory of today's Bosnia–Herzegovina)'.[1] Here, over the last few centuries and at the confluence of several empires, the Balkan states either expressed their national identity, or alternatively, watched it be, yet again, suppressed or erased from the map. The Ottoman Empire was an occupying force for over 500 years. The Austria–Hungarian Empire only ended with WW I, and Russian influence has only now abated with the collapse of the Soviet Union. Long-standing British, French and German influence continues, but in a weakened form.[2]

Now, the leaders of Serbia and Croatia, apt students of their former conquerors, continue the tradition of expansion and rule over others, attempting once more to realize 'conflicting dreams of lost imperial glory', but this time with an added ethnic twist.[3] Of the main contenders in the present conflict, Serbia, Croatia and Bosnia–Herzegovina, all have long histories of political and cultural uniqueness. The Serbs celebrate their Christian Orthodox heritage, and their defeat in 1389 on Kosovo Polje (Field of Blackbirds) in present-day Kosovo by the Turks has become a Serbian obsession. Catholic Croatia, the other major power in modern Yugoslavia, lost its independence in 1102. Despite claims of modern Serb and Croat nationalists that Bosnia–Herzegovina is an artificial entity, it has had consistent approximate borders from the thirteenth century, demonstrating 'more durability than any territorial state or unit assembled by the Serbs or Croats'.[4]

In the late nineteenth century, as Ottoman power receded, these nations emerged again. The Serbian state appeared in modern times with the settlement formalizing Turkish losses at the Congress of Berlin in 1878, and it gradually expanded its area of jurisdiction. Croatia was recreated when the new state of Yugoslavia emerged in 1918 after World War I, while Bosnia–Herzegovina became a republic in Tito's Yugoslavia after World War II.

THE CREATION OF YUGOSLAVIA

The ideas of freedom and self-determination introduced by Napoleon were given a further impetus with the end of World War I and Woodrow Wilson's promotion of national self-determination. Out of Serbia and the remains of the Austria–Hungarian Empire, the new Kingdom of the Serbs, Croats and Slovenes emerged. The creation of this new state was a balancing act from the beginning, and maintaining the balance got increasingly difficult. Serbian influence was disproportionate and conflict and violence led to the establishment of a dictatorship by King Alexander (a Serb) in 1929 (when the new state was renamed Yugoslavia). With the coming of World War II, Serbia joined the Allies, and Croatia, including most of Bosnia–Herzegovina, became a German-created independent state, while Slovenia was part of Germany.

Some of the fiercest fighting anywhere in World War II took place between Serbian guerrilla fighters known as Chetniks (loyal to the exiled Yugoslavia government in London) and Croatian Ustashi (fascists). Comparison of the atrocities and the intensity of hatred and barbarism during that period with current events yields many parallels, and naturally the memories of that period have done much to fuel the present fighting. Serbs and Croats engage in endless debate over the allocation of blame and the correct number of fatalities on both sides in World War II. That period has become a major reference point for the demonization, historical distortion and ethnic stereotyping that is central to ethnic conflict.

After the war, Tito, a Croat, made a second attempt to create a viable Yugoslav (South Slav) nation based on the record of his partisans in fighting the Germans and establishing power, with the Yugoslav League of Communists. In 1948, Tito had a bitter break with Stalin, a powerful incentive toward Yugoslav unity, since Tito's defiance brought the full wrath of Stalin and the Soviet propaganda apparatus down on Yugoslavia. Yugoslavia then became of special interest to the United States as a buffer between East and West and a thorn in Stalin's side.

Before the recent wars began, Serbia, Croatia and Bosnia were the three large republics in Yugoslavia. Croatia and Bosnia each had a population of between four and five million, while Serbia, including the autonomous provinces of Kosovo and Vojvodina, was approximately nine million. The smaller republics of Slovenia and Macedonia each have populations of approximately two million, while Montenegro is considerably smaller. The southern areas tend to be poor, and the north richer. The ratio in per capita income between the extremes of Slovenia (rich) and Bosnia and Macedonia (poor) are of the order of two to one. An even more destitute population exists in impoverished Kosovo.[5] Serbs are Christian Orthodox and Eastern, and they use the Cyrillic alphabet, while the Croats use the Roman script, but the language is essentially the same. Croats are Catholic and Western, while the Slovenes are at least as Western as the Croats, with the highest standard of living in Yugoslavia. Since the Slovenes declared independence, were invaded by and quickly repulsed the Belgrade Serbs, they are no longer part of the equation in the former Yugoslavia.

Tito's scheme was to create six national republics which theoretically had autonomy, but owed primary loyalty to Tito and the party. Within this framework, Tito established pre-war 'Southern Serbia' as the republic of Macedonia, and created two autonomous regions within Serbia itself – Kosovo in the south, with a large Albanian population, and Vojvodina in the north, including various minorities, but especially Hungarians. Montenegro, mostly Serbian, was also made a republic.

Tito's biggest problem, however, was what to do about Bosnia–Herzegovina. Claimed by both Croatia and Serbia, with the citizenry including Croats and Serbs as well as those of the Muslim religion, Tito made it into a republic in its own right, but Muslims were made an official nationality only in 1964. In keeping with its role in the war of defending a multi-ethnic state, Bosnia had a high degree of intermarriage between ethnic groups, and it stood out in 1990 and 1991 with the largest percentage of explicitly Yugoslav-oriented and liberal democratic parties, possibly because its citizenry was very aware of the need to preserve inter-ethnic harmony in a potentially explosive environment.

REFORM AND DECENTRALIZATION: NATIONALIST APPEALS AND DEMOCRATIZATION

Yugoslavia, which had fueled growth during the 1970s with foreign borrowing, hit rough economic waters in the 1980s. As late 1970s oil price rises rippled through the world economy, recessions hit Western countries, and Europe came increasingly to be divided into those who would become part of a more closely knit European Community and those who would not. After 1981 Yugoslavia was hit by rapidly increasing rates of unemployment. The disappearance of the Cold War accelerated those forces, promoting trends toward political democratization, economic reform and decentralization. The citizens of Yugoslavia increasingly became dependent on the republics when the weakened Belgrade government could no longer guarantee economic prosperity and political stability. They were thus susceptible to nationalist republican appeals, whether the blatantly crowd-pleasing speeches of Serbia's Milosevic, or the more subtle separatist rhetoric of Slovenia's Kucan. As Yugoslavia's middle class became more insecure and increasingly aware of their dependence on the republics to guarantee their well-being, the stage was prepared for Yugoslavia's demise. And in the view of Susan Woodward, the pressure toward liberalization and austerity from international institutions contributed to the weakening of central institutions and encouraged on all sides the notion of being 'victims of economic exchanges by others'.[6]

The reforms were introduced and promoted by President Ante Markovic, who took office in the spring of 1989. They were intended to transform Yugoslavia from an authoritarian relic of the Cold War into a modern efficient and productive state that would fit in with the emerging united Europe. The reforms included measures for trade liberalization, privatization, full convertibility of the Yugoslav dinar, the creation of capital and labor markets, an overhaul of the banking sector, and the promotion of small and medium-sized enterprises. Markovic successfully cut inflation and removed controls on hard currency savings by citizens. He became the most popular political figure in Yugoslavia, and his reform package was loudly applauded in the West and by international institutions.

But Markovic's efforts seemed to find little useful support except among ordinary Yugoslavs. In the West, he got applause and strong verbal support, but little else. In Yugoslavia, he was caught between the Slovenes and the Croats on one side, who criticized his promotion of a pluralistic, democratic federation as being too centrist and pro-Serb, and by the Serbs on the other side who were critical of the speed and methods of implementing his market reforms, claiming the reforms made the Serbian economy suffer the most. Markovic was hurt by his decision to form his own all-Yugoslav Reform Party. He was criticized on all sides for abusing his prime ministerial position to form a political party. The party was formed too late to participate in the Slovenian and Croatian elections, which made the Serbs suspicious of his wanting to participate in their republican elections. His party did well in Macedonia, and not badly in Bosnia, the two republics most sympathetic to Markovic's views on what the future of Yugoslavia should look like.[7]

On the political stage, two sets of events in 1987 were harbingers of the growing nationalist fragmentation in Yugoslavia. In Slovenia, at the end of September, there was a growing tendency to promote Slovene sovereignty by opposing all federal institutions that seemed to interfere with republican rights and were not based on parliamentary and republican supremacy.

The parliament passed constitutional amendments that initiated a process of disassociation from the federation, declaring the 'complete and unalienable right' to 'self-determination, including the right to secession' and indicating the conditions under which federal authority would be invalid in Slovenia. Slovenia's Milan Kucan, discreet and low key when compared to Milosevic's style of playing directly and personally to the crowds, nonetheless showed a disturbing tendency to promote national objectives at the expense of Yugoslavia, even if the cost was high. Rather than engaging in consultation to ameliorate the Slovene criticisms, the federal government pushed ahead with its own reform proposals.[8]

On the Serbian side, Slobodan Milosevic staged an inner-party coup in November 1987, replacing liberal party and state leaders with his party faction by defeating the more moderate faction led by his mentor, Ivan Stambolic. This was one more step in a disturbing trend in Serbia toward a hard line nationalism that showed a high degree of intolerance toward other nationalities. A trend toward authoritarianism in Serbia could be traced through a whole series of events in the 1980s. In 1981 Albanian-student-led demonstrations in Kosovo (which is 90 per cent Albanian) were forcibly suppressed; in 1984 trials of intellectuals who took part in unofficial debating societies were held, and in September 1986, the Serbian Academy of Sciences published a manifesto which described the Serbs as victims in Tito's Yugoslav Federation; claimed that Serbia was weakened by the provincial autonomy given Kosovo and Vojvodina; that the Albania majority threatened genocide of the Serbs in Kosovo; that Slovenia and Croatia conspired to keep Serbia poor; and that Tito unjustly left many Serbs outside Serbia. This latter assertion, especially, provided a basis for later Serb claims on those areas populated by Serbs but lying outside Serbia.[9] This manifesto by intellectuals became a central rallying cry for Serb nationalists and the Milosevic forces in the years ahead. Milosevic, responding to the success he had in Kosovo in mobilizing Serbs by appealing to large crowds with fiery rhetoric about the persecution of the Serbian minority in Kosovo, increasingly relied on this tactic to build his political movement and to gain allies in Vojvodina and Montenegro as he had done in Serbia proper. The demonstrations began small but expanded to crowds numbering up to 1 million. The demonstrators were often paid by their employers to attend, but the crowds increasingly drew on the unemployed.[10]

After taking power, Milosevic led an increasingly strident Serbian nationalist movement in directions that were intolerable for the rest of the republics. Branka Magas suggests that as the Serbs became more intent on holding Yugoslavia together on their own terms, it became increasingly harder to do so: 'The more the Serb nationalists embraced the cause of "Yugoslavia", the more anti-federal that Yugoslavia of theirs became – and inevitably, the greater the resistance to it in other parts of the country.'[11] The other republics, especially Slovenia and Croatia, propelled by their own nationalist dynamic, had no desire to be part of a political union that was intent on integrating them into the kind of Serb-dominated polity which Milosevic was promoting. By mid-1991, Milosevic had promoted several developments that were not conducive to the continuation of an integrated Yugoslavia:

- governments in Vojvodina (October 1988) and Montenegro (January 1989) were replaced with governments favorable to Milosevic
- constitutional autonomy was ended for Kosovo (March 1989).

But it was not only the Serbs who were growing more nationalistic. Liberalization in the 1960s particularly encouraged Croat nationalism, complete with fascist symbols from the wartime period; it alarmed the Serb minority, who began arming themselves. Tito suppressed the Croat movement in 1972, but Dusko Doder, driving through the Serb-populated areas of Yugoslavia in 1974, found that the ethnic tension had intensified. As Milosevic's movement developed and Yugoslavia began to come apart, it became possible to mobilize these minority Serbs, especially since the Croats were lax in protecting them.[12] Croat nationalism developed slowly with Croats showing remarkable restraint in the face of the displays of Serb nationalism. They 'watched the rise of Milosevic in silence ... The vast Serb processions and mass rallies, teeming with Serbian imagery and symbolism of domination, were often to be seen, but, as late as 1990, the Croatian counterpart was cowed and furtive.'[13]

But the Croat leader, Franjo Tudjman, although lacking the stridency of Milosevic, was a match for him in cunning. He was a master of taking advantage of the opportunities that the rise of Serbian nationalism presented, for expanding his own power by building on and stimulating the Croatian reaction. The leaders of Serbia and Croatia, as the two powers that counted in the increasingly disintegrating Yugoslavia, naturally thought in terms of expanding their spheres of influence in the new order of things. As Tudjman was later to admit, he and Milosevic met secretly several times early in 1991 (and perhaps earlier) to work out the details of a division of Bosnia between them. Their counterparts in Bosnia, the Serb Radovan Karadzic and the Croat Mate Boban met a little over a year later for the same purpose.[14]

In the conflict between the advocates of decentralization (and eventually independence), Slovenia and Croatia, on the one hand, and the advocate of centralization, Serbia, on the other, Bosnia and Macedonia were caught in the middle. They worked hard for a compromise solution to the organization of Yugoslavia, but with little success. Bosnia was the most democratic of the three republics, but as the system liberalized, ethnic identification was important there as elsewhere. Izetbegovic's Party of Democratic Action (SDA) was the first to be organized along ethnic lines, promoting Muslim interests, and the results of the November 1990 elections reflected the division according to ethnic parties. The Bosnian Serbs and Croats soon followed suite and established their own parties, and Izetbegovic angered them when he announced that the SDA opposed the principle of national parity, and that the government would be formed on the basis of one-man one-vote. This led two observers to comment that Izetbegovic was attempting to dominate Bosnia just as Milosevic was attempting to dominate Yugoslavia.[15] But perhaps the most damning charge that can be leveled at Izetbegovic is that of naivety about the likelihood of war and the future of Bosnia. He consistently underestimated the ethnic turmoil and the Serbian threat. Hoping to avoid war, he had not created a Bosnian territorial army. He asserted at one point that, 'It takes two sides to have a war and we will not fight.' But, as David Rieff points out, it does not take two sides to have a slaughter.[16] Izetbegovic, a moderate and well-intentioned leader, tended to pursue business as usual without sufficient regard for the 'combustible environment' in which he was operating.[17]

In 1990, all the republics held elections, the first meaningful post-communist elections. They were for the most part free and fair, but with some restrictions on access to the media, especially in Serbia, the last republic to hold elections. The results of the elections further legitimized the nationalist cause in all the republics, with the possible exception of Macedonia where a divided vote made it difficult to form a coalition. In Serbia, Milosevic's Serbian Socialist Party (SPS) won 78 per cent of the parliamentary seats and 47 per cent of the popular vote, handily defeating his main rival and nationalist, Vuk Draskovic. In Croatia, Tudjman, who had run an aggressively nationalistic campaign, won 58 per cent of the parliamentary seats and 41.5 per cent of the popular vote with his Croatian Democratic Union (HDZ). The Croat parliament immediately amended the constitution, declared 'political and economic sovereignty' over Croatian territory, adopted a new and provocative flag and coat of arms, and sent the interior security police into neighborhoods to replace local police and reservists of Serb nationality with Croats. This antagonized the Serb population and led to violence with Serb radicals. In Bosnia, three nationalist parties gathered votes reflecting roughly the ethnic make-up of the republic. Izetbegovic's Party of Democratic Action (SDA) received 33.8 per cent of the vote, the Serbian Democratic Party (SDS) 29.6 per cent, and the Croatian Democratic Union (HDZ–BH) 18.3 per cent. although all winning parties appealed to the electorate on nationalist grounds and the elections were widely interpreted as a vote against Markovic, his standing remained high in the polls, 80–90 per cent in many republics, thus suggesting considerable ambiguity in voters' attitudes about the future of reform and Yugoslavia.[18]

Indeed, two observers have argued that the elections in Bosnia demonstrated a surprising degree of historical continuity with previous Bosnian multiparty elections in 1910 and the 1920s. And despite their avowed nationalist principles, the leaders of Bosnia elected in 1990 briefly restored the 'historical pattern of coalition politics' in the Bosnian parliament, in an effort to provide a workable solution to the ethnic fragmentation. This effort is consistent with a tradition among the Bosnian Muslim leadership of supporting 'broader, multinational political entities that would protect the interests of the Bosnian Muslims'.[19] Izetbegovic, who had been imprisoned by the Communists for advocating an Islamic state, later became an advocate of a multi-ethnic Bosnia. Indeed, Izetbegovic often seems of two minds, finding it difficult to choose between a multiethnic solution to Bosnia's problems or a defense of his traditional Moslem constituency. This ambiguity is illustrated by his stance on the Lisbon plan to partition Bosnia. His movement from an early defense of a multi-ethnic Bosnia to an increased emphasis on defending Moslem interests later in the war is consistent with the historical ambivalence of Bosnian Muslim leadership, which has tended to defend multinational entities when possible, with a fall-back position of defending Muslim interests when survival is at stake. Thus when it became clear in 1993 that the West was not going to intervene to support their cause, and as Muslim–Croat warfare raged, Izetbegovic began to consider a partitioned Bosnia that would be based on a Muslim state, even flirting with acceptance of the Owen–Stoltenberg plan which moved a great distance in that direction.

The status of the Serb minorities in Croatia and Bosnia was the most important issue standing between peace and war. The Croatian government was willing to concede cultural autonomy, the right to a Serbian media, and so on, but they were opposed to any form of Serbian political autonomy. The Serbs, on the other hand, were willing to acknowledge Croatia as their 'homeland', but only in a Croatia that was part of Yugoslavia, not an independent or confederal Croatia. It was the failure to resolve this fundamental difference that made it hard for the Serbs to let the Croats go peacefully when they seceded.[20] A similar dilemma existed in Bosnia, where the Serbs proclaimed their unwillingness to remain in a Bosnia that was not part of Yugoslavia, and the Bosnian government, supported by the referendum on independence in February 1992, was unwilling to continue in a Serb-dominated Yugoslavia that did not include Slovenia or Croatia.

As the national disintegration of Yugoslavia progressed, the Bosnians were clearly in the most difficult position, victims of the complex ethnic make-up of Yugoslavia and the vexing question of how political organization could be fashioned to provide an acceptable solution to the various ethnic demands. Both the Serbs and the Croats were fanning the flames of discontent, and the loser, caught in the middle, would be Bosnia. There was no adequate solution for the problem of national identities and state borders in the former Yugoslavia. No group wanted to have minority status in a larger polity, but it was also impossible for each group to have its own state given the complex patterns of population and ethnic group location. The ethnic mix in Bosnia precluded a clean separation of groups and the creation of homogeneous communities short of large-scale population movement. But at the same time, the trust, good faith and ethos of cooperation needed to construct arrangements that would allow cohabitation were also lacking.

> Croatia's President Tudjman and Serbia's President Milosevic actively cultivated the discontent of their fellow nationals in neighboring republics. Both of them hoped to gain by dismembering Bosnia and Hercegovina. This involved each of them in a fundamental contradiction: Milosevic argued for the partitioning of Croatia and Bosnia to accommodate their Serbian inhabitants, while simultaneously insisting that no one interfere with his continued repression of the Kosovo Albanians. Similarly, Tudjman demanded that no one interfere in Croatia's treatment of its Serbs at the same time that he sought to annex portions of Bosnia and Hercegovina in the name of its Croatian inhabitants. These contradictory stances seemed to bother neither of them in the least.[21]

As we have seen, Izetbegovic was not above some inconsistency of his own in claiming a commitment to multi-ethnicity, while furthering Muslim dominance, but in terms of ruthlessness he was not even playing in the same league as Milosevic and Tudjman. This fact would become painfully evident to all in the next few years, especially those citizens of Bosnia who suffered the trauma of war and atrocities.

THE DISINTEGRATION OF YUGOSLAVIA

After the elections, the movement toward republic autonomy, and the flight from the Yugoslav federal structure, continued. Reflecting the centrifugal forces at work in areas outside Serbia, on 23 December, 1990 a plebiscite in Slovenia authorized the parliament to declare independence in six months if negotiations did not produce a new confederal framework that would allow autonomy for Slovenia, even though a European Community summit declared support for a unified Yugoslavia in October. On 30 May, 1991 Croatia declared its intention to secede if a confederation agreement was not reached by June 15. On 25 June both Croatia and Slovenia declared their independence, in spite of a last moment trip by US Secretary of State James Baker to Belgrade where he declared support for a united Yugoslavia and said the US would not recognize Croatia and Slovenia as independent states.

On 26 June, Milosevic and the Yugoslav army began actions in Slovenia. But Milosevic was in for a surprise. The Slovenes were prepared, and in less than two weeks the Serbs were forced to withdraw. This incident has been cited by those favoring a more forceful US strategy in Yugoslavia as an indication that Milosevic and the Serbs would respond to a more assertive Western strategy.[22] While this may well be the case, and there is other evidence to support that position, Slovenia occupies a unique position in the Serbian cosmology. Unlike every other republic, Slovenia contained no vocal Serbian minority which would invite Serbian interest. In any case, Slovenia had successfully repelled the Serbian thrust and was no longer a player in the Yugoslav denouement.

Croatia, however, was a different story. In mid-July, Milosevic invaded Croatia, and in response the UN Security Council in September passed Resolution 713, supporting an arms embargo on Yugoslavia at the request of its Serb-dominated government.[23] Serbia was well on its way to attempting to implement its version of a Greater Serbia, a concept that had been advocated by many Serbs throughout the 1980s. Although not well-defined, it presumably included the 32 per cent of the Bosnian and the 12–14 per cent of the Croatian population made up of Serbs prior to the start of the war. The war against Croatia, fought partly by proxy by Croatian Serb paramilitary forces and partly by the Yugoslav People's Army (JNA), was a major Serbian initiative. At the same time, while Croatia claimed to be in favor of a confederal solution, it was determined to destroy Yugoslavia. The rhetoric of Croatian president Franjo Tudjman during the election 'conjured up images of a fascist spirit stalking that land'.[24]

The war in Croatia quickly picked up steam. From September through the end of the year, Croatian cities such as Vukovar and Osijek were shelled. Zagreb was attacked in October, and the historic town of Dubrovnik in December. A ceasefire was arranged in January 1992, by Cyrus Vance, and a UN peace-keeping force was deployed in March. The next Serbian offensive was to occur in early April, when Radovan Karadzic declared a Serb republic of Bosnia–Herzegovina, the early clashes between Bosnian government troops, on the one hand, and the JNA and Bosnian Serb paramilitaries increased, and the shelling of Sarajevo began. At that time, the EC and the US recognized the Republic of Bosnia. Germany had recognized the independence of Slovenia and Croatia several months earlier in December, followed closely by the EC in January.

The opening of the war in Bosnia began the final and most compelling drama of the conflict in the former Yugoslavia. The war escalated quickly, from the initial stages when combatants fighting at the barricades in Sarajevo wore face masks to hide their identify, to all-out war. The Bosnian Serbs at first relied heavily on the JNA, since they otherwise had only a few light arms. In January Milosevic had quietly begun to transfer JNA personnel born in Bosnia to serve in Bosnia, and those born in Serbia and Montenegro to service there. When the fighting began and the Yugoslav army pulled out of Bosnia, those born in Bosnia remained there. Izetbegovic, for too long, naively viewed the army as neutral. When Izetbegovic finally succeeded in getting the army formally to leave, it not only left arms and soldiers behind for the Bosnian Serbs, but also removed production facilities it deemed useful. Then it destroyed anything that would be useful to the Bosnian government, including an airport that cost up to $2.5 billion to construct.[25] From then on, while much of the fighting was done by Bosnian Serbs, there was a constant flow of materials and personnel across the Drina River and other borders, the flow slowing from time to time as Milosevic professed to be withholding support (in both the spring of 1993 and the spring of 1994) from Radovan Karadzic and General Mladic, the civilian and military leaders respectively, of the Bosnian Serbs.

The Bosnian government did not get the benefit of the kind of ceasefire negotiated in Croatia. In Bosnia, the stakes were higher since the Serbian minority made up a larger percentage of the population, the Bosnians were weaker and therefore more vulnerable, and both the Serbs and Croats felt that Bosnia lacked legitimacy, giving each of them a right to a piece of it. As the war continued, the Serbs and the West engaged in a game of 'cat and mouse', with the West attempting to shame and threaten the Serbs to halt their aggressive war and the Serbs testing the West to see what they could get away with. Both sides soon adjusted to the rules of the game, and it became clear that under those rules the war could go on for a long time. The West put up ineffective resistance. Economic sanctions were tried first, then peacekeeping forces were sent and attempts made to inject some Western military presence into the conflict. But movement was painfully slow and it was clear that the Western governments did not have their hearts in it. The six months of debate before a decision was made to enforce already existing 'no-fly' zones over Bosnia is symbolic of the lack of will to deal with the problem of Serbian violations of the UN resolutions.[26]

After the 1992 US election, it appeared that Bill Clinton might be willing to raise the price of war for the Serbs, but in the end he bought into the same broad policy guidelines that had underlain US policy from the beginning. It was only in the summer of 1995 that he began a new approach, used significant force to bring the Serbs to the peace table, and then committed American troops to peacekeeping in Bosnia.

RESPONSIBILITY FOR THE WAR

Yugoslav specialists are not able to agree on the origins of the war nor the responsibility for it.[27] It is useful, therefore, to get a feel for some of the differences that divide them and what the implications for analyzing the war that follow from the different assumptions might be. A good place to start explaining the demise of Yugoslavia is a set of propositions suggested by Warren Zimmermann. He examines five factors which are relevant to understanding that demise.

1   Serbs and Croats are ancient enemies, with different religions and historical experiences. But this gives no explanation of how the two groups coexisted in relative peace in both Croatia and Bosnia for so long.

2   Nationalism also arose because of the economic/political differences between north and south. Slovenia and Croatia resented having to subsidize the poorer south. The Serbs, to the south, had a grievance because Josip Broz Tito, leader of Yugoslavia from 1943 to 1980, had denied Serbia its formerly predominant role.

3   Tito, in preparing for his death, framed a constitution in 1974 that made Yugoslavia ungovernable from within. A territorial and political base of the kind of nationalism that Tito had been trying to stifle sprang up in the republics.

4   Nationalism arose from the ashes of communism and built on its cultural assumptions: it is collectivist – the group, not the individual matters; exclusivist – people outside the group are enemies or traitors; and militant – the enemies and traitors must be eliminated. Milosevic and Tudjman are examples of the link between communism and nationalism.

5   Finally, Milosevic's nationalism was decisive and the most dangerous because it lashed out against Albanians, Slovenes, and Croats. In this way it differed from other nationalisms in Yugoslavia which were either non-threatening (Muslim), had no particular target (Slovenian), or were in large measure a reaction to Serbian nationalism (Albanian, Croatian).[28]

Zimmermann thus suggests a multifaceted explanation of Yugoslavia's disintegration, with the rise of Serbian nationalism as the proximate cause.

Putting more stress on economic and institutional factors, Susan L. Woodward, in her massive study of the tragedy in Yugoslavia, stresses first the effect of the end of the Cold-War international system on Yugoslavia's disintegration. She argues that the viability of the Yugoslav regime depended on its foreign position and a policy of national independence and nonalignment in the Cold-War international system. Yugoslavia's access to foreign credit and capital markets was made possible by Yugoslavia's strategic position and its independent foreign policy. The West's view, after the collapse of the Cold-War system, that political and economic liberalization, privatization and cuts in public expenditures were what was needed in former communist countries, exacerbated what was already a deteriorating economic situation in Yugoslavia. The deteriorating economic situation, already a breeding ground for authoritarian movements, was further worsened by the West's willingness to accept growing emphasis on national rights and exclusiveness, as long as it was accompanied by political democratization and liberalization. The diminishing authority of the central Yugoslav institutions further accelerated the authority of the nationally-exclusive republican governments, and left the individual ever more dependent on a national movement, in effect forcing a national (non-Yugoslav) choice. Woodward's approach thus stresses the elements of the situation common to all the republics (and in her view many elements common to other East European and former Soviet states and nationalist movements after the Cold War), downplaying specific Serb responsibility for the evolving situation and emphasizing the role of the West in contributing to the growing conflict.[29]

Woodward's approach is useful for suggesting the impact of the changing economic and political situation on the average citizen, the way in which increasing insecurity and powerlessness prepares citizens to respond to nationalist appeals. The breakdown of central Yugoslav institutions and their capacity to deal with economic and social problems can explain the increasing opportunities that politicians at the republic level found to mobilize the citizenry for their nationalist movements. But her approach leaves out the other half of the equation, the appearance of political leaders with the motivation, ideology and skills to build and institutionalize nationalist movements. An approach that stresses the income, unemployment and economic growth figures falls short of explaining the rhetoric of Milan Martic, a Serb police inspector in Knin, who wrote a letter to the Federal Interior Ministry in Belgrade to inform them that he and his officers would refuse to wear the new uniforms of the Croatian police, which he associated with Croatian atrocities. When the Croatian Interior Minister was sent to resolve the situation, the Minister argued that the question of the new national symbols on the uniforms was a matter of little importance. He reminded the Serbs that the Tudjman administration had, early on, increased the salaries of the police. Some officers were earning ten times what they had earned under communism. Martic said he was insulted by the Minister's words, which he saw as an attempt at bribery, an effort to persuade the police to sell their national dignity for higher salaries. 'Gentlemen', he told them,

> you have forgotten one fact. Yes, it is nice to live well, to have good pay, to have good clothes, a good car. However there is something which money cannot buy. What cannot be bought is our Serb dignity. We would rather go hungry, as long as we are together with our Serb people. We will eat potatoes and husks, but we will be on the side of our people. We will remain human.[30]

An approach that can capture the role people like Milan Martic play in the violence that developed in the former Yugoslavia must stress the role of ethnic feeling and the ability of political leaders to harness those sentiments for their purposes of promoting ethnic separatism. V.P. Gagnon, Jr believes that the situation that developed in the former Yugoslavia can best be explained as the deliberate act of nationalist leaders determined to save their own positions and defend their interests in the face of the challenges of reform. 'The Serbian leadership from 1987 onward actively created rather than responded to threats to Serbs by purposefully provoking and fostering the outbreak of conflict along ethnic lines, especially in regions of Yugoslavia with histories of good inter-ethnic relations'.[31]

Gagnon argues that threats to the status quo and the ruling conservative leadership, including the emergence of a political system where elections played a key role, the reforms of Prime Minister Markovic, and the growth of opposition forces in Serbia, led Milosevic to develop a purposeful and rational strategy of violent conflict along ethnic lines to counter threats to the structure of economic and political power as a result of the changes being advocated by reformists within the ruling Serbian party. Downplaying both the historical antagonism and conflict between ethnic groups and spontaneous tendencies to engage in ethnic conflict, Gagnon notes that the case for Milosevic's arguments about a security threat was destroyed by nationalistically-oriented elites in Serbia who denounced the war and claimed there was no need for it. Furthermore, in both Bosnia and Croatia, forces allied with Belgrade went to great lengths to destroy the long-standing harmony between Serbs and non-Serbs. Although the Croatian regime had resorted to nationalist rhetoric and actions worrisome to local Serbs, both sides were willing to negotiate over key issues until Belgrade began terrorizing moderate Serbs.

Dissenting Serbs have been silenced and even killed by the extremists in power, to create a domestic political situation where 'ethnicity is the only politically relevant identity'. Gagnon attributes the salience of racial animosity that leads to violence almost wholly to this kind of mobilization of ethnic sentiment, and the evidence indicates that ethnic hatreds are not the 'essential primary cause' of the conflict in the former Yugoslavia. He points out that Yugoslavia never experienced the kind of religious wars so much a part of the Western and Central Europe experience and that Serbs and Croats never fought before this century. He also bolsters his case for the extreme and violent nature of the Milosevic movement by noting that Milosevic's Socialist Party of Serbia (SPS) began an open alliance after the spring of 1991 with the neofascist Serbian Radical Party of Vojislav Seselj, and that until August 1991 when Croats went on the offensive, Serbian guerrillas and the Yugoslav army committed by far the most egregious human rights abuses.[32]

Yet another observer focuses on multiple causes of the conflict and stresses the role of 'deep interethnic "fears"', with each of the three ethnic groups fearing to some degree those outside their community. Lenard J. Cohen, drawing on the analyses of various scholars familiar with violence in the former Yugoslavia, argues that it is too simplistic to attribute the origins of the war to externally inspired aggression by one ethnic community, or to argue that historically Bosnia was a 'model of intergroup coexistence' until ethnic hatreds were stirred up by opportunistic or fanatical politicians or intellectuals. But he also rejects the notion that the violence in Yugoslavia stems from the 'spontaneous continuation' of the interethnic conflict of World War II, or that the area is constantly 'seething' with ethnic hatred.

Cohen suggests that in an environment where there is a complex pattern of ethnic relations and reciprocal fear, the potential for ethnically and religiously-based violence is greatest in periods of regime crisis and breakdown, an appropriate characterization of Yugoslavia in the late eighties and nineties. Here his analysis complements that of Woodward who describes the nature of that crisis. Because of the long history of resistance to conquering forces, an orientation toward rebellion rather than conformity is an important part of Yugoslav culture, especially those areas subject to Turkish rule. An individual may harbor ethnic or religious resentment for a lifetime with no real opportunity to express it. When that opportunity comes along, the expression may take an extreme form that seems completely contradictory to the orderly and staid life the individual previously lived.[33]

The purpose here is not to resolve the differences among specialists on the causes and origins of the war, but rather to suggest that the differences in perspective are important and they are bound to affect the way one evaluates policies of outside powers toward the war. The interpretation the US and Europe put on the motivations, objectives and behavior of the various actors in the war were important in determining their actions. Beneath most of the basic policy disagreement on the war, between the US and many European views was a different interpretation of the causes of the war and who was responsible for it. Such assumptions color the approach one takes to the war and the judgement made on the actions of the participants. Woodward's approach, which attributes the war to the breakdown of the Yugoslav system and de-emphasizes the role of any particular national group tends to be more congruent with a British or French policy prescription for the war which treats all warring parties more or less impartially and believes an even-handed approach is most likely to achieve a settlement. Gagnon's assumptions may be more compatible with the American approach which blames the Serbs for the onset of the war and believes that the conflict can best be ended by putting pressure on them.

A lively debate can also be generated over the constitutional violations in the break-up of Yugoslavia and who was most responsible for departures from constitutionality. An interesting controversy from the standpoint of constitutional law, such a discussion is of limited use in analyzing the issues with which this book is concerned. Constitutions are primarily of use when a polity is functioning in a democratic manner. When a country gets to the point at which a break-up brought on by an authoritarian movement is imminent, no matter how admirable the constitution, it is not likely to be of much use in holding the country together. In Yugoslavia, the Serb demand for a centralized federation that accommodated their demands met resistance from Slovenian and Croats' preferences for a loose confederation or less, with the Bosnians caught in between the two sides. In pursuit of these goals, both sides violated the constitution, the Slovenes in both the preparation and the execution of their independence, the Federal (Serbian) authorities by their illegitimate use of force. Nonetheless, the 'Yugoslav constitution was sufficiently imprecise to allow both sides to read and interpret it in the way that suited them best'. And as Crnobrnja points out, the objective should have been to settle the conflict, not to win debating points. While there may have been a constitutionally valid justification for the use of force when Slovenia left Yugoslavia, the use of force further embittered the parties in the conflict.[34]

One may ask why it was legitimate to recognize the independence of the Yugoslav republics, as the US did in 1992, but at the same time to insist on the territorial and political integrity of the Bosnian state, as the US has occasionally done. One answer is that, because of Serbian action and obstructionism, Yugoslavia could only have been preserved if the non-Serb republics were willing to accept a substantial amount of non-democratic and Serb-dominated rule.[35] In Bosnia, on the other hand, there was a substantial government commitment to universal democracy and the equality of all citizens regardless of ethnic origin. It was precisely this structure that the Serbs were unwilling to accept. As democratic reforms took hold in the Yugoslav secessionist states, the Serbian formula for governing therefore became increasingly unacceptable to the other republics. But Serb nationalism and suspicion, both fueled by Milosevic's movement, ensured that Serbs, both in Serbia and elsewhere, would find it impossible to accept a governing framework which cast them as a protected minority.[36] The institutions and atmosphere in Bosnia were conducive to ethnic coexistence and tolerance prior to the war. As the government became increasingly embattled and population from rural areas replaced much of the Sarajevo population which had fled the war, government policy became more oriented toward preservation of a Muslim state and less concerned with preserving a multi-ethnic society. The attempt to preserve Bosnia as a multi-ethnic state forced upon it a conflict so difficult to pursue that the leadership's primary objective became survival as a Muslim state.[37]

Furthermore, the willingness of the Serbs to use force to achieve their aims, both to prevent Slovenian secession *and* to abet separation of the Serbian communities from both Croatia and Bosnia indicates the weakness of the Serbian case. It suggests that Serbian actions were driven not by any principle upon which the ethnic problems of minorities in Yugoslavia might be solved, but rather by the unilateral pursuit of immediate Serb goals. This contrasts markedly with Izetbegovic's willingness to talk and his reluctance to arm for the conflict, and they anticipated the outbreak of war much more clearly than he did. Finally, Serbian culpability for their willingness to use force was further exacerbated by the large responsibility they must bear for the perpetuation of atrocities in Bosnia.

4 The Nature of the War

STRATEGIC OBJECTIVES

The dynamics of the war in Bosnia can be understood by examining the general objectives of the three warring parties, how they attempted to accomplish them, and the strategic interaction between them during the war. The Bosnian Serb effort is most important, since the Serbs were the initiators of military actions and had by far the largest arsenal of artillery, planes, tanks, and other heavy equipment, supplied primarily by the part of the JNA left in Bosnia after independence was declared, and by the men and materials that continued to come across the border with Serbia. The Bosnian war was by far the largest effort in which the JNA engaged during the period of Yugoslavia's disintegration, after a brief foray into Slovenia, and a second larger war in Croatia. In Croatia, as in Bosnia, the war was conducted both by the JNA and by irregular paramilitary recruited from the local population. Fighting raged throughout Croatia from the northern areas to the Adriatic port of Dubrovnik.

Many observers viewed the Serbs, once it was clear that Yugoslavia would not remain intact, as motivated by the creation of a Greater Serbia which would encompass in one contiguous area, all those areas containing sizeable numbers of Serbs. This was a view widely held in the US, but one on which Yugoslav specialists did not agree. There was important involvement by Belgrade in the wars in both Croatia and Bosnia, and Belgrade was an important source of aid in both cases. Belgrade's control of the situation in Bosnia, however, was also far from complete and local leaders, specifically Karadzic and Mladic often defied Milosevic, especially in the later stages of the war. Belgrade's most important role may have been in encouraging the kind of ethnic extremism that started the war, and it created a momentum that Milosevic later found hard to shut off.

Primary Serb objectives in Bosnia included Sarajevo, of enormous symbolic value and viewed by the Serbs as the legitimate capital of the Serbian Republic of Bosnia. They hoped to divide the city and place their capital in the Serb-held city. The long siege of Sarajevo thus had symbolic significance as well as the military objective of breaking the hold of the government troops on the city. The eastern lands of Bosnia–Herzogovina, just across the Bosnian border were also an early priority of the Serbs. Being contiguous to Serbia itself, they were easier to defend logistically and presented an ideal means of extending Serb influence into an area that could be unified with Serbia. The Serbs spent much effort expanding to the north the belt of Serb controlled territory contiguous to Montenegro. In August of 1994, the Bosnian Serb parliament proclaimed that for the first time in 500 years, Serbs west of the Drina River were free.[1] The problem with these areas of course, was that while there were communes where the Serbs had absolute majorities, they also contained large numbers of Muslims, especially in the cities such as Tuzla, Srebrenica, Gorazde and others. But by the time of the cease-fire in the fall of 1995, the Serbs controlled a wide belt in eastern Bosnia all along the border with Serbia. A good share of the ethnic cleansing was concentrated here and in northern Bosnia, but even though several 'safe area' cities fell to the Serbs, pockets of Muslim control such as Gorazda continued to exist.

The Bosnian Serbs also concentrated on expanding the areas under their control in north and northwest Bosnia. Bihac is strategically important for constructing a Greater Serbia, since a vital but long unusable rail line connecting Knin to Banja Luka and Belgrade runs through there.[2] While they made considerable progress in all areas in 1992 and 1993, the north and northwest sections were considerably diminished by the fall of 1995 after a Bosnian offensive coinciding with the NATO bombing. Of primary importance to the Bosnian Serbs, especially in the later peace plans, was maintaining a passage that allowed travel between Serbia and the eastern area of Bosnia and the northwest section through an area retained in the Dayton Agreement and known as the Posavina Corridor.

In the early stages of the war, the Vance–Owen peace plan determined strategy to a degree, as the maps of the plan served as blueprints for expansion in a way that would maximize a protagonist's negotiating advantage.[3] As the Bosnian forces became stronger and more effective in 1993, the Serbs were forced to use their resources to consolidate and hold their gains, as they did through much of 1994. An ultimatum by the allies temporarily ended the siege of Sarajevo in February, and the Serbs spent much of 1994 on the defensive since the government had by now become much more capable on the battlefield as compared to the first eighteen months of the war. This fact, combined with the increasing recklessness of the Serbs in overrunning safe areas and confronting the UN/NATO troops, would lead to disaster for the Serbs, who were first subjected to two small NATO bombing raids and then to a massive series of 800 allied bombing sorties in the late summer of 1995. Following the previous rout of the Croatian Serbs, the Bosnian Serbs finally agreed to a settlement proposed by the outside powers, resulting in the Dayton Agreement.

After the breakdown of the Croat–Muslim alliance in the fall of 1992, and with even greater intensity after spring 1993, the fighting in Bosnia assumed a complicated three-way pattern compared by one analyst to the confusing intermittent warfare and shifting alliances of the city states of Renaissance Italy, where each side continued to 'skirmish wherever and whenever it seemed profitable, and cooperated with whomever seemed at any time and place the appropriate ally'.[4] The Bosnian Croats, strongly supported by Tudjman, sometimes directly with Croatian troops, engaged in a serious effort to carve out a separate Bosnian Croat state. Croatian objectives included retaining arms factories in central Bosnia, contested by the Muslims, securing their position around Mostar, which endured a long and devastating siege, and other towns in the Herzegovina (southern Bosnia–Herzegovina) region, and ensuring that the Serbs did not resume shelling of the Dalmatian coast. Retention of Kupres in central Bosnia allowed control of the highway to the important Croatian seaport of Split.[5] Much of the bloodiest fighting took place between Muslims and Croats in western Herzegovina after the spring of 1993, and some of the worst war crimes committed in the whole of the former Yugoslavia were committed by Croats. The extent of Croat aggression, received inadequate attention.[6] Even so, the military showing of the Bosnian Croat forces was not impressive.[7] An agreement signed in Washington in March 1994 put an end to the worst of the Croat–Muslim fighting and led to more cooperation against the Serbs. Increased Serb shelling of cities and their confrontation with the allies corresponded with preparations by Tudjman to test the mettle of his rebuilt military, in a test offensive in West Slavonia. This successful offensive showed an army better trained and with more equipment, a weak Serb response, and a benign international reaction.[8] A military offensive from Zagreb at five different points in the Krajina in the summer of 1995 followed and resulted in the recovery of all of the Serb held territories within Croatian boundaries (except for East Slavonia) within a week. Widespread ethnic cleansing led to a massive exodus of 150 000 Serbian refugees, and Croat atrocities including summary execution, shelling of refugees and systematic torching of homes and villages.[9] But the offensive also weakened the Serbian position in Bosnia, not least because it suggested the vulnerabilities of the once invincible Serbs.

Bosnian government objectives, at least through 1993, were primarily defensive. Unprepared for war, the Bosnians were the victims of initial successes by the Serbs that left them defeated and demoralized. Possessing many more men than either the Bosnian Serbs or the Bosnian Croats, the government suffered from a virtual absence of heavy arms and equipment, and lack of training and organization. When war did come, a spontaneous 'ragtag force' made up mostly of gangsters and Muslim townspeople rose up to defend the city. While the defense of Sarajevo was an inspiring story, the irregular nature of the fighting force meant that ideals, corruption and profiteering became intertwined. It was only when Haris Silajdzic became premier in late fall of 1993 that the hold of the gangster guerillas over Sarajevo was broken.[10] The Bosnian Muslim leadership also entertained hopes of Western intervention on their behalf long after more cynical observers had reached more realistic conclusions. The government was reduced to possession of a few cities and small areas of land holding them together, and by August of 1993 some were predicting that the Serbs were on the edge of a complete victory.[11]

But as significant number of arms began to reach the Muslims, they sharpened their organization and discipline, eliminated renegade commanders, and employed more appropriate tactics, and their fortunes began to improve. By the late 1993 they were challenging the Croats in central Bosnia, an area important for its arms factories and industrial production,[12] and in August 1994 the Bosnians overran Bihac. But a later counter-attack by the rebel Abdic Muslim forces, allied with both Bosnian and Krajina Serbs, soon reversed the gains. The offensive, although short-lived, was sufficiently impressive that the Croatian government threatened to intervene. The Washington Agreement between the Croats and the Bosnian government signed in March 1994, had played a key role in relieving the Bosnians of the need to concentrate resources on fighting the Bosnian Croats as they had been forced to for the previous year. In September the government troops around Sarajevo had become sufficiently aggressive that UNPROFOR threatened air strikes against them if they continued to violate the cease-fire, and by early November they were showing the first major gains since the war started in April 1992.[13] In mid-1995, as the West concentrated on the threatened safe areas of Srebrenica, Zepa and Gorazde, the renegade Muslim Abdic launched an attack on Bihac. This time, Croatian government troops came in to repulse him.[14] Still, it was observed that in spite of the changes, the overall military balance was relatively unchanged, and no military victory could have been reached by any party without substantial outside assistance.[15] Such an awareness no doubt contributed to the government's acceptance of the Dayton settlement, in spite of the major Bosnian gains in the northwest, once it was made clear that the West expected the Muslims to sign.

EXTREME NATIONALIST MOVEMENTS AND THE BOSNIAN WAY OF WAR

The ethnic cleansing, atrocities, and wanton destruction that took place in the former Yugoslavia is best understood in the context of group behavior and institutions that accompany the development of extreme nationalist movements, and should not be viewed as just the work of autonomous individuals. Here we can make only brief suggestions of the kind of dynamics that may have been at work to produce the war crimes and atrocities that people assumed could no longer occur in Europe. Various explanations of the outburst of ethnic violence can be given. As suggested in the previous chapter, one explanation is that these feelings typically surface in time of regime and institutional breakdown. Another is that political leadership is responsible for fanning the flames of hatred and divisiveness which eventually leads to violence.

Whatever the origins of ethnic movements, once they are established a group dynamic takes over which encourages a kind of violence which is hard to imagine in normal times. When a threat, unjust treatment, or violation of one's rights is perceived, opinion crystallizes, slogans are formulated and measures are organized to deal with the perception. Whether the threat is real or imagined is irrelevant, since perceptions drive the image of an enemy who is portrayed, in the most extreme movements, as the incarnation of evil. But the 'threatened' individual, movement or nation-state assumes a posture of self-righteousness. The assumptions behind this self-image, which serves the purpose of transcending the threat by elevating the self to a position of moral superiority, tend to 'produce grandiose feelings of power, invulnerability, and strength vis a vis the enemy'. Further, the individual may lose the distinction between himself and the group, and become so dependent on the group that there is a loss of individuality and the individual becomes dependent on others for a definition of who he is and what to think. A final step, depersonalization of the enemy (as the incarnation of evil), makes it possible to carry out atrocities that could not previously have been contemplated.[16] These kinds of dynamics facilitate (1) the definition of the enemy by drawing a line between the in-group (your group) and the out-group (the enemy), (2) stereotyping the two groups, which exaggerates the power and potential of the in-group while deprecating those of the out-group, and (3) depersonalizing the enemy which breaks down the usual human defenses against barbarous behavior and legitimizes it by caricaturing the enemy.

While manifestations of this kind of behavior and characteristics could be observed of many groups in the former Yugoslavia, they were most strongly evident among the Serbs. Even those observers opposed to stigmatizing the Serbs as aggressors acknowledge a high degree of paranoia that should be taken into account in formulating the peace settlement.[17] Milosevic's movement developed in an authoritarian system and with authoritarian methods that allowed the image of the enemy to be created. There has been much comment on the lack of choice for the viewing public and the paucity of broadcasts giving an alternative view of the war in the Serbian media. The Serbs (Belgrade and Pale), with the most authoritarian systems and leadership, have been responsible for the most aggressive foreign policy and the greatest number of atrocities and crimes against civilians in the former Yugoslavia. The Bosnians, the most democratic of the warring parties, have had the most restrained foreign policy and the smallest number of casualties, while the Croats fall in the middle on all counts. While all parties have committed atrocities, the Bosnian government has usually repudiated these kinds of actions, while they were an integral part of the Serbian way of war, and were almost certainly sanctioned at the highest levels.[18] 'Ethnic cleansing' is a practice that can only flourish in an authoritarian environment, and most intensely in a proto-fascist setting.[19]

Shelling of cities

The Serbian reliance on the heavy use of artillery emerged very early as a fighting strategy. Disdaining the heavy casualties that direct assaults and close-in fighting would bring, the Serbian method of taking a city has been to lay siege to it and continue pounding it with artillery until it is destroyed, the population has fled, or both. This method of war, summarized by one observer as 'never sending a man where a bullet can go first', is combined with a predilection for targeting hospitals, water treatment plants and refugee centers, and has the effect of producing the maximum amount of terror in the population.[20] When necessary, the Serbs have displayed infinite patience in using this method: witness the siege of Sarajevo which began in the spring of 1992 and continued until late summer 1995 (with less intensity and one long lull after a NATO ultimatum). A more extreme example of destruction was the leveling of Vukovar, a Croatian town of 46 000. Vukovar in 1991 was a town of mixed ethnic population – 43.7 per cent Croat, 37.4 per cent Serb, and 7.3 per cent Yugoslav, and a few other nationalities. JNA and Serbian militia forces laid siege to Vukovar and shelled the city incesantly for three months. Over 2300 people were killed and thousands wounded in this assault alone. Both sides were alleged to have committed atrocities against their civilian and military rivals. Vukovar was completely destroyed and emptied of inhabitants. It was reported that not a building was left habitable.

Moreover, hundreds of civilians were executed as they emerged from the basements of houses that were under assault. For some, such as Vuk Draskovic, a Serbian opposition leader, this episode stands as a 'monument to insanity', but to Serbian ultranationalists the 'liberation' of Vukovar is a landmark in the struggle for Serbian unity. Other cities were victims of the vicious artillery assaults, including the historic Croatian city of Dubrovnik on the Dalmatian coast, and various 'safe areas' in Bosnia. Such indiscriminate shelling and firing on populations centers continued throughout the war.[21]

Aside from the obvious advantage of minimizing Serb casualties, this method of taking the offensive toward population centers is explained by the Serb objectives and methods of ethnic cleansing, to drive the non-Serb population from the area so that there is left only the Serbian ethnic group. Laying siege to cities not only destroys any potential military opposition, but also forces the population to evacuate, most likely into non-Serb-held areas. I was once asked what the military objective was in the bombardment of Sarajevo. To someone viewing the conflict through the lens of a conventional war, this is a sensible question. But through Serbian eyes, bombarding the non-Serb areas of Sarajevo serves not only a military objective, but if successful, the objective of the whole conflict, to drive the enemy population out so that the city will belong only to the Serbs. This method quite naturally produced a very high rate of civilian casualties, not to mention refugees. Cyrus Shahkalili, the UN Director of the Office of the UN High Commissioner for Refugees, reports that what characterizes this conflict is the willingness of armies to attack civilians as the main form of warfare. He went on to say that he had never seen anything like it, not even in Afghanistan or the attacks on the Kurds in Iraq.[22] Reliable figures for casualties of the conflict in Bosnia ranged from 90 000 to 145 000. Population relocation was being discussed in the Yugoslav media even before the wars began, and even then population movements had begun. Massive population transfers swelled as fighting intensified among the groups. Within a month of the Bosnian declaration of independence on 3 March 1992, 420 000 had fled Bosnia or were forced from their homes. According to the UN High Commissioner for Refugees, by the end of July the number of displaced persons was 2.5 million.[23]

The refugees included many Serbs, especially from Croatia, and the movement of people on all sides was intensified by the fears of ethnic retaliation. Serbian military tactics were very important in contributing to these numbers.

This particular strategy, however, was hard on civilians for another reason. Because of the lack of foodstuffs, medicine, fuel for heating and other necessities of life which could not be obtained once access to the encircled population was cut off, widespread suffering and death occurred. Thus the necessity for the UN supply convoys, the airlifts of supplies into beleaguered cities, and the airdrops over Bosnia.

Rape and atrocities

The rapes and atrocities committed by the Serbian military and paramilitary groups also had a specific political purpose. Rape, atrocities and torture were viewed as a means of driving the non-Serb population away from the areas Serbs claimed as their own. Rape is a brutal and humiliating experience, especially in a Muslim culture. If the victim became pregnant, she was forced to carry the child of the person assaulting her. EC investigators concluded that in 1992 at least 20 000 women and girls, some as young as 10 years old, had been raped by Bosnian Serb soldiers as part of a deliberate effort to terrorize people, drive them from their homes, and shatter communities in Bosnia. Often accounts indicate women were raped in front of their families, they were raped repeatedly and over long periods of time, and the rape and abuse often resulted in death. For the Serb perpetrator, it was often a means of extending his racial 'superiority' through progeny.[24] Threats of torture, death and imprisonment were also systematically used as a means of getting the non-Serb populations to move from the areas the Serbs were liberating.

The same catalogue of torture and atrocity with which the Nazis made us familiar is in evidence here. Included are the transport of victims by boxcars to camps and other holding locations, arbitrary killing and torture by every conceivable method, the apparent relish with which the perpetrators carry out their 'work', and the seeming complete lack of normal humanitarian impulses in most of the perpetrators. The nature of this behavior can best be absorbed by quoting reports on the atrocities. These accounts come from a series of eight State Department reports given to the United Nations. The incidents are arbitrarily selected to give an overview of the kinds of things reported, but inasmuch as these things can be judged, they are typical of the severity and type of the atrocities reported in other incidents.[25]

May 1992: An American citizen, in the custody of Serbian forces after serving in the Croatian army, said that he saw Serbian soldiers torture a Croatian soldier to death in a camp near Bileca, Bosnia. He saw the same soldiers torture another group of Croatian prisoners. He saw one die being [sic] carried away (Department of State, cited in first report, *DSD*, 28 September 1992, p. 733).

21 August 1992: More than 200 men and boys were massacred by Bosnian Serb police on a narrow mountain track at a place known as Varjanta, near the confluence of the Ugar and Ilomska rivers about 15 miles north of Travnik, according to at least three reputed survivors. Semire, a 24-year-old man, told reporters that he was one of the last off the bus:

I saw three Serb policemen standing there, and in front of them were big pools of blood. I decided at that moment to jump. I rolled a long way down, until I was caught on a tree. I heard shooting up above for about an hour after that. Bodies were tumbling past me. There were a lot of them.

'Cerni', a 31-year-old Muslim, described how the prisoners were taken off the buses:

I jumped as soon as they started. I protected my head and arms and tumbled down. When I stopped, the other bodies were falling on me. The blood was all over. The other people ... were all killed at this place.

Semir, who lost a brother and a 16-year-old nephew during this incident, said he had recognized several killers because they were from his home village, Corakovo. He recognized two brothers in particular – naming them as among those who had rounded up this group of Muslims in Corakovo. A third

witness threw himself over the edge of the cliff as his guard
turned to speak to another soldier. He had seen a Serbian
soldier put a pistol in the mouths of several men and fire.
(Department of State; The *Washington Post*; The *New York
Times*; Reuters, cited in second report, *DSD*, 2 November 1992,
p. 802.)

March 1992: A 17-year-old Bosnian Muslim girl gave details of
her detention with about 60 women and girls in a forest motel,
where the prisoners were raped over a period of 4 months.
Serbian forces on 3 March 1992 captured the witness's town in
the vicinity of Teslic. She said the soldiers talked with a strong
Serbian dialect, including colloquialisms. Some had the White
Eagle insignia on their uniforms. Some of the Serbian forces
who burned and looted the houses in the town were drunk.
One of the drunk soldiers hit the witness's mother, calling out
that Muslims would regret the day they were born. On depart-
ing the town, the soldiers fought over the bottles of wine that
had been left behind in the central marketplace.

The prisoners were taken to a motel complex of small
cabins located in the forest about five hours away on foot from
their hometown. Some of the cabins were used as sentry
boxes. The whole motel complex perimeter was fenced off
with barbed wire. Hundreds of old men, women, and children
were prisoners at the motel complex.

Upon arrival, the witness was separated from her mother
and sister. She never saw them again. She said the soliders
'raped us every night'. Most nights 20 soldiers came to the
motel. The female prisoners were forced to strip, then to cook
for the soldiers and serve them. Each girl or young woman was
raped by several soldiers, with several victims in one room at a
time. The witness experienced so many rapes that she could
not give an estimate of the number. One night, the Serb
brother of one of the girls helped twelve girls, including the
witness, escape the motel complex. Two of the escapees were
later found and returned to the prison. The ten others spent
several days hiding in improvised underground shelters in the
forest. The witness identified the most ruthless of the rapists, a
man who raped 10-year-old girls 'as a delicacy'. She saw many
of the younger females die from the rapes. (Department of
State, cited in the sixth report, *DSD*, 12 April 1993, p. 248.)

24 September 1992: Muslims from Kamenica reportedly killed more than 60 Serb civilians and soldiers in Serbian villages near Milici on September 24–6 (Department of State).

An American freelance writer reported that he saw the bodies of mutilated and tortured Serbs from the villages of Rogosija and Nedeljiste at the St Paul and Peter Serbian Orthodox Church in Vlasenica after the lids on about ten of the coffins were removed by soldiers for viewing. Some bodies were burned to a charcoal, others had fingers cut off on their right hand, which the Orthodox use to bless themselves, some were circumcised as a final affront (Serbian Orthodox males in Yugoslavia are not circumcised, whereas Muslims are), some had their eyes gouged out, gaping knife wounds everywhere, and heads were battered beyond recognition, arms and legs broken and severed. (Serbian American Media Center, Chicago, cited in the third report, *DSD*, 16 November 1992, p. 825.)

May–September 1992: A 53-year-old Bosnian Muslim described the ethnic cleansing of his district, Obrevena. The witness said the Rudo district (opcina) originally had a 28 per cent Muslim population and two mosques. In April 1991, the Serbian Democratic Party (SDS) candidate, a Serbian language teacher, was elected president of Rudo. Ethnic relations were fine until the beginning of May 1992, when the police chief fired Muslim policemen and the district government called up the local reserves, excluding Muslim reservists.

In May 1992, the witness saw Serbian soldiers burn the Muslim village of Polmilje and, in July, he witnessed the burning of the Muslim village of Bisevic. Also in July, the police started arresting Muslim men and interning them in a military warehouse in Rudo and at the Gojava military installation. Some were transferred to KP Dom, a criminal rehabilitation center.

On 2 August 1992, local Serb soldiers came to Obrevena. The witness recognized many of the Serbs who were dressed in camouflage uniforms with Serbian flag and SDS insignias, wearing headbands, and heavily armed. The soldiers collected nine Muslim men from the village and marched them two kilometers to a field by the Sokol Pasa mosque in Sokolovic. After the men waited there for two hours, the soldiers' leader told the men, 'If you can run, then run', and released them.

The men fled toward Prijob, the closest town across the Serbian border, but were not allowed to cross the bridge over the border. They then forded the river and traveled by foot for two months through the woods until they arrived in Novi Pazar, the capital of the Muslim-controlled Sandzak area of Serbia. (Department of State, cited in the seventh report, *DSD*, 19 April 1993, p. 266.)

Concentration camps

Concentration camps were widely used in Yugoslavia, predominantly but not exclusively by the Serbs. Again, they are all too reminiscent of the Nazi camps, but apparently lacking the means for systematic extermination. They also seem to have been rather temporary. Omarska camp, in northern Bosnia, for instance, was closed down and its inmates moved elsewhere. Since the international community quickly became aware of the presence of camps, the Serbs were somewhat sensitive to the outside world's reaction to the detention of individuals, often under inhumane conditions, and with rape, torture and arbitrary killing the common fate of the victims. There is plenty of evidence that the camps were often staffed by brutal personalities who enthusiastically used harsh methods of suppression and liquidation. The camps also were part of the strategy of ethnic cleansing. Men were held in the camps, and women were presented with an ultimatum: the men will be released from the camps if the women flee the area. Some 5000 Muslim families 'expressed' a desire to flee, according to the Bosnian Serbs.[26] Although some of the 'hawks' on Bosnia, such as Jeanne Kirkpatrick, recommended that the West demand that the camps be emptied, backed up by a threat to empty them by force if necessary, the UN troops never had the backing or the mandate to undertake those kinds of actions. As recently as early 1994, the US government estimated that as many as 70 000 prisoners were being held in 135 camps in Serbia proper.[27] Occasionally the Bosnian Serbs deported inmates by the trainload. According to the UN, these were not isolated incidents. The victims were either forced to board the trains or had no choice since living conditions in their home area had become intolerable.[28]

Destruction of homes and culture

Another characteristic of Serbian warfare was the destruction of the enemy's living quarters, property, and religious and historical buildings and monuments. These policies also were aimed at making an area uninhabitable, or at least less attractive, and forcing or encouraging the population to flee the area. Gutman speaks of an 'assault against the Muslim religious and cultural tradition'. Clergymen are dispersed, imprisoned or killed. Many clergy were forced to violate cultural and religious norms in front of their communities. National libraries and religious seminaries have been destroyed. By September 1992, it is suggested, over half of the mosques, historical monuments and libraries in Bosnia had been destroyed. One estimate was that by mid-June 1993, 800 mosques had been destroyed, and in most instances the sites leveled and the rubble removed. Many saw this as a systematic attempt to eliminate a six-century-old religious and cultural heritage. The attacks on historical cities and monuments were widely reported, while numerous ancient and magnificent mosques have been destroyed specifically because of their cultural significance. The well-known stone bridge in Mostar, however, was destroyed by the Croatians rather than the Serbs.[29]

But the destruction was aimed as well at the habitat of ordinary people. In Banja Luka, in north central Bosnia, not even in a war zone, tens of thousands of people were driven from their homes in a 'massive wave of "ethnic cleansing"', creating a landscape of exploded Muslim and Croat houses abutting the trimmed hedges of untouched Serb homes'. Of a prewar population of approximately 400 000 Muslims and 100 000 Croats, fewer than 50 000 Muslims and 20 000 Croats remained. The reason for the wholesale destruction was given by the vice president of Banja Luka municipality in an interview with a Serb reporter. Mosques and [Catholic] churches had been destroyed, he said, because that is the only way to 'teach minorities to respect Serb law'. In nearby Baljvine, it was reported that one mosque remained of the 202 in the region before the war began in 1992, including sixteenth and seventeenth century masterpieces. More than half of the Roman Catholic churches were reported destroyed and the rest damaged.[30]

Part III

US Interests in and Perceptions of Yugoslavia

Introduction

The national interest is a subjective concept that is difficult to define and often a matter of controversy. What are perceived to be national interests vary according to the state of the international system, domestic affairs and the public mood, and the definition of the national interest given by a national leadership. The sudden changes in the international system following the end of the Cold War deprived the US leadership and the public of the guidelines and landmarks they were accustomed to using to formulate policy. Without a second superpower, against which interests had to be defended, it became difficult to know what our interests were and which ones were worth defending militarily. Moreover, the public was weary of foreign-policy burdens and was looking inward, the result of more than four decades of Cold-War tensions and the consequent neglect of domestic issues. The sense of urgency that had characterized foreign policy during the Cold War was lost.

US national interests in Yugoslavia at the time of the break-up can best be understood by distinguishing between security interests and humanitarian interests. Security interests, thought by realists to be the only justification for intervening militarily in a conflict, are for most people the most important aspect of foreign policy. Security interests are seen as the first priority in formulating a foreign policy, and justify the highest foreign-policy costs. Pursuit of interests perceived as solely humanitarian is often considered a luxury of which a nation can avail itself only if security concerns are satisfied and there are no other pressing demands on monetary or political resources. The end of the Cold War changes the context in which non-security interests are considered, but does not necessarily make it easier to determine the priority which they should be given. Although post-Cold-War security interests are generally less urgent and allow more leeway for consideration of humanitarian policies in foreign policy, the diminished importance of foreign policy in general affects the priority given to international humanitarian issues in the political agenda of the nation.

Having distinguished between security interests and humanitarian interests, however, it is still easy to be sympathetic to Stanley Hoffmann's view that 'the distinction between interests and values is largely fallacious'. Noting the traditional distinction between what were called possession goals and what are termed milieu goals, he points out that national security deals mostly with the former. Foreign policy, however, often is concerned with more indirect concerns, such as shaping an international environment that will provide a modicum of order and where a nation's citizens will feel both secure from attack and 'morally at home'. To provide such an environment, a great power is concerned with nurturing a world order that goes beyond strict national security concerns, and its definition of order is therefore 'shaped by values'. To the extent this is true, it becomes harder to distinguish between 'security interests' and 'humanitarian interests' or values.[1]

I will continue to distinguish between security interests and humanitarian interests in this book because I believe it is a useful device for understanding the situation in the former Yugoslavia and US interests there, but the reader should be aware that terminology may sometimes imply more separation between the two concepts than is warranted. This is especially the case in the former Yugoslavia, since most commentators believed that both security and humanitarian interests existed there, but they disagreed on whether there was a sufficient interest of either kind to warrant the likely costs of engaging there. But if one spends any substantial amount of time analyzing those interests, it becomes clear it is very often difficult to cleanly separate the two categories.[2] Perhaps the best example is the question of intervening to prevent atrocities. Commentators agreed we had a humanitarian interest in minimizing atrocities; some believed we also had a security interest preventing the commission of atrocities which would encourage such behavior elsewhere and could seriously threaten world order. As Margaret Thatcher pointed out, preventing the creation of large numbers of refugees can be seen as having both a humanitarian and a security dimension, since refugees may affect adversely the countries that accept them, and may constitute a group that will later disrupt the status quo in order to gain an acceptable status.

It is clear that humanitarian interests are sometimes given priority even when they conflict with security interests.[3] In the case of Bosnia, however, where the potential costs of pursuing humanitarian interests were considered to be high, two administrations declined opportunities to intervene, even though security interests could also have been served by intervention. Intervention was rejected on the assumption either that the price was too high, or alternatively that, Vietnam style, the result would have been deleterious to security interests as the US became stuck to the Bosnian 'tar baby'.

5 Security Interests and Other Interests

SECURITY INTERESTS

As the crisis developed in Yugoslavia, few people believed that vital US security interests justifying substantial sacrifice or cost existed there. There was considerable sentiment that the war was undesirable from an American perspective, and that the US might be justified in some low-cost intervention in order to protect US interests. But few were willing to argue for more. Only a small minority of foreign-policy specialists advocated putting troops into the Yugoslav theatre.[1] A somewhat larger group advocated limited and less-costly alternatives such as air strikes, lifting of the arms embargo against Bosnia, or a more assertive UN presence. All of these options were thought (or at least hoped) to be low risk/low cost policies appropriate to the limited security stakes, or the humanitarian goals.

A traditional concern of US foreign policy has been to avoid single-power domination of a region by a hostile power. Both world wars were fought in Europe, among other reasons, to prevent German domination of the continent. The Cold War and the United States' forty-plus-year standoff with the Soviet Union were based on the same concerns. In Asia, the US objective has been to prevent the domination of East Asia by Japan, and after the war, by China. Similarly, the US has attempted to ensure that the Middle East is not dominated by a hostile power, a goal that involved a continuous duel between our proxy states and those of the Soviet Union during the Cold War.[2]

Yugoslavia was a small and relatively weak country, however, and its importance in the European power equation stemmed solely from the intense competition for allies and proxy states between the superpowers during the Cold War. Once the superpower rivalry ended, Yugoslavia's international significance diminished considerably, and the successor states are even less significant militarily. Serbia, the most powerful, is certainly in no position to dominate Europe, or even the Balkans. A small country with a population of less than ten million, even including all the Serbs scattered throughout the former Yugoslavia, it has very limited military capabilities. While the Serbs have managed, until the summer of 1995, to run fairly successful and strategically coordinated military campaigns, the autonomy and independence of some of the military units, and the undisciplined, bloodthirsty, and bullying behavior of troops had led some to suggest that in close-in, difficult and trying fighting conditions the Serbian war machine might turn out to be much less invincible than it had appeared to some. This verdict seemed to be validated in the highly successful Croatian offensive against the Croatian and Bosnian Serbs in the summer of 1995. 'Barely viable states of little consequence,' was one description of the military importance of the states hatched from the once intact Yugoslavia.[3] Ironically, a continued Russian interest in its historical and Christian Orthodox Serbian ally served to discourage Western action in the Yugoslav conflict. During the Cold War, direct Soviet involvement would have increased Western interest in the fate of Yugoslavia. But in a post-Cold-War world when the West is trying to work out a cooperative relationship with the Russians and to encourage that country's experiment in democratic government, it prefers not to confront the Russians by escalating military involvement to stop the Serbs.

It is easy to see why the United States and Western Europe have not been fast to suggest quick and massive involvement to settle the conflict in the Balkans. In line with historical judgements, the Balkans, with its weak and underdeveloped countries, has been rated a backwater rather than the mainstream of European politics.[4] Events there were historically judged not significant enough to merit a major involvement, but too important to be ignored completely. This is precisely the approach that led to the half-hearted Western involvement. The West in effect ignored the defense of its modest security interests, but the US was ultimately persuaded to make the costlier commitment of troops when the Bosnia problem would not go away.

One of the concerns that continued to trouble the West was the possibility of the war in Bosnia spreading to the rest of the Balkans. The potential involvement of other former Yugoslavian republics seemed significant in the early phases of the Bosnian War. Kosovo, with its large Albanian population, could explode in spite of Serbian attempts to maintain tight control. Newly independent Macedonia, caught between Serbia and a hostile Greece with Serbian sympathies, might well be invaded by either of these neighboring powers. In those circumstances, involvement by Bulgaria, which has a long-standing interest in Macedonia's fate, could not be ruled out. These concerns led to the stationing of a UN peacekeeping force and first 300, then 500 US troops in Macedonia – an attempt to ward off such a possibility. Within the former Yugoslavia, once the center of the war shifted to Bosnia, clashes between Croatia and Serbia tended to take place in Bosnia. But the right conditions could lead to a resurgence of conflict in Croatia. Mistreatment of a significant Hungarian minority in Vojvodina could draw Hungary into the conflict.

But the net effect of the fears of a wider war and its impact on the Balkans may have been to decrease the likelihood of greater involvement on the part of the West. While some argued that the prospect of expansion should drive intervention to stop the conflict, no large power had been prepared to send in the requisite number of troops to do the job. On the other hand, prescriptions for less drastic measures such as air strikes and a lifting of the arms embargo were ruled out by the Europeans, in part because they feared that the effect would be to provoke precisely what it was intended to avoid: a widening of the war.

Another concern has been the effect of a weak Western response in Bosnia on the coherence and credibility of NATO. The argument goes that if NATO shows that it is not up to the challenge of an appropriate response to the Yugoslav crisis, then it will not have a future as a military organization. If NATO cannot demonstrate a long-term goal, if the US does not demonstrate leadership, then NATO will cease to have the authority or pretensions to leadership that it has had thus far. While few may quarrel with the substance of this argument, the problem is that concern about the effect of Bosnia on NATO itself was not sufficient to convince the NATO countries of the need for intervention. It was rather NATO's disagreement over the proper strategy in Bosnia that was preventing action and hurting NATO. The argument is circular. Calls for an active

NATO role were heard because it was believed something should be done. But the main reason nothing effective was being done was that Britain and France could not agree on such a strategy, and without their cooperation, NATO was paralyzed. Strong US leadership might have galvanized them into action, but that leadership was hampered by domestic restraints and doubts about an effective course of action. Under those conditions, strong action to 'save NATO' did not materialize. But NATO could only be energized when there was a goal that resolidified its purpose. The foreign-policy elites of the United States and Europe could no longer agree on NATO's purpose, on how far it should extend and who should be in it, or what it should do in a European conflict with the worst fighting since World War II. Under those circumstances, it did little good to suggest that NATO should be saved until some conceptual coherence could be found on which to base its resuscitation. That conceptual coherence came when the situation on the ground and elsewhere changed enough that military action began to appear preferable to passivity.

It can be conceded, however, that after the Dayton Agreement and the multitude of international commitments it includes, failure of any of the major parties (Britain, France, the US) to participate in the implementation of the accord would harm NATO's credibility. This statement is made notwithstanding the criticism of the importance conventionally attributed to the idea of credibility in Chapter 8. When, after so much war, a comprehensive agreement is concluded, the effectiveness of which rests on the willingness of the alliance to commit troops to reinforce it, an inability to follow through would seriously diminish the effectiveness of the organization. This is one case where the very act of commitment to the agreement makes it imperative that the NATO powers follow through in implementation if NATO is to retain coherence as a military organization.[5]

Finally, the argument was made that the effect of inaction in Bosnia would have deleterious effects on Eastern Europe and the Muslim world. The example of Western inaction in Bosnia would harm our credibility in Eastern Europe, make it appear that the West was giving a green light to ethnic fragmentation, brutality and war, and further exacerbate an already-tense situation with numerous minorities living in a volatile environment similar to Yugoslavia.[6] While the claim of establishing

credibility in foreign policy is often overrated (see Chapter 8),
it is possible that the paralysis of the West may be interpreted
as permission to promote ethnic agendas without paying
a price. It is also possible that seeing the cost to the Serb
economy and to the members of the former Yugoslavia, other
Eastern European ethnic actors may look for an alternative
route to nationalist goals. But in order to discourage repeti-
tion of the Serb performance, it is certainly desirable to send
a signal that a price will be paid for aggressive and criminal
international behavior.

Still another argument, that failure to respond in Bosnia
would alienate Muslim countries, was based on the fact that the
main defendant against both Serb and Croat aggression was the
predominantly Muslim government of Bosnia. Muslim countries might well conclude that the West fails to react to
aggression against Muslims as it would to the same actions
against a Christian country. This perspective is given credence
by contrasting the West's reaction in Bosnia to the strong action
taken by the West in the Gulf against Iraq (a Muslim country),
which took place only months before Milosevic moved into
Slovenia and Croatia. Further evidence of these biases can be
seen in the concern in Western Europe over the existence of a
Muslim state in Europe (see Chapter 10). A related concern has
been that continued fighting in Bosnia will lead to a widely scattered number of alienated Muslim refugees similar to the
Palestinian diaspora, laying a foundation for terrorist activity.[7]

The case for intervention in the Balkans solely on the grounds
of security interests is a difficult one. Security interests certainly
exist, but they are not the type that provide an immediate rallying point for either foreign-policy specialists or the general
public.[8] There was a pervasive feeling that US security interests
did not justify sending ground troops to Yugoslavia, and opinion
was divided on whether security interests justified any other kind
of intervention, and whether it would have worked.

A brief survey of opinions on the most urgent reasons
for intervening justifies that statement. Peter Tarnoff, US
Undersecretary of State for Political Affairs in the Clinton
administration gave three reasons the US had an interest in
events in Yugoslavia: to prevent the spread of fighting and the
resultant instability that could threaten our allies or Russia; to
stem the flow of refugees, provide humanitarian relief and

stop the slaughter; and for the US to maintain a leadership role in European affairs. Anthony Lake, National Security Adviser under Clinton, cited the need to maintain the balance of power that could be threatened if the war were to expand and draw in Greece and Turkey, the need to contain Muslim extremism, and the need to stop ethnic cleansing. Former British Prime Minister Margaret Thatcher cited as factors justifying Western intervention: the fear that the Serbs would expand the war; the need to maintain the credibility of the US, the UN, and NATO by demonstrating resolution to would-be aggressors waiting to see how the West reacted to Serbian actions; and the dangers from the flood of refugees. She added that feeding or evacuating the victims of the war rather than helping them resist aggression 'makes us accomplices as much as good samaritans'. Finally, analyst Charles William Maynes argued that in the event the UN pulled out of Bosnia (mid-1994), failure of NATO to act to fill the power vacuum would destroy its credibility. None of these arguments emphasize the immediate threat to the balance of power or Balkan order from the actions of the Serbs or other actors in the war area. The stress is almost entirely on the threat that would be posed if the war expanded to bring in other powers, threats to the credibility of US or NATO leadership and the impact on future similar actions by other expansionists. One of the perplexing ironies of this war is that those who worried about what effect not punishing the Serbs would have on other aggressors almost never mentioned the Croats, the group most likely to imitate the Serbs if they thought they could get away with it – and by the Spring of 1993 they were doing just that. The other concerns of these analysts tended to humanitarian, or second-or third-level security concerns, such as ethnic cleansing or the flow of refugees.[9]

HUMANITARIAN INTERESTS, AMERICAN INTERESTS AND MILITARY INTERVENTION

The Western argument over the Yugoslav situation has not been over whether Western values have been violated in that area, or whether the public would like to do something to remedy the situation, or even whether the West could do something to further humanitarian values. Even the staunchest critics of intervention concede that the answer to these questions is yes. The catalog of atrocities documented in Chapter 4 is offensive to numerous American values, including the value of settling problems through peaceful means rather than violence; both American and international standards on the limits of the means by which warfare is carried out and the need to limit its impact on civilians; prohibitions against torture; values against offensive warfare and values that specify that racial and ethnic tensions should be discouraged and dampened rather than exploited and fanned.

But the debate has been rather over the price we are willing to pay to intervene in order to influence the situation, and whether we would have the perseverance to complete the job once it was started, and over what the nature of the conflict is and what could be done to stop it. Far from being controversial, the revulsion against the violation of humanitarian (and American) values in the former Yugoslavia has been sufficiently strong that it has provided substantial pressures for the Bush and Clinton administration either to talk about intervening, or at the least to continue diplomatic efforts and to focus continually on the conflict. Without this pressure, the war would have suffered from 'benign neglect' to a greater degree than it did from 1992 to 1995. Neither has the principled opposition of the international community nor the stricture of international law been an obstacle to intervention. Prior to World War II, human-rights issues rarely appeared on international political agendas. The modern international system, since its founding in the seventeenth century, had focused on the sovereignty of individual nations and the international norm of nonintervention. But in recent years more attention has been paid to conditions within countries, from human-rights to civil war, mitigating somewhat the principle of national sovereignty.[10] The holocaust drew international attention to the issue of human rights and became a catalyst for attention and action on the issue. When the UN was founded, there was a greater focus on these issues than under the League of Nations. Whereas the Preamble to the UN Charter reaffirmed faith in fundamental human rights, the League of Nations charter had not mentioned them. In 1948, the Convention on Prevention and Punishment of the Crime of

Genocide was opened for signature, and the UN General Assembly unanimously passed the Universal Declaration of Human Rights, an extensive list of internationally recognized human rights.

But it was not until the 1960s and 1970s that the UN began to discuss and monitor human rights violations. In the 1970s, US foreign policy began to link foreign policy and human rights, President Carter promoted a human-rights agenda, and by the end of the Reagan Administration human rights had a secure and institutionalized place in US foreign policy. The end of the Cold War has eliminated the chief rationale for not focusing on human rights, and has seen at least one invasion of a neighboring country (Haiti) where the rationale was heavily based on the need to restore democracy and human rights. Unlike many Cold-War interventions, where the local population had distinctly mixed feelings about US intervention, in Haiti the overwhelming majority were very receptive to the US intervention.

In the present international system, most states have explicitly endorsed the Universal Declaration of Human Rights and other documents that contribute to a world-wide standard of behavior. Increasingly, UN resolutions and the UN Charter have provided the basis for foreign policy and military actions that support democratic and human rights, even if there is curtailment of the sovereignty of the nation in question. One observer has noted that 'the Helsinki Final Act and subsequent documents negotiated by all participants in the Conference on Security and Cooperation in Europe (CSCE) have made a government's treatment of its citizens a matter of proper international concern'. On the other side, the limitations and ambiguities of any international norm favoring intervention in a state's internal affairs or in favor of a democratic state, can be noted. First, the same documents that seem to sanction these new standards also often endorse the norm of nonintervention in the internal affairs of states. Second, the documents that bestow the blessing of the international system on certain human rights for all individuals, do not provide for enforcement of these rights. Finally, the real disagreement among the various nations about the nature of these universal human rights suggests that the consensus is more on paper than a question of real belief or practice.[11]

These qualifications do not invalidate concern with human rights; they rather point out the complexity of the issue and difficulty of formulating satisfactory policy. While intervention in the former Yugoslavia can be justified on the basis of resistance to aggression, for which the UN Charter does provide guidance and legitimation, the issue of international human rights may also arise, as for instance in questions of whether Bosnia should have been given special consideration on the basis of its relatively more democratic political system, or the kinds of rights that should be accorded to certain minorities in a settlement. Since governments routinely make decisions based at least in part on these criteria of universal 'rights', it is no use pretending they are irrelevant, even if the extent of their legitimacy is open to question.

The situation in the former Yugoslavia provided no exception to this. Since the Serbs have been widely accused of aggression against internationally recognized countries and UN resolutions have condemned 'grave, massive and systematic violations of human rights', both legal and moral legitimation for military action existed. The United Nations Security Council had given specific legal authority for military action in Yugoslavia. Resolutions 781 and 816 (adopted 31 March 1993) authorized action to enforce a ban on flights over Bosnia. Resolution 819 (16 April 1993) authorized treating the city of Srebrenica as a safe area and this protection was later expanded to other cities in eastern Bosnia. While resolutions authorizing more stringent measures might have resulted in a Russian veto, legal prohibitions were not the limiting factor for undertaking military action. In international relations, a legal justification for action can almost always be found, particularly given the circumstances and the nature of the war in Bosnia. Some suggested that sufficient legal authority for intervention could be obtained though invocation of Article 51 of the United Nations Charter, setting forth the 'inherent right of individual or collective self-defense if an armed attack occurs against a Member of the United Nations, until the Security Council has taken measures necessary to maintain international peace and security'. Since there was strong support in the General Assembly for opposition to the aggression in Bosnia, use of the 'Uniting for Peace' Resolution, used during the Korean War to circumvent a Soviet veto, and which authorized the General Assembly to make recommendations for action to member states, could also be used to legitimate military action in response to aggression in Bosnia if Russian opposition had developed. A strong Western alliance with the political will to take meaningful action in Bosnia would have had no trouble finding the resources to provide the legal justification.[12]

INTERVENTION IN BOSNIA AND INTERVENTION ELSEWHERE

Other interventions and opportunities for intervention by the US military offer points of comparison with the Bosnian situation that may help in evaluating the advisability of our involvement there. In discussions on Bosnia, it was sometimes argued that the US could not intervene everywhere and that there were other trouble spots where US intervention was more important or more feasible. UN Secretary-General Boutros Boutros-Ghali argued, for instance, that Yugoslavia is a 'rich man's war' and that there are much more pressing problems around the world to which the UN should give priority. Others have argued that Yugoslavia has received disproportionate attention in the media and elsewhere because it is European and white, even though the number dying and the scope of the disaster is much greater elsewhere. In Rwanda, for instance, many more (some estimates are as high as 1 million) and roughly a tenth of the population died in a few months. In comparison to this catastrophe, the 'bloodletting in the former Yugoslavia measures up as little more than a neighborhood riot'. For the Rwanda disaster, the US was able to muster only a contingent of some 2300-odd troops to help deliver food, water and sanitation to refugees after the main event (the mass killings) was over.[13] When there are limits to the political and economic capital that can be committed to foreign affairs, especially true in the case of humanitarian ventures, it is appropriate to examine other situations where intervention might be either requested or desirable, and to suggest priorities.

Most other post-Cold-War intervention opportunities have much in common with the Bosnian situation. Like many foreign-policy issues in the post-Cold-War international system, most of these cases touch significant humanitarian issues, but do not pertain to major American security interests, and sometimes touch no security interest at all. But if we assume that the United States sometimes should make decisions to intervene on a humanitarian basis, in light of the lack of useful guidelines for determining when to intervene, it is useful to put decisions on Bosnia in context.

In Table 5.1 we compare intervention opportunities along the same dimensions emphasized in the discussion on Bosnia. Vietnam and the Gulf War, conflicts thought to involve a security interest, are discussed later in Chapter 8. This choice of cases suggests a realist bias, given the implication that security interests should take precedence over purely humanitarian interests in choosing foreign policy priorities. This is precisely the emphasis I intend, but decisions on intervention for humanitarian reasons also require evaluation. All opportunities for intervention in countries that were part of the former Soviet Union have been ignored, on the grounds that the US would not risk intervention in countries so close to Russia.

Table 5.1   Intervention opportunities

Conflict	Security interest	Humanitarian interest	Chance of success	Cost	Public support
Bosnia	minor	yes	modest	modest	modest[3]
Haiti	no[1]	yes	poor[2]	modest[2]	no
Somalia	no	yes	modest	low	yes
Sudan	no	yes	poor	low/modest	no
Rwanda	no	yes	modest	low/modest	no
Panama	minor	minor	modest	low	yes

1 A social/economic rationale for invasion to stem the refugee flow undoubtedly played a major role in promoting the invasion.
2 These values reflect the common perception before the invasion, rather than after it.
3 Air strikes only.

The cases of Haiti, Somalia, Sudan and Rwanda certainly meet a standard of being among the most urgent humanitarian cases, involving nations in some of the direst straits in the world. All four of these countries are among the poorest as measured by GNP per capita and economic growth rates, have high rates of population growth, have the worst health conditions as measured by life expectancy and infant mortality rates, and all have high illiteracy rates. In addition, perhaps most importantly, they lack the stable social and political infrastructure that is required for economic growth and provision of solutions to the problems of violence and misrule from which they all suffer, and which suggested the alternative of intervention.[14]

Analysis of this sample of trouble spots, candidates for actual or potential intervention, suggests the plenitude of opportunities for intervention. Other cases could be mentioned, including for instance, the civil wars of long-standing duration and massive loss of life in Angola, Liberia and Sierra Leone. The likelihood is that the US will intervene in very few of these places, given the lack of substantial security interests and the present state of public opinion. Indeed, given the present public mood, there is a real question if a president would have intervened in a situation such as Somalia if a similar situation presented itself in 1994 or 1995, because of the adverse reaction among the American public to our difficulties there.

It is noteworthy that two of the three interventions on our list, Panama and Haiti, occurred in this hemisphere. This is congruent with historical trends in American foreign policy. The US has always been more likely to intervene in its own hemisphere because the problems are more likely to affect US citizens directly and are more easily comprehended than when they occur further afield. It is doubtful that the end of the Cold War will change this tendency.

It is also noteworthy that the invasions of Panama and Haiti had implications beyond the humanitarian issues of restoring democracy and humane government. In the case of Panama, the US was concerned about Panamanian President Noriega's role in the drug traffic and the long-standing feud with him, which if allowed to worsen, could have raised questions about the inviolability of the Panama Canal.[15] In the case of Haiti, the flow of refugees to the United States from Haiti had plagued the Clinton administration and the only way to solve that problem once and for all was to remove the Cedras government. Since the economic embargo had not been sufficient to do that, there was no alternative but to use military intervention. While the exception of Somalia, where we intervened to restore order and prevent starvation, shows that we may intervene for purely humanitarian reasons even outside of this hemisphere, the chances of intervention are certainly increased if the opportunity is close to the United States and if some economic or security interest is also involved.

In all three cases from our sample where intervention took place, in no case was there even the pretense of intervening against foreign aggression or interference. We made no excuses for intervening in either Haiti or Panama purely for the purpose of overthrowing one government and installing another. This supports the argument made above and in Chapter 7 that inhibitions against violating the sovereignty of a country are of little importance once a president is of the belief that intervention is justified. And in the case of Somalia, there was no government to claim sovereignty as a basis for opposing US intervention.

When compared to these cases, in Bosnia the humanitarian goals a successful intervention would have served appear to be greater than in Panama, where Noriega's authoritarian government trampled on democracy, but was not involved in widespread terror or killing. But the number of lives at stake in Bosnia was substantially less than in the case of Rwanda. It is difficult to compare humanitarian goals with the Haiti intervention, where sporadic terror and violence were stopped, but had never attained the status of civil war. The humanitarian values would certainly be high in the Sudan, where persecution of the South by the northern-based government has produced a civil war that has dragged on for years, but intervention there is not likely ever to be considered because of its remoteness from the American consciousness, ambiguity about what could be done, the size of the country, and the lack of physical and social infrastructure on which to build.

Bosnia, as in the case of Panama and Haiti, also had a significant security interest that helped to justify intervention. On the other hand, precisely because it is not in this hemisphere and because the situation was so complex and difficult to explain to the public, there was a tendency to let the Europeans take the lead. Intervention in Bosnia with air power only was considerably easier to advocate than intervention in Rwanda, or possibly even in Haiti, which was widely thought to be a very difficult undertaking. The use of air power to stop the momentum of the war early on in Bosnia, it could be argued, would have broken the momentum of the Serbian effort and prevented the development of a wider war at a relatively low cost.

There is also the argument that the focus of the media on Bosnia reflects the fact that the conflict is European and the people are Caucasian and that it receives more attention than it merits. But we have historically given more attention to European conflict, not least because it was the cockpit of international politics, and to a great extent still is. Even were there no security interest at all in the former Yugoslavia, some greater interest and attention there reflects historical trends rather than a racist approach to deciding which victims should be aided. After all, the much touted 'special relationship' with the British is not attributed to racial sources, but to historical and cultural similarities.

In sum, intervention in Bosnia would seem to rank toward the top of our list of intervention opportunities, because of the value of the combined humanitarian and security purpose to be served, and because intervention with air power for modest objectives was easier and less costly than putting in troops, which all of the other operations would have required. In the case of Bosnia, public opinion had also been shaped somewhat to support intervention. On the other hand, if one believes that only troops could accomplish US objectives in Bosnia, then intervention there before the Dayton Agreement becomes a case more difficult to defend than Panama or Haiti because of the reluctance of public opinion to support such an effort, and perhaps more difficult to advocate than Rwanda. Rwanda is a much smaller place and a short-term US operation might have saved many more lives than intervention in Bosnia. At the time of the Rwandan massacre, General Romeo Dallaire, the Canadian commander of the UN force in Rwanda, stated that he could end the genocide with between five and eight thousand troops. Many others accept similar estimates of the ease with which the killing could have been stopped.[16] It is this reluctance to send troops abroad even for worthy causes that explains why the decision to send US troops to Bosnia came only after more than three years of trying alternative policies that failed, and why opportunities were missed that might have stopped the conflict at less risk to the US if used earlier.

CONCLUSION

Examination of numerous arguments about US security interests in Bosnia suggests that while security interests do exist, there is a consensus that they are not interests that should lead the US to costly expenditures of blood and treasure. At the same time, there is agreement that humanitarian interests do exist, and some support for intervention to defend them. There were few legal or moral impediments to such intervention. When compared to other opportunities to intervene, Bosnia was a less pressing case than some, such as Rwanda, but there is a good case to be made for intervention in Bosnia, when viewed in comparative perspective.

6 The Foreign Policy Mood in the United States

Two points will be made in this chapter, both of which have a bearing on our analysis of US intervention in Bosnia. First it will be argued that public opinion is important in influencing foreign policy. Recent reassessments of the importance of public opinion have led to a reformulation of the relationship between public opinion and foreign policy. Second, it will be argued that the impact of public opinion and the public mood has been a deterrent to intervention in Bosnia. The lack of a taste for a potentially costly involvement in a foreign land was one of several important reasons that two consecutive administrations were cautious about increasing our presence in Yugoslavia.

PUBLIC OPINION AND FOREIGN POLICY

Except in times of crisis, Gabriel Almond wrote in 1950, foreign policy 'has to shout loudly to be heard even a little'. He articulated a view prevalent then, that domestic policy was much more visible to the general public, and something that it was likely to feel more strongly about than foreign policy, due to the preoccupation of most Americans with their private material welfare. Articulating his famous 'mood' theory of foreign policy, he went on to argue that the foreign-policy attitudes of most Americans lack intellectual structure and factual content. Moreover, he argued that to the degree the public is interested in foreign policy, it tends to have a negative emphasis, focusing on avoidance of foreign involvement rather than increasing participation or wielding influence. For this contention, he cited pre-World-War-II data as well as evidence of the public's reluctance to confront the post-war problem of Soviet power and assertiveness. The public recognized the inevitability of US involvement in foreign affairs, but it was reluctant to become involved when confronted with the tedium, tension, threat, and frustration that was the reality of our relations with the Soviet Union.[1]

Almond was not alone in this general view of the public and its role in foreign policy. Walter Lippmann, George Kennan, and Hans Morgenthau were 'realists' who shared much of the opinion Almond articulated. These men not only emphasized the limitations of the mass public in influencing and shaping foreign policy, but saw intense public participation as something that was undesirable, since the complex issues of foreign policy could best be left to a trained elite of foreign-policy experts. In opposition to this position was the liberal school which welcomed an expanded role for the public as a means of improving foreign policy and creating a more peaceful world.[2]

The troika of foreign policy characterizations put forth by Almond and the realists about public opinion and its impact on foreign policy had spawned a consensus by the 1960s. Responding to general agreement that public opinion on foreign policy is volatile, that it lacks structure and coherence (foreign policy attitudes are 'non-attitudes'),[3] that in the end public opinion has little effect on policy, analysts either expressed apprehension about the potentially harmful effects of public opinion on foreign-policy formulation or, alternatively, expressed relief that the public really had little impact on policy. This consensus, however, was soon to be fractured as further research reassessed the role and attitudes of the public.

The reassessment resulted from the convergence of several factors, including the increasing availability of polling data, more sophisticated analysis and survey techniques, and perhaps most importantly, the trauma of the Vietnam War. While it was agreed that the public was not well informed on foreign policy and often lacked key information, still evidence emerged that opinion on foreign policy was as stable as on domestic issues, that attitudes were predictable and coherent. Contrary to the central thesis of volatility in Almond's study, it became increasingly common to see the public as a source of moderation and continuity. Lacking in-depth knowledge of foreign affairs, the public apparently uses simple heuristics to measure and evaluate foreign policy.[4] One striking example of this was John Mueller's study of public support for various wars, but especially the Korean and Vietnam Wars. He found a close relationship between increasing casualties and decreasing support for both wars that succinctly explained diminishing public support as the wars continued.[5]

Finally, the belief that public opinion has little impact on foreign policy has also been increasingly challenged. Various studies, including one of presidential campaigns and foreign policy indicate that the public is much less powerless in influencing foreign policy than previously supposed. The powerful example of Vietnam in forcing Lyndon Johnson's resignation and ultimately the withdrawal in defeat from Vietnam was especially telling of the public's impact in a time of crisis. Over a longer period of three decades and in a less eventful arena, one analyst found that policy toward China was remarkably consistent with public preferences.[6]

In sum, the relationship between public opinion and foreign policy has increasingly come to be seen as similar to that of opinion on domestic issues. Opinion is reasonably stable, changes and shifts can be explained by reference to events and issues, and it has a significant impact on policy. While many observers agree that foreign-policy opinion has become more partisan and polarized since the great trauma of the Vietnam War, it remains to be seen what effect the end of the Cold War will have on it. The polarization may moderate somewhat, but the end of the Cold War, the increasing importance of economic issues, and the growing awareness of Americans about the outside world, may accelerate the trend we have just observed: the increasing similarity between the politics of foreign and domestic policy making. Foreign policy will become, more and more, 'politics as usual'.[7]

THE DOMESTIC SETTING FOR BOSNIAN POLICY

To show the relationship between public attitudes on the war in Bosnia and US policy, attention must be given to the specific context in which Bosnian policy was made. During the long Cold War, the American people were asked by their leadership to support high defense budgets, they were subjected to often gloomy accounts of the US standing versus the Soviets in the Cold War contest, and they endured numerous crises and periods of tension, most notably several Berlin crises,

Soviet invasions of Hungary and Czechoslovakia and, most traumatic of all, the Cuban missile crisis. Moreover, limited wars in Korea and Vietnam led to widespread casualties over extended periods of time. It is therefore not surprising that once the public came to realize that the institutionalized competition between the two major superpowers had come to an end, or at the least had been transformed into a more traditional rivalry with one power having a much-diminished economic and territorial base, it welcomed a period of relaxation and a change of priorities. The end of the Cold War suggested to the public that they could lower their guard in foreign policy and escape the constant concern with watching and responding to the moves of the rival superpower, the essence of most crises and major foreign-policy issues, not to mention spy mythology and entertainment stereotyping, for the last four decades.

Nor was the relief limited to the general public. One official, noting the growth in the number of countries adhering to liberal democracy and the end of the struggle between the authoritarian and democratic countries, suggested the 'end of history'. Francis Fukuyama's formulation may have been extreme, but it suggests the revolution in expectations that accompanied the end of the Cold War.

> The United States and other liberal democracies will have to come to grips with the fact that, with the collapse of the communist world, the world in which we live is less and less the old one of geopolitics, and that the rules and methods of the historical world are not appropriate to life in the post-historical one.[8]

General relief over the end of the Cold War was heightened not just because the long struggle was over, but because the West had won. What other threat could equal that of Soviet Communism? The American people felt themselves entitled to some relief from foreign crises and a chance to concentrate on domestic issues.

The stage was set for a demobilization in both attitude and armament. At the end of an earlier struggle, World War II, similar attitudes led to drastic reductions in armaments, and the psychological disarming of a population that was then ill-prepared to meet the new threat of the Cold War. The sense of relief with which a more relaxed international scene was greeted complemented a growing concern with the need for domestic reform in the United States. The little attention given foreign policy issues in the 1992 campaign was remarkable. Reeling from a sense that the Reagan–Bush years had failed to deal with economic and social problems, the American people were in a mood to use the 'peace dividend' and newly freed-up energies to deal with the seemingly overwhelming problems of economic restructuring, international competition, crime and violence, welfare reform, health care, and education. In a recent survey of opinion on foreign policy in early 1995, not one foreign-policy concern appeared on the public's list of the top ten problems facing the country. Whereas in the mid-1980s, 20–27 per cent of the public polled by Gallup cited the US–Soviet standoff or other Cold-War challenges as the most important problem facing the country, in the latest poll on the question the number citing a foreign-policy problem had fallen to 2 per cent. The foreign-policy category of problems facing the country now comprises the lowest percentage of total problems ever among leaders (11.4 per cent) and the lowest since 1978 for the public (11.5 per cent).[9] A policy-making environment existed in which, if intervention abroad was to be undertaken, it had to be well planned and convincingly argued before the American public was likely to accept it.

Moreover, intervention in Bosnia faced another obstacle to public acceptance, no matter how convincing the case to be made for it. As noted in Chapter 1, the post-Cold-War world is less predictable, more violent, and less likely to be controlled by the major powers. As William Schneider notes, we learned from Vietnam that Americans prefer clear-cut wars where massive force can be used to win a clear-cut victory, after which the US can withdraw as the victor. We do not like to fight limited wars for political advantage.[10] Unfortunately, in the new decentralized, nationalistic world in which we now live, most wars in which we might get involved are precisely those wars that will be limited, have ambiguous and fluctuating goals, and will require constant cost–benefit analysis to determine whether the US should stay involved, and if so, how. The conflict in the Persian Gulf is the exception that proves the rule. President Bush argued that the degree of public support for the war showed that we had shed the 'Vietnam syndrome', when it actually confirmed it.[11]

Foreign-policy making from now on is likely to become more like domestic policy-making, the product of bargaining and negotiating between groups, as people are more aware that foreign policy affects them, but are less certain just how it does so. At the same time, uncertainty in the international arena will require subtle mixes of negotiation and force, and lots of patience. Debate over what is a US interest and what should be done if that interest is threatened will be less clear-cut and more difficult.

While the public was more willing to commit force abroad in 1992 than was the case soon after Vietnam, it was not as willing to do so as in the 1950s, and after the problems in Somalia it is even more apprehensive about foreign involvement. And it is more willing to commit force abroad to restrain aggression than it is to intervene in the domestic politics of an offending country.[12] The limited interest of the American public in an assertive foreign policy is shown in a 1992 poll by four newspaper editors from around the country, published in *Foreign Policy*. The domestic focus of most citizens is clear, and to the extent that foreign affairs are a concern, the focus is primarily on economic issues that are likely to be affected by foreign policy. There is intense concern with trade issues, with the effect on defense jobs as Pentagon spending is cut, and with new waves of immigrants and foreign investment. Cynthia Tucker of the *Atlanta Journal – Constitution*, notes that even in defense-conscious Georgia, the relative lack of interest in the Gulf War 'underscores the trend among voters to emphasize domestic concerns, rather than foreign policy issues, in this campaign'. She notes that Democratic senator Wyche Fowler, who voted against committing force for the Gulf War, had never once been asked, in 60 town meetings, about his vote on the war. One could summarize the findings of the four reports with Gerald L. Warren's (*San Diego Union-Tribune*) observations that 'San Diegans are not unique. In the absence of a direct threat to US strategic interests, they tend to look inward'.[13]

There is another way in which public opinion on foreign policy is coming to resemble that on domestic policy. Whereas

Americans often talk conservatively but vote liberally on domestic policy, on foreign policy they often talk international but isolationist tendencies intrude as one moves to policy. Voters in 1990 were quite interested in supporting democracy abroad, protecting humanitarian rights, and protecting weaker nations against foreign aggression, to the point of being more international than the foreign-policy elite. This reverses the usual relationship between the attitude of the mass public and elites, since the foreign-policy elites are expected to be more internationalist. What the public appears to mean, however, is that they are in favor of these policies as long as there is no substantial cost involved.[14]

PUBLIC OPINION AND BOSNIA POLICY

Political elites

The opinion of the foreign-policy elite and decision-makers is of decisive significance in considering support for intervention in Bosnia. Since the fracturing of establishment opinion on foreign policy as a result of the Vietnam War,[15] elite support for foreign involvement has been less predictable than it was during the early years of the Cold War. Never has that been more true than during the debate on US involvement in Bosnia. Partisan and ideological predictors of foreign-policy opinion were meaningless, since individuals took positions that seemed unrelated to previous positions.

In the US Congress, both the then Senate majority leader George Mitchell and minority leader Bob Dole supported stronger action in Bosnia. Liberals such as Senator Joseph Biden and Representative Frank McCloskey of Indiana also supported stronger action, but conservative Senators James McCain and John Warner opposed intervention. Among commentators, conservative Jeanne Kirkpatrick was a hawk on Bosnia, while William Hyland, a former editor of *Foreign Affairs*, was against intervention. Liberal columnist Anthony Lewis strongly favored intervention along with nuclear-deterrence-'superhawk' (in Cold-War days) Albert Wohlstetter. In my own case, I found that colleagues with whom I had usually agreed on foreign-policy issues during the Cold War now held different positions from mine on Bosnia. And as two commentators pointed out, not since the Vietnam War had a conflict aroused such passions as the war in Bosnia.[16]

The unfamiliar coalitions continued after the change in US policy in August 1995 which resulted in increased military action against the Serbs, the negotiation of the Dayton Agreement and the decision of President Clinton to send 20 000 US troops to Bosnia. After initial hesitation, now Senate majority leader Bob Dole decided to support the President, hoping to put some of his own restrictions on the mission, as did the until-then 'dove' on Bosnia, John McCain. Other Republican candidates for president, however, tended to be opposed to sending troops. Meanwhile, in the President's own party, Congress tended to support the sending of troops, but with many reservations and while feeling intensely the pressures against doing so from those back home.

The seemingly random relationship between partisan and ideological positions and opinion on Bosnia reflects the fact that the motivation for intervention was primarily humanitarian rather than security concerns, the lack of agreed-upon foreign-policy guidelines for intervention, and the volatile nature of public opinion. Policy making on Bosnia was taking place in a new foreign-policy universe.

The general public

Public opinion on Bosnia is not easy to interpret. *New York Times* data showed consistent opposition to involvement when the public was asked a simple question: 'Should the US get involved in Bosnia?' Consistently negative answers were obtained throughout the war. In January 1993, only 24 per cent answered yes and 67 per cent no. By mid-year those answering yes to involvement had climbed to 37 per cent, and no had dropped to 51 per cent. With some fluctuation, these figures were representative of feeling on this question through April 1994.[17]

More specific questions on the US role in Bosnia, however, give a somewhat different picture, depending on which poll one uses. After initially cautious responses, a plurality in favor of US action was visible in 1993. When asked in a July

1992 Gallup poll whether the US should take the lead in seeking UN-backed air strikes if Serbian forces continued to block the delivery of relief supplies, 35 per cent answered yes while 45 per cent said no. By August, however, sentiment had shifted and 53 per cent supported US participation in either UN-backed air strikes or ground action against Serbian forces. Support for intervention remained stable through the rest of the year and well into 1993, but there was also a stable minority of approximately one-third who continued to oppose intervention.[18] In January, 1993, 63 per cent favored the US sending aircraft to enforce the no-fly zone, while only 28 per cent opposed it. But in February, when voters were asked about the 'Clinton plan' for Bosnia, defined as negotiations followed by peacekeeping troops on the ground to enforce a peace treaty, 44 per cent said there was too much involvement, 43 per cent that involvement was about right, and 8 per cent that there was not enough.[19] As Serbian intransigence and attacks on Sarajevo increased, an August Gallup poll showed majorities of 51 per cent and 60 per cent in support of air strikes against Serbs, but in conjunction with European allies, although earlier polls following the rejection of the Vance–Owen plan by the Serbs showed a majority against US air strikes (62 per cent in April; 56 per cent in May).[20] Further adding to the confusion is strong support for policies that do not involve military action. A May Gallup poll showed 48 per cent approval, 35 per cent disapproval of President Clinton's handling of the war.[21]

When questions were asked about participation in a multilateral operation or a peacekeeping operation, results were more positive. A January 1993 poll showed 57 per cent favored sending US troops to restore peace and humanitarian aid, with 35 per cent opposing. And support for a UN operation to deliver relief supplies in December 1992 was 57 per cent; support rose to 68 per cent in May and 73 per cent in April 1994 if the operation was also part of a peacekeeping force. Reinforcing this preference for consensual action is the response that air strikes should be conducted only with congressional approval (85 per cent) with only 15 per cent favoring them without congressional approval.[22]

While a core of public support for stronger actions than either Bush or Clinton had taken could be discerned, there

was frequently not a majority and sometimes not even a plurality in support of such a course. The ambivalence of public
sentiment was easy to spot. To a question in February 1993 of
whether the US was too involved or not involved enough,
30 per cent answered too involved, 14 per cent not involved
enough, and 49 per cent about right. In a pattern that was-
consistent throughout 1993, the public favored more military
involvement while simultaneously affirming that the present
level of involvement was about right. When asked in January
whether, if the US sent troops, the war would turn out more
like the Vietnam War or more like the Gulf War, 41 per cent answered it would turn out like the Vietnam War and 47 per cent
like the Gulf War, while 4 per cent said neither. This pessimistic view of the likely outcome of US intervention in the
war remained firm, as a May poll reflected almost identical
percentages.[23]

Different groups showed various degrees of support for
involvement in the war. Those who claimed to be following the
war closely supported intervention in slightly higher propor-
tions. This finding is not unusual, however, since those citizens
more informed about international politics normally tend
to favor a more active foreign policy. Men tended to favor
intervention in substantially higher percentages than women,
and, in contrast to the Cold War period, liberals were more
likely to support intervention than conservatives. Throughout
the polling period, strong support continued to exist for
continuing relief operations in the former Yugoslavia.[24]

After the February 1994 shelling in Sarajevo which killed 68
people and wounded 200 others, Americans were split on
whether President Clinton should have ordered air strikes
against Serbian positions. Favoring air strikes were 48 per cent,
while 43 per cent were opposed. And in the same poll,
47 per cent believed that such strikes would not be effective,
while 42 per cent believed that they would be. This poll, taken
after probably the most dramatic incident broadcast on
American TV screens, indicates a plurality favoring stronger
action, but at the same time pessimistic that it would achieve
the desired results. In evaluating these numbers, however, it is
prudent to remember the extremely negative reaction to the
deaths of 18 Americans in Somalia in late 1993. Whatever
the public's opinion on Bosnia, the visceral reaction of the

public to events in Somalia could not help put any president on notice that support for foreign-policy interventions is potentially very shallow.[25]

The level of public interest in the war has been consistently low, especially considering the amount of media coverage. Those who followed news of the conflict 'very closely' climbed above 20 per cent only once, in May 1993 when US military action appeared likely. At the start of the conflict, fewer than 10 per cent were paying close attention. The figure hovered around 15 per cent during 1993, dropping to 12 per cent in 1994.[26] While this indifference could be interpreted as giving the administration latitude to devise its own policy, it also suggests that any military action that became costly would have very little public support since the public appears not to discern an important US interest. When asked in early 1993, 30 per cent of respondents said they were more sympathetic to the Muslim side, while only 8 per cent chose the Serbs.[27]

The reasons Americans gave for intervention also reflected the softness of support. In January 1993, when asked to give a reason why the US should consider involvement in Bosnia, 15 per cent chose a US national security interest, 19 per cent wanted to prevent the spread of fighting in Europe, while 37 per cent cited a moral responsibility to stop ethnic cleansing, and 16 per cent said no US interest was at stake. This emphasis on humanitarian motivation for intervening, downplaying the extent of US security interests in the former Yugoslavia, was consistently displayed in the polls over time, and followed closely the position of many of the US foreign policy elite. A poll in mid-1994 found 31 per cent agreeing that vital US interests were at stake in Bosnia. Similarly, the reasons given for displaying caution in opposing air strikes reflected conventional thinking including fear of casualties, eventual involvement of ground troops, US economic problems, ineffectiveness of air strikes, and a perception that the problem is a European problem.[28]

Following the significant change in NATO policy in August 1995, the substantial bombing of Serb positions and infrastructure, and the negotiation of the Dayton Agreement, the American people were faced with the fact that American troops would be going to Bosnia to serve with other NATO troops as peacekeepers to enforce the agreement. Widespread resistance to this policy, by constituents contacting their representatives in Congress, in focus groups which the media assembled and so on, was reported. Polls reported a substantial majority opposed to the sending of troops even though a peace keeping task is usually better accepted by the public than a peacemaking mission.[29] These reports are quite consistent with earlier data on public opinion and President Clinton clearly took on the challenge to explain the policy to and shape the opinion of both the foreign-policy elites and the public, to allow him to implement the policy. A year after US troops began to be dispatched to Bosnia, opposition has been muted. Just as in the Haitian involvement, the public tends to accept the involvement so long as there are few human costs and no major incidents.

CONCLUSION

The tenor of public opinion during the war in the former Yugoslavia reflected the changed priorities and the lack of moorings that afflicted foreign policy in general. Old guidelines were obsolete, and old cleavages among the foreign-policy elite as well as the public were no longer apparent. A president wanting to prosecute this war inherited an environment which offered significant opportunity to mold public opinion in the direction he wished to go,[30] but it was also an environment where an aggressive effort to intervene would have substantial risk. Support for US involvement in Bosnia varied over time and depending on the question asked, but there was clearly significant support, usually a plurality, sometimes a majority, for air strikes, and in some cases for the use of troops. At the same time, the public was obviously cautious, somewhat anxious, and not convinced the war represented a vital interest or merited close attention. They were apprehensive about a Vietnam-type involvement, and wanted presidential actions to be coordinated with the Congress. Any successful effort to gather support for intervention would be in peril once the conflict became prolonged or the costs escalated. A low-cost option such as air strikes could have been successfully presented to the public as a viable policy, at least through most of 1993.

While television images were instrumental in stimulating support for intervention they did not compel the close attention of the public to the war. Both in the US and in Europe, they were a two-edged sword that could have quickly dampened support for involvement in the war if the costs (casualties) had started to rise. There is no doubt that the ambivalent state of public opinion was one of the major factors in determining the position of the political leadership on intervention in the war in Bosnia.

7 American Perceptions: Civil War and Ethnic Hatred

This chapter will discuss some aspects of how Americans, both leaders and ordinary citizens, perceived the war in Bosnia and what impact those perceptions had on US foreign policy. The complexity of the situation in Yugoslavia and the environment in which foreign-policy decisions were made (a post-Cold-War world in which policy guidelines were not agreed upon) increased the importance of perceptions. Without established policy guidelines or an agreed-upon approach to the problem, initial and sometimes misleading impressions of the war were disproportionately important.

The American perception of the war in Bosnia must be viewed in the context of the relationship of its citizens to the outside world. The American public is not well informed about foreign languages, cultures or institutions. Isolated historically by oceans from the affairs of Europe and Asia, Americans exhibit a kind of provincialism that has not been erased by modern communications technology. At the same time, the United States, in large part due to its generous funding of higher education in the social sciences, humanities and area studies, has produced a small group of people who are well travelled and extremely knowledgeable in foreign languages, cultures and institutions. When confronted with a foreign-policy problem like Bosnia, this knowledge and erudition is challenged to the utmost, but it is not clear that the reactions of the general public and the foreign-policy elite differed that much, in spite of the difference in their orientations. One reason for this may be that, unfortunately, knowledgeable Southeast-European specialists seem to have played, at best, a minor role in policy formulation. While foreign policy is too important to be left to the area specialists, they certainly should be heard. This chapter will discuss three aspects of Americans' perceptions that were important in shaping their view of the war and the preferred American role: the complexity and difficulty of comprehending the events, actors and context of the war, the stress on determining whether the war was civil or international, and the issue of ethnic hatred.

COMPLEXITY OF THE WAR

The Yugoslav conflict introduced a degree of complexity that is unusual even in religiously and culturally pluralistic societies riven with conflict and strife. Historically, Yugoslavia was at the crossroads of three different empires, the Ottoman, the Austria–Hungarian and the Russian, and the interaction and overlap of those empires over decades, if not centuries, left a rich historical legacy. As a result, in modern-day Yugoslavia, three major religious influences (Muslim, Catholic and Christian Orthodox) coexisted in a state with six republics (five republics after Montenegro was effectively absorbed by Serbia in 1989) that were united in a strong centralized state only as long as the force of Tito and the League of Communists of Yugoslavia continued to wield power. In the four republics involved in this conflict, Slovenia, Croatia, Serbia, and Bosnia–Herzegovina, four officially recognized nationalities dominate (Slovene, Croat, Serb and Muslim). Once Slovenia had successfully seceded, the remaining three republics each engaged in battle with at least one and sometimes two of the other republics. In addition, the conflict involved sizeable Serb minorities in both Croatia and Bosnia, all recognized by their 'home' republic, in rebellion against the government of the republic where they were located, and sometimes in collusion with each other. There was also a sizeable Croat minority in Bosnia, recognized by the government of Croatia. Moreover, Serbia had two autonomous provinces (Vojvodina and Kosovo) that ceased to be autonomous after the 1989 takeover by Belgrade, and while non-Serb peoples were important in both, in Kosovo the overwhelming Albanian majority was seen by the Serbs as a menacing threat.

One may add the last republic left over from the disintegration of Yugoslavia, Macedonia, which is a complex mixture of nationalities, as well as an object of external interest, especially from Bulgaria and Greece. Leaving aside most of the other outside foreign influences and interests, this sketch illustrates that the situation in Yugoslavia challenged the knowledge and understanding of even well-informed foreign-policy specialists, much less average citizens, or even Congressmen who might have had difficulty finding Yugoslavia on a map. I argue that the most important dynamic behind the events in Yugoslavia (Serbian authoritarianism and expansionism) is fairly simply characterized. But the manifestation of this phenomenon through various Serb groups and the overall complexity of the forces at work in the former Yugoslavia made it anything but easy for a non-specialist to make sense of what was happening, particularly in the early stages of the conflict.[1] The Balkans, although in Europe, was not an area that was frequently in the American news media, and was outside the area receiving the most attention for all but the earliest years of the Cold War. It was an area not well known by most of the American public.

CIVIL WAR VS. INTERNATIONAL WAR

The question of whether the war in Yugoslavia was a civil war or an international war assumed some importance in determining American attitudes toward the war. It would appear to be a question with minimal relevance, insofar as concerns about sovereignty have become less absolute in the practical act of making foreign-policy decisions. As we saw in Chapter 5, in the post-World-War-II period, the distinction between international conflict and civil conflict has lost some of its sharpness, as individual nations, regional organizations and the United Nations have all become more active in intervening in what were previously considered domestic disputes, and therefore not amenable to outside influence.

Furthermore, anyone familiar with the history of US foreign policy can attest that the US has shown little reluctance to intervene militarily in other countries' affairs during the Cold War. The most recent major intervention, in Haiti, occurred even as the Bosnian War was in progress, in a conflict that presented no security threat to the US, even though it did create a refugee problem and therefore a domestic problem.

Numerous examples of intervention in civil conflicts stretching back to the beginning of the Cold War can be cited: Greece (1947), Iran (1954), Indonesia and Lebanon (1958), Cuba (1961), Dominican Republic (1965), Chile (1973), Panama and the Philippines (1989) and many more. With the end of the Cold War and the reduced tension in the world there may seem to be less justification for intervention, but resistance to intervening in civil conflict is still hardly an important consideration if US interests or general humanitarian issues are seen to be at stake.

There is another factor, really an extension of the way our view of sovereignty and the legitimacy of intervention has evolved, that is now relevant in any assessment of civil-war situations. Leaving aside the niceties of international law, the weight of international opinion tends to weigh in against the use of violence against minority groups within a country, whatever the legalities of sovereignty. While the Russian intervention in Chechnya was underway, criticism grew that the US government was insufficiently critical of the Russian assault. The criticism was not based, however, on the legal right of Moscow to intervene (widely acknowledged in the US), but on the humanitarian grounds that the destruction and loss of life was terrible and that Moscow's ends could not justify the means being used against the Chechens. The US government conceded the Russian right to bring the area under control since Chechnya was part of Russia, but deplored the means being used. Critics and other governments went even further and deplored the lack of a resolute stand by the US.[2] The lesson is that, increasingly, it is illegitimate to use force against break-away groups, especially if there is no convincing moral principle on the side of the central power. In democratic polities, secession issues should be handled peacefully. As this sentiment grows, intervention to prevent violence comes to be more legitimate. As humanitarian concerns become more urgent and obvious, the number of US policy-makers willing to intervene becomes substantial. Almost all policy-makers will be willing to intervene in a civil war under some circumstances.

All these arguments detailing the decreasing importance of sovereignty in international and American thinking do not mean, however, that policy-makers or the public are not influenced by an argument that opposes intervention in a civil war, or conversely, favor intervention because it is a response to international aggression. Perusal of the morning newspaper can provide plenty of evidence that these arguments still have influence. Notions of sovereignty as the linchpin of the international order go back at least to the Peace of Westphalia in 1648, and will retain persuasive power for some time to come. But examination of the situation in the Yugoslav theatre exposes the declining usefulness of this concept for making decisions on intervention.

There are differing opinions on the legal basis for the break up of the Yugoslav state and we cannot resolve those differences here. But as of April 1992, Slovenia, Croatia and Bosnia–Herzegovina had all been recognized by the United States and Western Europe and many other countries. By this time, the conflict would legally have to be treated as an international conflict. By the time the Bosnian War really got going and American military intervention was seriously being considered, the issue was not whether Yugoslavia would stay together – that had already been decided. The issue had become whether or not Bosnia–Herzegovina would stay together. In this sense, the war had once again assumed civil war status.[3] The complexity described here best makes the case that trying to differentiate between the 'civil' elements of the war and the 'international' elements is a rather hopeless case. It is, or was, both a civil and an international war, and the progression of events is an elegant statement of the earlier argument that this formulation is increasingly outdated as a tool for analyzing wars in the late twentieth century.[4]

The definition of the war, however, had more to do with a policy-maker's state of mind and the need to justify policy than with the legal facts. Because of the strong reaction against the appeasement which took place prior to World War II, it is always difficult to explain in the West why one's government is not intervening to prevent international aggression. President Bush's success in using that theme to mobilize public opinion for the Gulf War indicates the strength of the appeal. It was easy to justify intervention in the Gulf because of the blatant Iraqi intervention in Kuwait. It is more difficult to explain why that principle does not also apply to international aggression in Bosnia. The reason is, of course, that the US was perceived as having a lesser security interest at stake in Bosnia. President Bush conveniently explained to the public that our intervention in Iraq turned back a case of obvious international aggression, but downplayed the fact that it was because that aggression was intertwined with the dependence of the West and Japan on oil in the Middle East that we were so eager to intervene. When a policy-maker confronts a Yugoslav situation, it is necessary to explain the discrepancy between US behavior in the Gulf and behavior in the Balkans. Rather than explain that the principle of responding to aggression is applied selectively depending on the kinds of US security interests that are at stake, it is tempting to be able to define the conflict as an internal war that is not the business of the United States.

Such a tendency was evident in the analysis of the war in Bosnia. With important exeptions, especially in the Bush administration, those who favored intervention stressed the international nature of the war in order to highlight Serbian aggression and the need to respond to it, while those who opposed intervention emphasized the internal aspects of the war, to downplay the existence of aggressive behavior and the extent of US responsibility. As argued above, most of the State Department, President Bush, and President Clinton during his 1992 campaign, consistently interpreted the conflict as a war of aggression, the results of which could not be allowed to stand. But this interpretation was not followed consistently by policy makers at the highest levels, nor by President Clinton and his entourage once they were faced with the problem of explaining their inaction in Bosnia. Not surprisingly, those who compared the response in Bosnia unfavorably to that of the United States in the Gulf or the British in the Falklands preferred to define the war as international, not civil. And the non-interventionist's preference for defining the conflict as a civil war limited to the United States. British Foreign Secretary Hurd was as consistent in referring to the war as a 'civil war' as he was in opposing military intervention by the West. Where one stood on intervention, therefore, tended to determine how one defined the nature of the war. We may suppose that to the extent the public perceived the war as internal, support for intervention was thereby reduced.

ANCIENT ETHNIC HATRED

Perhaps no buzz word has been more consistently used in the debate over the Bosnian war than the phrase 'ancient ethnic hatred' or some equivalent. It is instructive to ask what relevance the existence of ethnic hatred has to the war. Are wars fought because of hatred, or because of divergent interests? Is ethnic hatred the decisive factor that leads to ethnic violence? Or is the nature of the leadership the decisive factor? Is ethnic hatred worse than other types of hatred, for instance, ideological hatred? Are ancient hatreds worse than hatreds that originated more recently? These are hardly easy questions, but the abandon with which the terms are used in debate and declarations on the war would lead one to assume that they are. A little probing, however, indicates that the questions themselves and certainly the implications of the answers are anything but simple.

Was it the uniqueness of the ethnic antagonism in Yugoslavia that led to the violence? Or did the ethnic violence follow from campaigns by the leadership that stirred up the ethnic antagonism? Looking at other societies with the potential for inter-group violence, there is plenty of evidence that even though the objective conditions for ethnic or racial hatred and violence may exist, it does not necessarily materialize. South Africa is a good example of a country that has much potential for racial antagonism and violence. The Africans and the Afrikaaners are two very different people with contesting claims to the right to rule South Africa going back centuries. Over a period of decades, one group was subjected by the other in a rigid system of apartheid which resulted in unequal and harsh living conditions for the black Africans and could well have led to widespread violence. But the moderate leadership on both sides, President Nelson Mandela supported by the Blacks and F.W. de Klerk, the former president, largely supported by the Afrikaners, were committed to a peaceful solution to the problem of race relations and the development of democratic procedures. It is too early to say how the experiment will end, but great progress has been made, attributable in great part to the nature of the leadership. Similarly in the United States, the commitment of the political leadership (both black and white) over a period of decades to integration and racial equality has led to much progress toward those values, but the changes could have been in the other direction if different leadership had held power on one or both sides. Neither of these cases shows that an equally benign outcome could have been obtained in the Yugoslav case, but the burden of proof is certainly with those who suggest otherwise.

If the uniqueness of ethnic hatred in Yugoslavia is questionable, so is the significance of ethnic hatred compared, for instance, to ideological hatred. In the American Civil War there was no history of ethnic hatred between Northern whites and Southern whites, but the issue of slavery generated an intensity of feeling that pitted family member against family member, forced individuals to choose sides and led to long-term antagonism between the North and the South that is still detectable 130 years later. The similarities between these two cases may be greater than is at first perceived. As has been pointed out, there is little of what is normally considered ethnic differences between the Serbs and the Croats. Their racial origins are the same, the language differs primarily in the script that is used. With the Muslims, the confusion is even greater, since the Serbs and Croats cannot agree on where they fit. Both consider the Bosnian Muslims to be racially indistinguishable from themselves and to belong to their group, although in Tito's Yugoslavia, the Muslims were considered to be a separate nationality. Aside from historical experience, the main differences between the groups lies in the religion to which they are most likely to adhere. At the same time, it is claimed that Serbs, Croats and Bosnian Muslims are not very religious. As David Rieff points out, the differences between Croats and Serbs can better be described as cultural rather than ethnic.[5]

As for the historical existence of ethnic hatred, it is of more recent origin than many outsiders assume. Many Yugoslav specialists concur that the violent conflict between these two groups occurred primarily in the twentieth century, especially during World War II. There is no doubt that the bloodletting and the atrocities in Yugoslavia at that time were horrific, that these events are still a vivid part of the historical consciousness of the people living there, and that both sides still argue intensely over the numbers killed on both sides. One source estimates that between May and October in 1941, between

300 000 and 340 000 Serbs were killed by the Ustashi, the Croatian fascist organization. As part of a larger campaign by Germany and its allies, a total of 750 000 Serbs were killed, along with 60 000 Jews and 25 000 Gypsies. In revenge, at least 100 000 Croats were killed by the Serbs.[6] As one can imagine, the cruelty of the methods of torture and execution were every bit the equal of those being used in the former Yugoslavia in this most recent war.

What is the relevance of all this to policy decisions on Yugoslavia today? It is hardly a revelation that hatred accompanies war. A more difficult question is which comes first, the hatred or the war? If war breeds hatred, as it almost surely does, this hardly suggests we should give up trying to find a peaceful solution to individual wars. One may argue that the existence of hatred prior to this war further complicates the situation. Could one deduce from this that the further the hatred extends back in history the more difficult it is to negotiate peace in a given conflict? If so, the Arab–Israeli conflict would be difficult to solve indeed, because the antagonism there goes back at least 2000 years. The Irish situation should be comparatively easy, however, since the landmark event there is the relatively recent Battle of the Boyne in 1690. It is very doubtful that careful historical research on how long different nationalities in Yugoslavia have hated each other would contribute much to an explanation of how the conflict could be solved, any more than examining the history and nature of ethnic hatred between Jews and Nazis would have been useful in ending World War II. The primary problem in World War II was not ethnic hatred, but rather that Hitler had harnessed the hatred and other grievances to fuel his authoritarianism movement. Similarly in Yugoslavia, Milosevic and others have used grievances, ethnic and otherwise, to promote hatred, authoritarianism and military conflict. As Susan Woodward suggests, to explain the Yugoslav crisis as a result of ethnic hatred is to turn the story upside down and begin at the wrong end.[7]

The historical record shows that ethnic violence in the area of Yugoslavia prior to World War II was rather rare. Noel Malcolm, author of a history of Bosnia, points out that the Bosnian War 'was not caused by ancient hatreds; it was caused by modern politicians'. He notes that historical differences certainly existed, but

> the idea that such differences should be a basis for hatred is, historically, a recent innovation, brought in by intellectuals and politicians in the nineteenth century when they tried to impose the theory of the homogeneous state on their very heterogeneous homelands ... Today, when these myths are harped on so constantly in the service of modern political hatred, it is easy to misjudge their significance.[8]

He argues that it could hardly have been otherwise, since the groups were so thoroughly mixed that coexistence was essential to avoid continual violence. He quotes the anthropologist William Lockwood who did field work in Bosnia and found interethnic relations to have been generally good since 1878,[9] and argues that violence prior to 1878 was generally sparked by landlord–tenant issues rather than ethnic conflict. According to Malcolm, Lockwood found that in the countryside, the various ethnic groups lived 'elaborately parallel lives – intertwined, so to speak, but not interwoven'. Other observers of ethnoreligious antagonism put more stress on the ever-present potential for outbreaks of violence. Lenard Cohen summarizes the view that 'the potential for ethnically and religiously based violence in the Balkans was most evident during periods of regime crisis and breakdown'. At such times seemingly tranquil intergroup relations can explode into an orgy of mutual bloodletting. But there is no comparison between the amount of ethnic violence in Yugoslavia and what historically went on between the French and the Germans, or the French and the English, now all joined together in the European Union.[10]

The concept of 'ancient ethnic hatreds' is important because it played a role both in influencing American behavior toward the war and in rationalizing it. As in most foreign policies, a complex interaction exists between the impact of ideas on the policy and the use of ideas as a justification for what is going to be done anyway. One pernicious use of the ethnic hatred approach is to define the whole conflict as irrational and completely unresponsive to outside influences.

Here is Acting Secretary of State Eagleburger, who had served in Yugoslavia, on the nature of the war

> It is difficult to explain, but this war is not rational. There is no rationality at all about ethnic conflict. It is gut; it is hatred; it's not for any common set of values or purposes; it just goes on. And that kind of warfare is most difficult to bring to a halt.[11]

Eagleburger seems to be suggesting that the course of this kind of war cannot be influenced by outside intervention; outside action is useless against irrationality. In light of this it is interesting to note that the reaction to the war, as reflected in the Bush/Eagleburger policy and Western policy in general until late 1995, was to put energy and resources into continual negotiation, although that process yielded very little. One might suppose that when dealing with irrationality, it would make more sense to use force rather than negotiation. Isn't force the preferred method of influence when confronting forces that will not listen to reason, whether in police work or in the international arena?

But the more detrimental effect of this approach to ethnic hatred is to blame all parties equally for the situation. Here is Eagleburger again:

> It's Serbs, it's Croats, it's Bosnian Muslims, the whole panorama. If you're intent on killing each other, don't blame it on somebody else. We'll do what we can to help, but in the end you've got to have some sense that there are limits to your insanity.[12]

It's just one big cauldron of crazies fighting one another without any rhyme or reason; they won't stop for anything or anyone, and if we intervene we will just get chewed up and have no impact at all, seems to be the theme of what Eagleburger says. This approach is puzzling, since the mass of materials on the war coming out of Eagleburger's own State Department directly contradicted much that he was saying (see Chapter 9). That analysis showed that the bulk of the blame for starting and continuing the war was directly attributable to Serbia and the Serbs, as were the overwhelming number of the atrocities. From the beginning of the use of the military in Slovenia, through the war with Croatia and during the military activities in Bosnia, the State Department kept up a steady criticism of Serbia and its aggressive role in the war, and its failure to abide by agreements.

Both Bush and Clinton appeared to attribute considerable significance to the impact of ethnic antagonism on the war. The view that all parties were equally to blame appeared in presidential statements from time to time. A book by Robert D. Kaplan, *Balkan Ghosts*, has been credited with a decisive influence on President Clinton's thinking on the advisability of US intervention in Bosnia. The book has been criticized for its sensational approach and lack of perspective on the problem of inter-ethnic relations in the Balkans.[13] Reading it without any background on Yugoslav questions, one could certainly take away the impression that the Balkans is a uniquely conflict-ridden place with almost no tradition of negotiation or peaceful resolution of disputes. This travel account is an entertaining read, but perhaps not the best guide to formulating foreign policy in the Balkans.

It is with regret, then, that one reads that the book was a key influence in dissuading Clinton from the advisability of committing the US to the 'lift-and-strike' policy, a policy of lifting the embargo on the Muslims obtaining arms and using air strikes against the Serbs. Clinton was reading the book while Christopher was in Europe talking to our allies about adopting the lift and strike policy. Defense officials meeting with the President heard him discuss his impressions from the book, which included the Balkan people's historic propensity for war with each other, tribal and religious war that had been going on for centuries, and the Serb National Day, which commemorates the battle of Kosovo, the 1389 battle where the Serbs lost to the Turks at Kosovo Polje. The conversation with the President reportedly made a big impression on then Secretary of Defense Aspen, who concluded that the President had changed his mind about lift and strike, and accordingly began to alert other officials to that fact.[14] This change in policy may be attributable to Bill Clinton's lack of skill in assessing foreign policy information, or to the inadequacy of Kaplan's analysis or, most likely, to both. In any event, it is disturbing to those who think foreign-policy decisions should be made on more comprehensive grounds than a rehash of the genocide of the Second World War, Serbian perspectives on fourteenth-century history, and the rest of the rather steamy and impressionistic brew Kaplan produced. It is doubly ironic that more recently Clinton was reported to have read Noel Malcolm's contrasting (to Kaplan's) views on the role of ethnic conflict in Balkan history, and that reading was reported to have influenced the August 1995 shift to a firmer policy toward the Bosnian Serbs![15]

This leads us to the second role played by the 'ancient ethnic hatreds' approach to the war: rationalization for a policy which has already been chosen. There was a clear connection between the way the war in Bosnia was portrayed and the kind of policy that US officials were promoting. If, on the one hand, the US was pursuing a policy that appears to be responding to the crisis and having an impact on stopping the carnage and expansion, or even rolling borders back to previous lines, then it was safe to portray Serbia and Serbs as the aggressors, as the primary problem with which the US must deal. Something bad is happening, there is a remedy available, and we are attempting to supply the remedy, is the way this foreign-policy situation might be described. On the other hand, if the US is playing a passive or ineffective role which will probably not lead to a 'satisfactory' solution to the problem, then it is in the government's interest to portray the nature of the war as originating with 'ethnic hatred' rather than Serbian aggression, to distribute blame evenly rather than pinpoint a specific villain, and to abrogate responsibility for the likely outcome. The war is bad, but there are many causes of the conflict, everybody involved is to blame for it, and there is really nothing we can do in these circumstances, is how the reasoning might go under this less-favorable foreign-policy scenario.

Much of the Bush administration rhetoric, especially at levels below the Secretary of State, did blame the Serbs for the war while consistently refusing to intervene militarily. But Clinton administration rhetoric on the war changed once it took office and began to back away from activist campaign language. Contrary to the initial policy under which Clinton advocated and planned a firm US response, the administration became resigned to keeping the war within the boundaries of Bosnia, essentially giving up a leadership role. Whereas Clinton had, in the campaign and the early part of his administration, portrayed the war as a product of clear cut Serbian aggression and as an international war, now the analysis altered. In February Clinton explained what was happening in the conflict in Bosnia by saying that

> Serbian ethnic cleansing has been pursued through mass murders, systematic beatings, and the rapes of Muslims and others, prolonged shelling of innocents in Sarajevo and elsewhere.

But by late March he was explaining the same basic phenomenon with quite different language that seemed to spread blame equally to all parties and suggest that there was very little that the US could do about it.

> The hatred between all three groups ... is almost unbelievable. It's almost terrifying, and it's centuries old. That really is a problem from hell. And I think the United States is doing all we can to try to deal with that problem.

Christopher began portraying the war as a 'morass' of deep distrust and ancient hatreds among Serbs, Croats, and Muslims where 'there are atrocities on all sides', a three-way feud with no clear aggressors or victims.[16] On this later point, Christopher was challenged in private by another State Department official who cited the State Department's own reports to the UN on human rights as evidence that the overwhelming number of atrocities were committed by Serbs.[17] Just as Clinton had sharpened the analysis of the war to score points in the campaign and to highlight his proposed response to Serb aggression at that time, now, as the solution seemed to be slipping from his grasp, the definition of the war changed to make the policy more acceptable to the American people. Given the concern over Bosnia and the expectations that had been raised about a US response, the public could only be comfortable with a policy explanation that suggested that the problem of Serbian aggression no longer existed, and therefore required no solution. The administration not only could not offer an American policy to deal with the situation, it was now reduced to denying that a war of aggression against the Bosnians was even underway.

CONCLUSION

The complexity of the war in Bosnia made it a difficult war for the public to understand. Sometimes through ignorance, sometimes by design, the concept of ethnic hatred served to obscure understanding of the war and to justify inaction by the leadership. Labeling of the war as either civil or international sometimes also served to justify policy. These characterizations of the war by the foreign policy elite further confused a public not well-informed on the war.

8 Vietnam and the Debate on Intervention in Bosnia

Previous chapters have stressed the diminishing importance of Yugoslavia as a security interest with the end of the Cold War and the tendency of Americans to look inward to domestic issues and avoid foreign obligations and burdens. But the legacy of the Vietnam War also contributed to both the American public's lack of enthusiasm for a Bosnian involvement and the foreign-policy elite's perception that intervention in the former Yugoslavia would have the 'tar baby' effect of the Vietnam involvement. This thinking was particularly apparent during the Bush administration's decisions on Bosnia. This chapter will explore the nature of that impact and the problems connected with the attempt to use the Vietnam analogy for analysis of the Bosnian War.

Atrocities and war crimes in the former Yugoslavia evoked memories of World War II, and explicit parallels were frequently drawn between the two, as at the dedication of the Holocaust Museum in Washington, DC. Other analogies were sometimes cited the German experience in Yugoslavia in World War II, Lebanon and – by those who favored intervention – the Gulf War with its relatively easy 'victory' using high-tech weaponry. But none of these memories or images were salient enough to overcome the dominant images, fears, and influence on decision-making that stemmed from the Vietnam War and other foreign-policy disasters such as Lebanon. The American experience in Vietnam permeated the debate on Bosnia. The fearful images of Vietnam seemed more potent in the Bush administration and the Congress than with the Clinton people, which may partially explain why Clinton was always more inclined toward an American military response in Bosnia.

Vietnam was a defining, traumatic experience for a generation of Americans. That war had split the foreign-policy establishment, divided the country along ideological lines, adversely affected the economy, and raised persistent suspicions about any proposals for undertaking military actions abroad.[1] Twenty-five years later, that war still provided the reference points for the foreign policy debate on Bosnia, while the Gulf-War experience proved to be only a momentary respite from the grip of the Vietnam experience on the country's foreign-policy perspective. With national security interests not clearly at stake, and humanitarian intervention dependent on the mobilization of divided or indifferent public opinion, the residual impact of Vietnam was sufficient to ensure no obvious foreign policy risks would be taken in Bosnia for over three years after the war began in the spring of 1992.

COMPARISON OF BOSNIAN, VIETNAMESE AND GULF WARS

There was little comparison of the Bosnian War with the Gulf War either by policy-makers or commentators. The Gulf War had barely ended when the Serbs invaded first Slovenia, and then Croatia. The Gulf war was widely seen, both among foreign-policy experts and the general public, as a clear-cut victory for the United States, a morale builder, and an experience that helped to lift the cloud of self-doubt that the Vietnam defeat had inflicted on the American people. But analogies drawn to the Bosnian War have most frequently referred to Vietnam. This was more indicative of the continued grip of the 'Vietnam syndrome' on the American consciousness than it was of the similarities or differences in the wars. It is interesting, therefore, to note that the Bosnian and Gulf Wars have a surprising number of parallels.

Table 8.1 compares the three wars. A yes answer is given for a favorable condition for intervention, and each yes is given one point. Favorable factors for prosecuting a war include a consensus in the US on the question of who the aggressor was in Bosnia, motivated allied troops (Bosnian government troops), and international opinion favorable to intervention.[2] Bosnia is judged to be partially a civil conflict, and the allied Bosnian government is considered to be legitimate. This is a controversial position, because of the Serbian rejection of the referendum on independence, but the government at the

Table 8.1   Comparison of three wars

	Vietnam	Gulf	Bosnia
'Non-Civil war' type conflict	no	yes (1)	partial (1/2)
American consensus on enemy	no	yes (1)	yes (1)
Perceived security interest	partial (1/2)	yes (1)	no
Terrain favorable for bombing	no	yes (1)	no
Legitimate allied government	partial (1/2)	partial (1/2)	yes (1)
Motivated allied troops	no	no	yes (1)
Favorable international opinion	no	yes (1)	yes (1)
Cooperation from allies	partial (1/2)	yes (1)	no
Cold War in progress	yes (1)	no	no
Favorable characteristics	**2.5**	**6.5**	**4.5**

Note: All characteristics favorable to a decision to prosecute a war are given one point if present, one-half point if partially present. In all cases, a point is given for a yes answer.

start of the war was committed to respecting minority rights and did hold open elections.

On the negative side, since the perceived US security interest was minimal, a no answer is given to that factor. Much of the comparison of Vietnam and Bosnia centers on the terrain. In Bosnia, it was pointed out, the mountains and the forests were ideal for guerrilla warfare (similar to conditions in Vietnam), whereas in Iraq the barren deserts made spotting and eliminating the enemy easy. If one defines the Serbs as the aggressor, however, there is an important similarity with Iraq. Just as the war there was taken to Baghdad, the war in Bosnia could have been taken to Belgrade in the early months of the war. Targets in Belgrade, key bridges over the Drina River connecting Serbia and Bosnia, and supplies and industry in Serbia were significant targets in the summer of 1992. Nonetheless, a no answer is assumed for this factor. Other negative factors include limited cooperation from allies for military actions (before 1995), and there was no Cold-War atmosphere conducive to prosecution of a war as in the case of Vietnam.

In spite of similarities between the Gulf and Bosnian wars, the wars are perceived as being very different. To an important degree this is justified. On the one hand, the perception of a vital American interest was much stronger in the Gulf because of the oil interests. Moreover, the similarities in terrain between Vietnam and Bosnia and the difficulty of bombing, the absence of a Cold-War atmosphere, lack of cooperation from allies, and the public's perception of the number of actors and complexity of the situation made Bosnia a hard war to sell.

Comparison of the wars on this crude scale illustrates that as an environment for American intervention, Bosnia (4.5 favorable points) presented considerably better prospects than Vietnam (2.5), although not as good as in the Gulf (6.5). But the reluctance to intervene was as much a product of the lens through which Bosnia was viewed, a lens which added a heavy Vietnam cast to the images, as any reliance on factual analysis of the two situations. This is supported by examination of the themes that appeared repeatedly in discussions of intervention.

THE CONTEXT OF DECISION-MAKING

We all make decisions using devices and shortcuts that facilitate thinking and analysis but may also distort the end result. Using analogies to sort through policies and choose the best one is such a shortcut. The ideal decision involves emulating a 'naive scientist' ferreting out the facts and then drawing conclusions based on logic and evidence. In many cases, however, it is difficult or impossible to find the needed information, and to go through all the steps necessary to process the factual material. All of us, in other words, because of limitations of knowledge and abilities, fall short of being objective.[3]

Given this shortcoming, we tend to adopt the solution of sorting through difficult issues using analogies with past experience to explain and understand current dilemmas. Reasoning by analogy is probably essential because we 'cannot make sense of our environment without assuming that in some sense, the future will resemble the past'. Therefore, statesman turn to the past in dealing with the present. But reasoning by analogy, although useful, is also inadequate. Since a given event is almost never the same as a past event, and the environment in which events take place is changed and conditions are different, it is risky to assume that a past event or outcome can be used as an accurate model for a present one.[4] Moreover, one study found that the function served by apologies is psychological as well as intellectual, and once accepted the hold of an analogy on an individual is such that there may be considerable resistance to contrary or qualifying evidence.[5]

A tendency to use a widely accepted paradigm or set of assumptions and values to view the world is a second shortcut to decision-making. People working and acting in a certain field at a given time tend to accept some basic assumptions which comprise the dominant paradigm of that field. Those making foreign policy are no exception to this rule. These 'paradigms', it is argued, dominate foreign policy-making in each period, as most people assume the conventional wisdom of the paradigm is the only realistic way to view the world. The minority, with views held over from the previous paradigm, tend to be ignored by those adhering to the majority paradigm. Two basic paradigms, or conventional wisdom, have alternated in dominating US foreign policy in recent decades. An interventionist paradigm emphasizes the importance of events overseas, believes in a significant US involvement in international affairs and is willing to pay a significant price for that involvement. An isolationist paradigm, on the other hand, puts less emphasis on overseas issues, favors a more isolated United States, and is unwilling to pay a price for foreign involvement.[6]

Paradigms periodically shift, as one orientation gives way and an alternative perspective becomes dominant. Michael Roskin argues that an interventionist paradigm (Pearl Harbor paradigm) was dominant from the attack on Pearl Harbor in 1941, until well into the Vietnam War when a paradigm shift led to the ascendancy of the Vietnam paradigm. In both cases, traumatic events, Pearl Harbor in the first case, the Vietnam War in the second, led to the paradigm shift and the emergence of a new paradigm. Roskin traces conflicting paradigms in US foreign policy through five incarnations, going back to the civil war period.

The concept of a paradigm or conventional foreign-policy wisdom fits nicely with the concept of thinking with analogies. If foreign-policy-makers think with the aid of analogies, then they are most likely to use analogies from the current dominant paradigm. It is hard to say here to what degree the 'Vietnam paradigm' was accepted, but in the context of decision making on Bosnia it was very salient and certainly more important than any other paradigm, including any 'Gulf paradigm'. In the absence of appropriate foreign-policy guidelines for the current period, the Vietnam paradigm exercised dominant influence.

But the Vietnam analogy is unique in one respect: there are at least two interpretations of the lessons to be learned from the Vietnam experience. One school believes that the lesson is the need for caution in making decisions to intervene. For this school, 'no more Vietnams' means that the US should not intervene where there is limited or doubtful strategic value, where the means and the ends of the conflict will be questioned and where it will be difficult to win. The second school reject this stricture against intervention, and holds that the lesson of Vietnam is that the intervention was justified, but the mistake was in imposing restraints on the military and that steps should be taken in the future to make sure that a conflict is won.[7] In the context of Bosnia, both of these interpretations were at work, one impeding any attempt to intervene, the other ensuring that when and if intervention occurred, it would be of a sufficient scale to get the job done without too much cost. The first interpretation was probably the one most relevant to Bosnia decision-making, but the two interpretations are to some degree symbiotic. If one is already hesitant to intervene because of the salience of the Vietnam example of sinking in a quagmire, there is very likely to be careful scrutiny of any intervention that is eventually carried out to try to ensure the Vietnam results are not repeated. In fact, one reason there was a reluctance to intervene in Bosnia was that policy-makers and public did not believe a sufficiently important security interest existed to justify the kind of force that was presumed necessary to have the necessary margin of safety in accomplishing the goals of the intervention. The lessons learned from Vietnam may have diverged, but in the case of Bosnia, the effect on policy of both of them was the same: to impede intervention.

When one pivotal event results in a paradigm shift, there is a tendency for that event to continue to have influence and to play a role beyond the time when it is relevant. In such cases, the use of analogies may be misleading and detrimental to sound decision-making. That is exactly what happened on Bosnia. The generals (as well as the politicians) were examining the last war, as much or more than the current one.

MISUSE OF ANALOGIES

Stopping aggression in Vietnam

Thinking more relevant to Pearl Harbor and Munich was often used to justify the Vietnam War. The assumptions of the Pearl Harbor paradigm were interventionist, and they were enunciated by the interventionists after Pearl Harbor.

> If we do not nip aggression in the bud it will eventually grow and involve us. By not stopping aggressors immediately, you encouraged [sic] them. Apart from the moral issue of helping a victim of aggression, you are also setting up the first line of defense of your own country. Accordingly, altruism and self-interest merge.

These 'lessons' from Munich and Pearl Harbor were often applied indiscriminately in the Cold War following the allied victory.[8] If these analogies seemed to hold up in the early years of the cold war, however, they fared much less well when applied to Vietnam. The Pearl Harbor paradigm lost salience when the American foreign-policy establishment split over the war, and the war lost public support, Lyndon Johnson declined to run in the 1968 election, and it became clear that the troops would be coming home without securing their objective. A whole new conventional wisdom began to emerge. Not surprisingly, the new paradigm represented the flip side of the previous paradigm. Whereas heretofore foreign events were considered crucial to US security, now they were viewed as much less so. Whereas previously the US did not hesitate to intervene, now it was much more cautious and more prone to sponsor proxy troops to avoid US involvement in a local war. The US had tended to consider itself the 'world's policeman', now it was much less so inclined. After Vietnam, it would have fewer troops abroad, it would pare down its formal commitments, and the executive would suffer more Congressionally imposed restraints on decision-making.[9] Most notable from the standpoint of those studying paradigm shifts, now the experience that would constantly be evoked as a guide to policy-making was not Munich or Pearl Harbor, but Vietnam. This was especially true in the Bush administration's rhetoric on Bosnia.

Avoiding a quagmire in Bosnia

The Vietnam paradigm fits well with many of the explanations given by the Bush administration for not intervening in Bosnia. Clinton administration officials also mentioned analogies in explaining their views on the Bosnian War, but less frequently. President Clinton sometimes mentioned the World War II analogy and the difficulty both sides had in gaining control of Yugoslavia during that war.[10] But the decision-making atmosphere was suffused with the Vietnam paradigm, during both administrations. And this applies not only to the executive branch. Commentary from the Congress and the media also frequently focused on Vietnam. The policy of the Bush administration in Bosnia brings to mind Robert Jervis' line, reversing Santayana, that those who remember the past are condemned to make the opposite mistake.[11] Even though Bosnia was not Vietnam, the Bush administration treated it as if it were.

One of the themes repeatedly invoked by US policy-makers during the period after the Serbian invasion of Bosnia in April 1992 to justify the lack of military action on the part of the West was the fear that once military action was begun, it would have to continue in terrain and under political and military conditions that were not favorable to the United States. The result might well be an end point from which the United States could not achieve a victory, but from which it would also find it hard to extricate itself. In a similar vein, Senator McCain, expressing his reservations about Bosnia policy after the Clinton administration had begun a few tentative air strikes, talked of 'mission creep', which he defined as continual escalation which will ultimately force a choice between deploying ground troops to finish the job, or withdrawing in defeat. The latter, he suggested, 'could cripple all US foreign policy for the duration of this administration'.[12] In the Bush-administration handling of Bosnia policy, a defining theme was this fear of being irretrievably drawn into a quagmire once military action began. Relegated to a subsidiary place, in most cases seemingly completely forgotten, was the old decision-makers' obsession with the Pearl Harbor paradigm, the need to stop aggression before it is successful, the kind of reasoning that drew us into Vietnam, Cambodia, and other strategically marginal places. Now the aggression was deplored, but it was also made clear that military force would not be used to stop it.[13]

The most articulate Bush administration spokesman on the folly of following the Vietnam pattern was Acting Secretary of State Lawrence Eagleburger. On the MacNeil/Lehrer Newshour, after the London Conference on Yugoslavia in August 1992, Eagleburger was asked about the views of George Kenney, who had resigned from the Yugoslav desk of the State Department in protest over US policy there. Asked initially about the lack of substance in US policy, he rejected both a strategy of lifting the arms embargo against Yugoslavia, and the use of American military force. Assuming the lack of a US vital interest that would justify all-out war, he said military force leads you into a Vietnam-like situation, where there is no alternative that would be militarily effective without trapping us in a continually escalating situation.[14]

During the summer and fall of 1992, the President also made reference to Vietnam, with the clear implication that military involvement in Bosnia would lead to either a military quagmire or a withdrawal in defeat. In August, President Bush said he did not want to get 'bogged down' in guerilla warfare. We had lived through that once. Similarly, during the presidential campaign in October, he noted that

> I learned something from Vietnam. I am not going to commit US forces until I know what the mission is, until the military tells me that it can be completed, until I know how they can come out.[15]

It was frequently assumed by both officials and commentators that intervention could only occur if a clear exit strategy existed, which could be executed only after a clearly defined mission had been successfully completed. The alternative was a Vietnam-type quagmire.

AGGRESSION, DETERRENCE AND CREDIBILITY

Reading the government accounts of the situation in Yugoslavia, one is struck by the drastically lowered status of 'aggression' as a galvanizing factor compared to earlier wars. While aggressive behavior is prevalent, is roundly condemned, and the perpetrator, Serbia, is also condemned, it is made quite clear that the Bush administration intends to do nothing militarily in response.

In the Cold-War international system, no doubt deterrence was often overrated. The need to mobilize public opinion outweighed the need for balanced analysis and led to an over-dramatization of threats and the need to respond. Stopping aggression in one corner of the globe often had little relationship to preventing it in other corners. As some scholars have pointed out, successful deterrence is most likely when skillfully orchestrated with a clear understanding of the objective to be accomplished in a specific instance. It is more difficult to formulate a recipe for deterrence that is effective in a broad range of situations and instances, and in a post-Cold-War system this is even more true when one powerful and obvious enemy has been replaced by numerous despots with moderate capabilities and erratic foreign policies. As Fareed Zakaria notes, 'Generalized deterrence is impossible. It is an attempt to stop the clock of international conflict – a worthy but unattainable goal.' As Richard Ned Lebow points out, nations and their leaders often do things that are almost certain to fail and appear irrational. Even worse, action that is intended to deter certain behavior in some cases ends up provoking it. Such was the case with the American oil embargo on Japan prior to World War II.[16]

Nonetheless, most foreign-policy professionals assume that a permissive stance toward international outlaws will, in the long run at least, breed more aggression. It is not surprising that concern with teaching lessons to aggressive nations would diminish once the Cold War was over and the US was the only effective superpower, especially given the demonstrations of the futility of teaching lessons to aggressive powers. In a matter of months after the US had decisively dealt with Iraq and expelled it from Kuwait, President Milosevic began his wars against Slovenia and Croatia. The so-called Gulf lesson on aggression clearly was not fully absorbed by Milosevic and as subsequent events confirmed, his disregard of the lesson was prescient. Instead of replicating the Gulf lesson in Bosnia, this time the Bush administration preferred to react passively to the Serbs' military actions. Even allowing for the changed circumstances in the international system, the willingness to write off the Serbian actions as something too costly to deal with was striking, and indicated the degree to which the Pearl Harbor paradigm had fallen out of favor, especially once the the Cold War had ended.

In this case, however, there is good evidence that a stronger Western stance in Bosnia might have stopped Serb aggression. John Burns writes that Bosnian Serb leader Karadzic never seemed to doubt that if there was one force likely to frustrate his objectives, it was the United States. American reporters visiting the Bosnian Serbian headquarters at Pale were grilled about American intentions with a keenness the leaders rarely showed for the subtleties of European policy. The result, says Burns, was 'an almost arithmetical correlation between American leaders' statements on the conflict and the behavior of the Serbian forces'. As long as Serbian or Bosnian Serbian leadership took American threats seriously, they exhibited caution, but when it became clear that the threat was hollow, they moved ahead. They judged the seriousness of the threat primarily on the basis of immediate American intentions in Bosnia, not some general perception of past American behavior.[17]

Bush administration officials, despite their unwillingness to move against Serb aggression, manifested an extreme concern with credibility in Bosnia and took fastidious care to avoid any implication that the US was committing itself to the use of force or to the threat of force. In international politics, maintaining the maximum of uncertainty about one's intentions is often held to be a valuable tool for maximizing influence with minimum cost to the actor. During the Bush administration, however, American policy makers very often *a priori* indicated that they had no intention of using force, thus alleviating anxiety among the Serbs about potential threats to them. These kind of reassurances appeared repeatedly in the summer and fall of 1992, following the Serbian invasion of Bosnia in April, and they did not concern only the sending of ground troops. In July, the President was careful to assure journalists that movements of a carrier task force through the Adriatic signified no change of policy on Yugoslavia.[18] From an international perspective, these statements are puzzling since they seem to obviate all possible influence of the threat of military force. They can best be explained from a domestic perspective, however, as an attempt to soothe any public fears about possible military involvement and subsequent costs in lives and resources.

Policy-makers in the Bush administration were hypersensitive to the possibility that a statement would be taken by the Serbs as a threat. If it were then ignored by the Serbs, the reasoning went, it would harm American credibility because the US was not prepared to act. An extreme example of this kind of logic is Eagleburger's account of an incident in the Adriatic. During the war with Croatia when the Serbs were shelling Dubrovnik on the Adriatic coast, the President of Croatia asked the US government to sail the Sixth Fleet, already in the area, past Dubrovnik as a subtle hint to the Serbs of US concern. Eagleburger admitted he refused to do so, on the grounds that further action would be needed if the Serbs didn't respond to the message conveyed by the passage past Dubrovnik.[19] This is a remarkable statement given the ease with which any kind of hostile intent in moving the fleet could have been denied. Thus Bush administration officials were not only unwilling to commit force to the conflict, but they were also very careful to avoid specific threats of force, and to go out of their way to avoid leaving the impression that a threat was intended. Eagleburger seemingly had no misgivings about the value of American credibility unless some overt threat was made for which there was no follow-through. Complete inaction, in his view, did not compromise US credibility.

But for proponents of greater US involvement, inaction in itself signaled a lack of credibility and a squandering of the credibility already earned. For some, the prestige built up in the Gulf War and the Reagan–Bush years was being dissipated by the failure to stop the Serbs and take steps to stabilize the situation. In this view, the failure of the US to respond to a destabilizing action by Serbia in the NATO theater displayed a lack of American will and signaled a diminished American role as a great power, since it was clear we were no longer going to act as the policeman of the world, even if the cost was relatively low.[20]

It is hard to assign much importance to concerns with the effect of the war on American prestige or credibility, whether related to the concerns of the advocates or the opponents of military action. Most likely both sides are mistaken in assigning much importance to the long-term effect of an abstract quality like credibility, given the limitations of 'generalized deterrence'. The US has sometimes acted forcefully (Panama, Gulf), sometimes withdrawn in defeat (Vietnam, Lebanon), and sometimes unleashed fearsome rhetoric but done nothing militarily (Nicaragua). It is clear that the US will be less likely to act in a post-Cold-War world, since it is more difficult to perceive a vital interest when the US is no longer challenged over the globe by a superpower that is a near equal. Still, as the Gulf War showed, under certain circumstances the US will react decisively. Especially in a post-Cold-War type world where power is diffused and the threats to the US are numerous but limited, situations will be complex and the US reaction hard to predict. Such predictions will have to be done on a case-by-case basis, based on the circumstances and US declarations. The deterrent value of a specific foreign-policy action will therefore be even less than during the Cold-War period.

It is very hard to predict the deterrent effect of US intervention or the lack of it. Even though the US acted assertively many times during the Cold War and after, the impact was often ambiguous. As we have seen, Bush's spectacular victory over Saddam Hussein seemed to have no effect in intimidating Milosevic. Yet, there are numerous instances of both Milosevic and the Bosnian Serbs appearing to show restraint when the US made moves to carry out aerial strikes in Bosnia. Analysts' preoccupation with the abstractions of prestige and credibility now needs to be replaced with a more pragmatic evaluation of each individual military situation. If a powerful country like the US shows that it is serious about military action, notice will be taken.[21] Nobody doubts the ability to do damage if the will is there; the only unknowns are will and intent. In the present world, intent must be judged through assessment of the individual situation. Critics on all sides would be well advised to focus less on the mythic quantity of 'credibility' and base their arguments on current needs. Generally, the immediate impact of foreign-policy decisions in the immediate present is difficult to predict, let alone determining the effect of a decision on long-term credibility. If a decision improves credibility in the future, well and good, but the first question is the appropriateness of the decision for the problem at hand. Nowhere has the fatuousness of the claims for credibility as a meaningful concept in the analysis of international relations been more clearly revealed than in the debates on Bosnia. The preferences for using the term as an abstract entity to bolster one's debating position rather than one with meaning in day-to-day implementation of policy is evident in the way the debate has been handled on both sides. The proponents of a NATO role of active intervention have repeatedly cited a loss of credibility in countering ethnic violence as part of the price paid for doing nothing. But by this they appear to mean the loss of credibility as it would apply to some future Eastern European crisis, one in the former Soviet Union, or a third world country. But it was in its impact on Croatian behavior that any actions against the Serbs would most likely have an indirect deterrent effect. Both Serbs and Croats were carrying out military action in the same environment, the rules of conflict were roughly the same for both countries, and the US reaction might be presumed to be very similar for both parties. For these reasons, any serious action aimed at deterring Serb military aggressiveness would certainly have an impact on Croatian thinking, particularly if NATO had explicitly warned the Croatians of the likely consequences of military action. But the proponents of using force almost never mentioned the case where the response of an outside power was most relevant to credibility and deterrence: to help deter the Croats from carrying out the same actions that the Serbs did. Likewise, the European and other opponents of NATO military action against the Serbs almost never remarked on the kind of lesson that the lack of penalty for Serbian military action provided for the Croat opportunists, who acted, and very bloodily, on their knowledge that the West was unlikely to interfere. The opponents of military action against the Serbs (Bush administration) justified doing nothing on the grounds of the need to preserve credibility, and others (Europeans) complained that the 'interventionists' singled out the Serbs for condemnation while failing to criticize the Croats and Muslims. But it was their own failure to respond to the Serbs that encouraged military action by the Croats in 1993.

Moreover Eagleburger's assumption that if a threat fails credibility can only be maintained by carrying out continual escalation until the objective is achieved, is wrong. Air strikes in Bosnia, even if not successful in the end, could have been broken off without necessarily requiring the introduction of ground troops or totally damaging US credibility and prestige. Trying something, even if it fails, is not likely to have a very different effect on American 'prestige' than doing nothing.

A second fear, part of the Vietnam paradigm that encouraged inaction in Bosnia, was the fear that initial military action would lead to uninterrupted escalation from which there would be no escape. I have argued that to break such a pattern and withdraw from failed action is unlikely seriously to damage US prestige. But is it possible to withdraw? Is the escalator something which, once one has mounted the first step, you are doomed to ride to the top?

The assertion of mission creep or uninterrupted escalation is difficult to critique because there is seldom an explanation as to why this phenomenon occurs. During discussion of escalating the Vietnam War by putting American troops in, President Kennedy drew an analogy to taking a drink. As he put it:

The troops will march in, the bands will play, the crowds will cheer, and in four days everyone will have forgotten. Then we will be told we have to send in more troops. It's like taking a drink. The effect wears off and you have to take another.[22]

Plausible explanations for the demands for continual escalation are the result of military events, the pressure of public opinion, bureaucratic pressures, or some combination of all three. It is difficult to see how purely military pressures would result in uninterrupted escalation. There is no military imperative that pushes one inevitably from one technology, logistic mode, or action environment to another. While the introduction of ground troops may often follow the use of air power which has been used to 'soften up' the enemy, military actions should be used to accomplish political ends. Military escalation would presumably, therefore, be used only in pursuit of a political objective.

Political pressures may indeed lead to escalation. Often, such pressures are created, perhaps inadvertently, by the very officials who are pressured to escalate. During one of the rare instances of NATO exercising force against the Bosnian Serbs, Secretary Christopher, instead of justifying air strikes simply as a means of stopping the Serbs, presented the strikes as a means of preserving American military credibility.[23] Clearly such statements are likely to become a trap for the leadership. If an action is presented repeatedly as representing a test of American will or credibility, in the eyes of those both within the government and ordinary citizens, the veracity of the government will start to depend on avoiding 'defeat'.

If, however, the 'prestige' aspect of an action is de-emphasized and stress is placed on the immediate job at hand, some political cost may still be at stake in discontinuing a failed action, but an acceptable cost. As pointed out several times in this book, the world is now messier than it was. Instead of precise objectives, carefully calculated costs, and clear-cut victories, we are more likely to have shifting objectives, less predictable strategies, and elusive outcomes. Exhibit One of this phenomenon is the much ballyhooed Persian Gulf action, which turned out to be something less than the clear-cut victory many originally thought it was. As a result of that action, American planes still patrol two no-fly zones in Iraq. During the Clinton administration it was discovered that Saddam Hussein had planned an assassination plot against former President Bush, to which we felt compelled to respond, he has taken hostages which we were helpless to retrieve, and the Iraqi people still suffer. The outcome of that war, in short, is not exactly the advertisement for foreign policy clarity, resolution and victory that its proponents had hoped.

The lesson that the Bush administration took from Vietnam and tried to apply to Bosnia was that of avoiding the slippery slope of escalation by complete avoidance of military action. The lesson that should have been learned, and explained to the public, is that the costs paid to pursue foreign-policy object-ives should be proportional to the objectives being sought. More valuable objectives justify higher costs, and the cost one is prepared to pay should be adjusted as goals increase or decrease in value. Awareness of this principle should be the means of making foreign-policy decisions that avoid activating mission creep. The rationale of the Bush administration leads to complete inaction, since virtually nobody maintained that the US or the European countries had a vital interest in Bosnia that justified heavy involvement on the ground. It can be argued, however, that a limited interest, both security and humanitarian, existed. If the US subscribes to the now-obsolete doctrine that wars can only be fought all-out with objectives, costs, and end-points clearly defined and visible, then the US will play a far too limited role in shaping a world that needs a US military involvement.

It may be objected that in the real world, exact equation of cost and benefit is difficult if not impossible, military action cannot be initiated and terminated with the necessary preci-sion, and it is difficult to predict the consequences of military actions one is about to undertake. Of course, all these state-ments are true. But in the post-Cold-War world, the flexibility called for here is more suited to foreign policy making than the Cold-War obsession with deterrence and credibility. Policies proportionate to the interests involved and the costs that can be paid are the appropriate ones. The Bush adminis-tration, seeking the certainty of victory, but with limited cost, was reduced to a sterile rhetoric that was helpless before a Serbian leadership that had taken their measure, and acted accordingly.

Part IV

US Policy in Yugoslavia and Bosnia–Herzegovina

Introduction

The foreign policy interests of the United States in the former Yugoslavia during the Cold War were substantial, but less significant than in Northern Europe. Yugoslavia's defiance of Stalin and its continued independence from Soviet influence made it an important part of the Western strategy of playing autonomous East European countries off against the Soviets. The US therefore contributed sizeable quantities of aid to Yugoslavia, and supported its foreign policy independence, from both NATO and the Warsaw Pact. At the same time, the US did not have a commitment to defend that part of Europe as we did Central Europe, further north, where the US would certainly have become involved in the event of an attack against NATO. Aside from the US commitment to Greece and Turkey, the defense commitment in Southeast Europe was much less clear. In this area of the world the US could in a sense have it both ways. On the one hand it could encourage an independent policy by Yugoslavia (and Romania), but not worry about having to respond to Soviet retaliation. Southeast Europe was not considered a top priority area for control and influence for either superpower.

This contributed to the fact that US political leaders were less prepared to intervene when trouble developed once the central government in Belgrade began to weaken and Yugoslavia started coming apart at the seams. An area that had not been a top priority during the Cold War, and did not possess the oil which made the Gulf intervention so compelling, was unlikely to rate top billing as US post-Cold-War policy became less assertive and began to show signs of the emergence of pre-Cold-War isolationism. Despite the brave assertions of a 'new world order' by George Bush, neither US leaders nor the public displayed the will to carry out a policy consistent with that kind of grandiose vision. And the venture in Iraq turned out to be not the beginning of a new assertiveness, in a world where the main obstacle to US military dominance, Russia, was now prostrate, but more like the last crusade of an increasingly timid and uncertain American civilian and military leadership. Yugoslavia was not the focus of US attention, and few imagined that the disaster there would continue for years and become so intractable. While Yugoslavia was not important enough to be a priority for US policy, at the same time it was an area that was too important to be left alone to resolve the conflict itself. It is in that post-Cold-War twilight zone of low-profile involvement that two US presidents have struggled with the most difficult foreign-policy problem to appear in the post-Cold-War world, the dissolution of Yugoslavia and its aftermath.

US policy in the territory of the former Yugoslavia during the period of disintegration displayed more continuity (if not rigidity) than innovation. US pronouncements consistently contained criticism of the way events unfolded, often including sharp moral condemnation. But for three years the dissatisfaction with the course of events did not result in military action that could have made a difference in the outcome. The gap between what the US desired and what was actually transpiring on the ground was a constant, from the beginnings of the disintegration of the country and during the coming years of conflict. It is difficult to think of another foreign-policy case where there was such a gap between American demands and pronouncements and actual American action. Only in the most recent developments has that cycle been broken.

In this part of the book I will outline US policy in the various stages of the war during the Bush administration. I have divided US policy into six stages, which are constructed to capture the broad outlines of policy, not to account for every nuance, twist and turn of a policy. Table I.1 delimits the time period for each stage, and indicates the goal of US policy during a given stage, the means for obtaining the goal, and the desired outcome. Stage I is the period prior to the first Serbian military attacks against Slovenia after it and Croatia proclaimed their independence from Yugoslavia in the spring of 1991. The first stage goal was to maintain the status quo, a unified and peaceful Yugoslavia. When this was rejected by the republics, the Bush administration switched to supporting peaceful change and even independence if all parties could agree on the terms (Stage II). As the conflict in Bosnia heated up, the Bush administration finally moved to

Table I.1 Stages in US policy

	Goal	Means to end	Outcome	Date
Stage I	Keep Yugoslavia together; status quo	Diplomacy	Serb attack on Slovenia	Before July 1991
Stage II	Allow border adjustments in framework of intact Yugoslavia; ceasefire in Croatia	Accommodate change to preserve Yugoslavia	Worsening of war in Croatia	July 1991–April 1992
Stage III	Support independent republics; prevent deterioration	Recognize republics to avoid further war	War in Bosnia	April 1992–February 1993
Stage IV	End conflict in best way possible; 'just' solution	Find negotiated solution acceptable to Allies and Yugoslav parties	Continued conflict; Serb gains	February 1993–June 1994
Stage V	End conflict through negotiation	Pressure parties to accept variation on situation on the ground	Continued conflict; Bosnians strengthened; Croat offensive	June 1994–August 1995
Stage VI	Use coercion to force Serbs to table	Pressure parties to accept variation of situation on the ground	End to conflict; less than optimum outcome (Dayton Agreement)	August 1995–

recognize the independent republics (Stage III), just prior to a massive escalation in the war. But the Bush administration, despite its rhetoric condemning Serbian actions, consistently and accurately denied it would intervene militarily to influence the situation.

The Clinton administration, coming to power in January of 1993, talked frequently of using air power against the Serbs and lifting the arms embargo on Bosnia, but because of European opposition and US indecisiveness, until 1995, it had managed only a few minor military strikes or productive threats of force. Included among these were the shooting down by NATO of four Serbian planes and the successful ending of the siege of Sarajevo through the threat of force in February 1994, and some other minor bombing from time to time. Implicit in a policy proclaimed during the campaign of using military pressure to extract Serb concessions, which I call the 'American option', was the presumption that a settlement could come only when the Bosnians were able to roll back at least some of the Serb gains, and that their citizens, driven out by Serb shelling and 'ethnic cleansing', could return to their homes. As long as the Clinton administration talked about using military power against the Serbs, there was hope that some kind of rough justice, or an approximate restoration of the pre-war situation would be attained before the war could stop, and that a multi-ethnic state of Bosnia would be preserved. Inherent in this reasoning was the assumption that it was more important to find a justifiable solution to the conflict than to have peace at any price (see Table I.2).

An alternative policy competing for the attention of the Clinton administration, however, was what started as a 'European option' (most strongly supported by the British and French) that would accept many of the Serbian gains, attempt to reach a settlement without taking sides militarily and, *de facto*, concede the principle of political organization according to ethnic division. These principles were clearly visible in the Vance–Owen, Owen–Stoltenberg, and Contact Group plans for ending the war. The Dayton Agreement also accepted the principle of ethnic division and some Serb gains, but was arrived at only after the use of force against the Serbs. The Dayton Agreement, therefore, and the process by which it was arrived at, combined aspects of both the 'European' and

Table I.2 'European' and 'American' approaches to the war

	'European' option	*'American' option*
Nature of war	Civil war	Serbian aggression
Preferred Western reaction	Treat warring parties as equals	Lean on Serbs
Differentiate: Serbs/Bosnian Serbs	Early	Late
Acceptable settlement	Variation of partition	Prewar state; multi-ethnic Bosnia (*status quo ante*)
Means to end war	Negotiations	Military force plus negotiations

the 'American' perspectives. (American and European 'options' as used here reflect an ideal type, not a rigorously consistent policy.)

This stage of oscillation between the two approaches, the 'American option' and the 'European option', a period when the Clinton administration was trying various approaches and trying to decide which policy to pursue, I have labelled Stage IV. Clinton finally chose the European option, when he endorsed a negotiated settlement plan created by the so called 'Contact Group', the US, Russia and the European nations, that would give the Bosnian Serbs approximately 49 per cent of Bosnia, with the rest controlled by the Croat–Bosnia federation and the autonomous area of Sarajevo. Rejecting the risks of military intervention in favor of compromise and negotiation, however, proved to have its own risks. In spite of the best efforts to stop the conflict, none of negotiators were able to find a solution acceptable to all sides. Stage VI, the final stage, was characterized by the substantial use of force by the West, the use of bombing while still retaining at least the formality of the arms embargo, to bring the Bosnian Serbs to the negotiating table. While the basic outlines of the Dayton Settlement differed little from earlier plans, especially that of the Contact Group, it is clear that without the pressure of NATO bombing (and the Croat offensives) a settlement would not have been reached. It can therefore be considered a fundamental change in policy.

9 The Bush Administration: From Status Quo to Immobility

STAGE I   KEEP YUGOSLAVIA TOGETHER: POLICY
BEFORE JULY 1991

It has been charged that the US leadership prior to the break up of Yugoslavia underestimated the seriousness of the situation, underestimated US interests in Yugoslavia and did not take adequate action to avoid a crisis.[1] It is true that analysts had long predicted the demise of Yugoslavia after Tito's death, and there was plenty of evidence that that time was rapidly approaching.[2] According to David Gompert, a former Bush administration of official working on the issue, the US did urge the European Community to provide leadership in dealing with the crisis in Croatia, in the belief that the allies had more leverage then the United States to head off a catastrophe. American attempts in 1990 to get the European involved were brushed aside. An American proposal for consultations in NATO was declined, with the French accusing the United States of overdramatizing the problem. Ultimately, the US deferred to the Europeans' desire that the crisis be handled by the EC rather than by NATO. The alliance was thus kept out of the crisis until the Bosnia conflict had grown beyond the capacities of non-military organizations.[3]

A Croatian referendum on independence held 19 May 1991 was approved by 93 per cent of the 83.6 per cent of the electorate which voted – most of the Serbs of the Krajina autonomous region boycotted this referendum, but had voted in their own referendum held 12 May, to join the republic of Serbia and remain within Yugoslavia. Hostilities had been simmering between Zagreb and the Krajina Serbs since August 1990 and had escalated by March 1991 to violent local confrontations among police, paramilitary group, and citizens in

towns of ethnically mixed population in Croatia near the
borders of Serbia and Bosnia–Herzegovina. The Krajina Serbs
had declared their intention to seek autonomy in August 1990
and again in October. By September, however, the conflict had
become an open war between Croatia and the Yugoslav army.[4]
The Slovenian and Croat declarations of independence, and
the subsequent Serb attacks on those countries, were preceded by several months of constitutional crises that under-
lined the irreversible nature of the breakdown of meaningful
negotiations. While the Croats and Slovenes stressed the hope-
lessness of maintaining the federal structure and wanted to
move toward independence, Serbs kept the emphasis on the
unity of the federal state and maintaining the rights of Serbs
throughout the federation. Several months of discussions,
begun near the end of 1990 in order to resolve outstanding
differences among the republics, tried to find a formula to
resolve the differences between the centralized structure advocated by the Serbs, the independence or a decentralized confederation promoted by the Slovenes and Croats, and the
middle ground occupied by Bosnia and Macedonia, failed.

At this point, however, the differences were already un-
bridgeable, as was made clear by incidents during the period
March through May 1991. The president of the Yugoslav
collective presidency, Borisav Jovic who had a reputation for
holding inflexible positions on change deterimental to the
Serbs, presented the collective with a plan drafted by the
military, demanding that Croatia and Slovenia comply with a
decree ordering that all illegal paramilitary units be dis-
banded. This plan was rejected by the collective presidency,
whereupon Milosevic stated that Serbia would no longer
recognize the authority of the collective presidency. Jovic resigned, and according to one observer, the incident was en-
gineered to heighten the putative crisis and thereby to
provoke the support of the army. Jovic later withdrew his resignation. March also saw large demonstrations by the opposition in Belgrade for more access to the media. Jovic put
these down with tanks, and arrested the main opposition
leader, within the parliament building. The actions accentuated doubts that accommodations could be reached with the
Serbs on Yugoslavia's dilemmas. In May, the Serbia bloc of
the presidency blocked the regular rotation of the chair to

Stipe Mesic, the Croatian representative, an action that left in question the constitutional authority of the federal presidency.[5]

These events dashed any hopes that the Yugoslav federation could still function as a normal state. Prime Minister Markovic, who worked for the Yugoslav ideal and the reform policies that would make it possible, had already been rendered ineffective by the growing impossibility of using the existing constitutional structure to work out a compromise among the republics.

Typical of the Bush administration's attitude toward Yugoslavia, prior to the Serbian invasion of Slovenia of late June, were the positions expressed by a State Department official in February 1991. He noted that Yugoslavia had not made a clean break with its Communist past. In 1989 a democratic and revolutionary fervor had swept Yugoslavia. In five republics, democratization was successful, but in Serbia the process was marred by violations by democratic procedure. These included manipulation of electoral procedures and laws, intimidation of voters, manipulation of the media, and a boycott by Albanians of the elections in Kosovo. Moreover, Kosovo had seen ethnic tensions for the last ten years, local self-government eliminated in July 1990, and the closing of Albanian language schools. The US, he stated, would work with those working for democracy, and call the attention of the Yugoslav authorities to the situation.[6] Applying these themes directly to US policy, President Bush in May expressed his concern over growing violence in Yugoslavia, and affirmed support for Yugoslavia's political and territorial integrity. One reason for the firm US position on maintaining Yugoslav territorial integrity was concern about the example an unraveling of the country would set for the Soviet Union. Later in May, a spokesperson for the President reaffirmed the US interest in democracy, human rights and market reform, and stated that 'any dissolution of Yugoslavia is likely to exacerbate rather than resolve ethnic tensions'. Furthermore, the US blamed the Serbs for efforts to block the constitutional transfer of authority within the collective Yugoslavia presidency, and held the Serbian leadership responsible for the crisis. The spokesperson also was critical of human rights violations by Croatia.[7]

Economic aid to Yugoslavia was suspended 6 May under the Nickles amendment, which required a suspension of economic aid to a country after six months if human rights abuses continued. But Secretary of State James Baker allowed the aid to resume again after twenty days. He had chosen to let the sanctions go into force by default, but they were suspended because they penalized all of Yugoslavia rather than just Serbia. Suspension of aid was based on a resolution submitted to the Senate by Robert Dole calling on Milosevic to cease all repressive measures against the Albanian population.[8]

Concerned by the burgeoning crisis, Secretary of State Baker visited Belgrade on 21 June, just days before the deadline set by Slovenia and Croatia as a secession date. At that time, Serbian Prime Minister Milosevic reportedly told Baker that there might be a few problems in Slovenia, but Belgrade would quickly restore order. According to the then Slovenian Prime Minister, Lojze Peterle, Baker believed him.[9] While in Yugoslavia Baker emphasized the gravity of the situation, stated that everyone is interested in finding a way to 'craft a new basis for unity in Yugoslavia' and endorsed the devolution of additional responsibility and authority to the republics. He also reiterated US support for maintaining the territorial integrity of Yugoslavia, and stated that the US would not recognize Slovenia.

While the US continued to insist it would not recognize independent republics, US policy on the maintenance of Yugoslavia's territorial integrity showed signs of softening. In a statement on 24 May, Deputy Secretary of State Lawrence Eagleburger had stressed US opposition to the 'use of force or intimidation to settle political differences or change external or internal borders, block democratic change, or impose a nondemocratic unity'. Unlike past statements, however, this one omitted any reference to the inviolability of borders, and stated that US policy toward Yugoslavia is based on support for the 'interrelated objectives of democracy, dialogue, human rights, market reform and unity'.

By Baker's own account, at variance with that of Lojze Peterle, he stressed that either succession by Slovenia or the use of force against Slovenia would be disastrous, the match that lights the explosion. He also candidly told Milosevic that his policies were 'the main cause of Yugoslavia's present crisis' and that he was propelling Yugoslavia toward civil war and dis-integration.[10]

Baker's insistence that under no circumstances would the US grant recognition to independent republics ignored the well-known fact that the Serbs were starting to talk about borders, and both Croatia and Bosnia had said they would follow Slovenia out of the Yugoslav federation. Thus, while some have maintained that it was recognition of the independence of Croatia and Slovenia in December 1991 by Germany and by the EC on 15 January that encouraged the dissolution of Yugoslavia, a convincing argument can be made that earlier recognition would only have reflected reality and would have given the non-Serb republics additional stature and support to resist Serbian encroachments. The Badinter Commission, set up by the European Community to arbitrate issues of succession among the republics, found on 7 December 1991 that Yugoslavia was in the 'process of dissolution'.[11] But the US was critical of German recognition and resisted EC recognition when it did come. The State Department argued that postponement of a final decision on the recognition of Slovenia and Croatia would allow more time for the UN Secretary General and Lord Carrington, the EC negotiator, to find a political settlement for the crisis.

STAGE II   ACCEPT ARRANGEMENTS RESULTING FROM PEACEFUL CHANGE: JULY 1991–APRIL 1992

In the second stage, US policy moved from insisting on a united Yugoslavia with no border changes, to a willingness to accept changes, including the independence of individual republics, that could be worked out peacefully. When the Yugoslav army intervened in Slovenia in late June following Slovenia's declaration of independence, they were confronted by a Slovenian army that was well prepared. Milosevic, surprised, and realizing that he was in for a long hard struggle in a republic where there were very few politically active Serbs, reconsidered and withdrew the bulk of his troops in two weeks.

On 26 June, the day after both Slovenia and Croatia announced their succession from the Yugoslav federation, both

the United States and the Soviet Union issued statements
rejecting these moves and indicating their intention of continuing to deal with Belgrade. Britain and France issued
similar statements. But confronting the reality of his rout in
Slovenia, Milosevic declared that Serbia had nothing against
Slovenia's secession, which 'does no harm to our interests
and we have no reason not to accept their separation if it is
conducted in a peaceful way'. Later, US Secretary of State
James Baker issued a statement to the effect that the United
States was prepared to accept any new political configuration
acceptable to the Yugoslavs, even if it meant changes in internal or external borders, provided it was done peacefully
through negotiation. This statement can be interpreted as a
concession to Milosevic, the only party interested in changing
borders, and an affront to the non-Serb republics, which
wanted to preserve their borders.[12]

The US was willing to let the Europeans have the lead in the
former Yugoslavia through 1991. Former Secretary of State
James Baker reports that US officials felt comfortable with the
EC handling the Balkan crisis. After the end of the Gulf War in
February 1991, where the US had led decisively, Baker went to
the Middle East to try to jump-start the peace process. The
Europeans were feeling a little left out and the US had been
engaged in political battle between the Western European
Union (the EC's defense arm) and NATO where the Americans
asserted their belief that the US should continue to play a substantial role on the continent even though the Cold War was
over. After all, 1992 was to be a landmark year in integration of
the European Community, the Soviet Union was in decline, and
there was talk of an emerging European superpower. There was,
Baker reported, an undercurrent in Washington that Yugoslavia
was as good a place as any for Europe to step up to the plate
and show they could act as a unified power. This conflict
seemed to be one they could manage.

But equally important as these reasons for not getting involved was the hubris the Europeans displayed in taking on
the role of dealing with the Yugoslav problem. As David Owen
put it

There was a feeling that Europe could do it all on its own …
Europe wanted to stand on its own feet – Yugoslavia was the

virility symbol of the Euro-federalists. This was going to be the time when Europe emerged with a single foreign policy and therefore it unwisely shut out an America only too happy to be shut out.

This eagerness of both sides to play their assigned role thus led to what Joshua Muravchik calls 'the great experiment'.[13] To deal with the Slovenian crisis just after Baker's visit, the EC froze arms sales and financial aid and dispatched three foreign ministers to Yugoslavia to help promote negotiations.[14]

The misplaced optimism of the EC officials was reflected in remarks by Jacques Poos, Foreign Minister of Luxemburg ('This is the hour of Europe, not the hour of the Americans') and Italian Foreign Minister Gianni De Michelis who pointed out that the United States and the Soviet Union had not been 'consulted' but merely 'informed' of the mission. EC Commission Chairman Jacques Delors added: 'We do not interfere in American affairs. We hope they will have enough respect not to interfere in ours.' And American diplomacy was sympathetic to keeping diplomatic activity and transatlantic coordination out of NATO and the UN.[15]

But the seeds of division that would plague the allies throughout the Yugoslav drama were already painfully obvious. In March the European Parliament had passed a resolution stating that the Yugoslav republics and autonomous regions must have the right to determine their own future, in a peaceful and democratic manner, and on the basis of recognized international and internal borders. Moreover, in most European countries, public sentiment was disproportionately in favor of respecting democracy and self-determination, including possible independence for the republics, as opposed to preserving Yugoslavia's territorial integrity.[16] These sentiments were not congruent with the policies that Britain and France were to follow in the coming months and years. In early July, Germany and Denmark wanted to warn Serbia that the EC would recognize Slovenia and Croatia if they came under fresh attack. But the overwhelming majority of the countries preferred to say only that the EC would 'consider their position again' if an attack occurred. Roland Dumas, France's Foreign Minister, warned Denmark and Germany that their proposal would 'throw oil on the flames' and led the opposition to the move. He warned that if this course were followed: 'Tomorrow, what we have done would be applied to other cases.' Nonetheless, the Brioni agreement negotiated by the EC recognized a Slovenian victory and made Slovenia and Croatia the *de facto* subject of international law.[17]

The unique situation of many European countries made them particularly wary of supporting any case that involved assisting minority secession. The existence of nationalist groups in France, Britain, Italy and Spain demanding greater regional autonomy made these nations particularly reluctant to recognize the breakaway republics of Slovenia and Croatia. While the ostensible worry is the precedent this would set for the dissolution of the Soviet Union and Eastern Europe, in fact, a main concern is the problem of fragmentation in the countries of Western Europe.[18]

In the United States, the opposing philosophy with policy implications closer to those favored by Germany and Denmark, was laid out by William Safire. Decrying America's timid stance toward national autonomy, he compared the break-up of Yugoslavia to the dissolution of the Soviet Union. It is fine to talk about peaceful resolution, he said, but America's diplomats should not intervene on central power's behalf

> or threaten to not recognize withdrawing nations, in the sterile name of stability and order ... we should get creative: we should stop mumbling vaguely about 'loose confederation' and propose serious global talks on semi-sovereignty.[19]

But the allies did not take Safire's advice; they continued to maintain a cautious course and the results of their efforts were appropriately modest. After a promising beginning, they secured the agreement of Slovenia and Croatia to suspend their declarations of independence for three months and Serbia's agreement to allow the Croatian Stipe Mesic to take his turn as president of Yugoslavia.[20] And the fighting ended quickly in Slovenia, but intensified in Croatia with direct participation by Belgrade, with the army joining rebellious local Serbs to end Croatian authority in Serb areas. The EC undertook a seemingly endless series of efforts to negotiate ceasefires in Croatia throughout the summer. Each ceasefire was violated in a matter of days if not hours, requiring the whole process to begin over again. In August, the EC countries discussed the need for 'interposition' forces if they were to be effective in achieving a ceasefire. This concept was supported by Luxemburg, the Netherlands, France and Germany. Since there were no forces existing as an alternative to NATO, consideration was given to creating a Eurocorps with French and German troops as the nucleus. This proposal met firm and immediate opposition by the US.[21] By November, in a Croatia where battles raged from the Adriatic coast to the Danube valley, the EC announced the twelfth ceasefire, and Lord Carrington, chairman of the EC peace conference, issued a stern warning directed primarily at Serbia that the peace conference could be suspended if violations continued.[22]

In August, an EC observer had first confirmed the increasingly important role of the Yugoslav army in the fighting. Milosevic blamed the violence on incessant attacks by the Croatian military and paramilitary units on Serbian villages and towns. But the EC observer pointed to heavy ground and rocket fire and air-force attacks that were being flown, as evidence of major army involvement. The level of force inflicted by the federal army, the observer dryly noted, 'seems difficult to reconcile with the role it claims [of] an interposition force between fighting factions'.[23] But the army did exercise a kind of curious self-restraint, except when it indiscriminately pounded cities. On the other hand, units of the various ethnic militia waged an 'all-out war of hatred and revenge, committing atrocities hard to believe possible in our times'.[24]

Prodded by British warnings of the danger of involvement in Yugoslavia, in September the EC backed off from the idea of sending a peacekeeping force to Croatia. Referring to Britain's experience of getting bogged down in Northern Ireland, British Foreign Secretary Hurd was able to prevent action on sending a force in spite of a favorable stance by the Netherlands, France, Germany and Italy.[25] In early December, some European diplomats leaked a report by the EC peace monitors (approximately 200 were present in Croatia) that came down 'unequivocally against the Serbs and the [Yugoslav] army'. Among their recommendations were the 'selective show and use of force – to intimidate and hit the [Yugoslav army] in places where it hurts'. The report seemed to pacify rather than galvanize the EC. A month later a helicopter carrying five of the EC monitors was shot down by a Yugoslav air-force fighter plane. The white helicopter was clearly marked and had given notice of its flight plan but its downing triggered no military action by the EC.[26]

The response to this incident reflected a puzzling pattern that would become well-entrenched during the war in the former Yugoslavia. In spite of the evidence of the widespread promulgation of similar kinds of violence, the incident was treated as a routine diplomatic problem. Considering the kind of response such an incident would have stimulated during the Cold War, one can only conclude that in some cases old habits die quickly. It was a harbinger of the tolerance for the use of force and the willingness of the Great Powers to tolerate humiliation that was to form a new habit for Europe and the US. It has been argued that the EC defined the problem in terms of the use of force, and that to do so was a mistake. What needed attention was the 'ambiguity over the political issues at stake'. The EC, this argument goes, ignored the origins of the conflict – the economic decline, market reforms, and the failure to implement political reforms – and limited itself to the political solutions offered by the nationalist movements increasingly ascendant in the various republics rather than fashioning a strategy to deal with the problem of minority rights, borders, and sovereignty.[27] Such advice is good as far as it goes, but what was missing from Western policy throughout this conflict was an admission that the willingness to use military force needs to match and complement the diplomatic process. This was not Cyprus, where you can put pressure on a couple of NATO powers to reach a solution that affects a small number of people and where stability is relatively easily maintained. The problem in Yugoslavia was created by multiple actors motivated by intense nationalism, deploying paramilitary groups, and under no other power's authority. In the environment in the former Yugoslavia, reliance solely on negotiations was no longer an effective strategy.

But by early January a ceasefire was in place in Croatia, and by mid-February an agreement to send a UN peacekeeping force (14 000) had been negotiated and had the commitment of all parties. The president of Serb Krajina, Milan Babic, acquiesced in the peacekeeping force only after the Milosevic forces organized an abortive coup against him. His capitulation demonstrated who was really in control in the Krajina. With more than a quarter of Croatia's territory still under the control of the Yugoslav army (JNA) and Serb irregulars, the basic military situation with troops in place at the time of the ceasefire would hold until the Croatian roll back of Serb control in the summer of 1995.[28]

As for the US, it clearly identified Serbia as the aggressor and the main problem in Yugoslavia in 1991. As the war with Croatia developed during the summer and fall, the State Department was adamant that most of the blame for the crisis in Yugoslavia rested with the Serbs. But there were no US actions to match the rhetoric.[29] Slow to recognize the reality that Yugoslavia was finished as a nation-state, the US treated all republics as morally equivalent rather than formulate policy consistent with its words. Whereas the EC imposed sanctions only against Serbia in the fall of 1991, the US imposed them against all six republics, lifting those sanctions only with recognition of the republics in April 1992.[30] But the US role until then had been minor, as it continued to defer to the Europeans.

STAGE III   RECOGNITION OF REPUBLICS: APRIL 1992–JANUARY 1993

Recognition

In April 1992 the focus of activities in the former Yugoslavia shifted from Croatia to Bosnia–Herzegovina as the army and Bosnian Serb paramilitaries fought government forces. The start of hostilities in Bosnia also marked an increase in US involvement, and a formalization of the policy of recognizing independent republics. No longer entertaining hope for the survival of the state of Yugoslavia, on 7 April the United States recognized the independent states of Slovenia, Croatia and Bosnia–Herzegovina, following European recognition of Bosnia by a day. The Germans and the rest of the European Community had recognized Slovenia and Croatia in December and January, respectively.

Discussions over the role of Western recognition of the independent republics in precipitating the war have been among the most contentious disputes in this conflict. Some of these arguments suggest that Germany and Austria played the key role in bringing about early European recognition of Croatia and Slovenia and thus the destruction of Yugoslavia. Bogdan Denitch, for instance, deplores the 'bitter irony ... that Germany and Austria were prime movers of the formal destruction of both Yugoslavias' (referring also to the German role in World War II). Bosnian President Izetbegovic appealed to German Foreign Minister Genscher in early December not to recognize Croatia until Bosnia's political relations were more settled, and Lord Carrington, the British Chairman of the EC Conference on Yugoslavia, claimed that early recognition of Croatian and Slovenian independence seriously weakened his leverage to work out a lasting ceasefire among the various parties.[31] These arguments rest on the premise that once the West began to recognize independent republics, it started a chain reaction that led to the unraveling of the rest of the country. Once it became clear to all parties that some republics would gain independence, it was difficult to halt a movement for all nationalities to seek independence. The disintegration of Bosnia was therefore accelerated as the Bosnian Muslims and Croats, upon completion of a referendum on independence which the Bosnian Serbs boycotted in February, decided to secede from Yugoslavia, and the Bosnian Serbs, declaring their inability to live within an independent Bosnia, announced their own Serbian Republic of Bosnia–Herzegovina in early April.

But while this argument has some validity, it attributes a kind of omnipotence and influence to Western actions that is questionable. To allege that by virtue of recognition, Germany and Austria were prime movers in the destruction of Yugoslavia underestimates the already well-advanced disintegration of Yugoslavia, an event that some had predicted as early as 1990. The criticism ignores not only the rapid degeneration of the relationship between the republics that had occurred over the years prior to 1991, but it also overlooks the evidence that the whole thrust of Milosevic's movement, with the cooperation of the Yugoslav army, was to move Serbia toward a centralized Serb-dominated structure that the other

republics could not live with, and which they would not tolerate. While the critics are probably correct that recognition at
the time it came accelerated disintegration, this falls far short
of a compelling argument that non-recognition would have
ensured the continued political integrity of Yugoslavia.
European recognition of Slovenia and Croatia came, after all,
near the end of the Serb–Croatian phase of the war, not at the
beginning. It is worth remembering that on 23 June 1991, the
members of the European Community had voted unanimously, consistent with James Baker's message of preserving
Yugoslavia, not to recognize unilateral succession but to no
effect. On June 25 Slovenia and Croatia unilaterally declared
their independence, beginning the chain of events that led to
Serb–Croatian hostilities which lasted until January 1992. To
rely on the West's ability to influence events by granting or
withholding recognition in the spring of 1992, in a conflict
that in almost every phase, including the three years of war
since the spring of 1992, has defied attempts at negotiation,
peacemaking, and diplomacy, suggests analysis sharply at variance with the real world. The evidence of the way the conflict
has proceeded for the last four years suggests that those who
advocated *de facto* recognition of republics in the spring of
1991, with full recognition upon fulfillment of certain conditions or guarantees of democracy and individual rights, made
a case that might have been preferable to the course that was
followed and more effective in dampening the conflict that
developed.[32]

A second argument, more defensible than the first, is that
recognition should not have been given without first obtaining
some guarantee for the rights of Serbian minorities in the
seceding republics, especially Croatia. While the original
federal structure of Yugoslavia could not have been preserved,
such guarantees might have helped to retain the loyalty of the
Bosnian Serbs and prevent the war in Bosnia, since the Serbs
would not have felt the urgency to take military action to
ensure the integrity of their compatriots in Bosnia. It is widely
believed that the secession of Croatia and Slovenia and then
moves toward independence in Bosnia convinced the Bosnian
Serbs that they could not continue to live in Bosnia independent of Yugoslavia, and led directly to the outbreak of the war
in Bosnia.[33] President Izetbegovic asked for postponement

of recognition on those grounds, and the United States specifically delayed recognition, holding out for guarantees for Serb minority rights.[34]

No doubt a highly visible offer from the West to exchange recognition for constitutional arrangements for minority rights would have been a good idea, but it should have come much earlier in the game. As Sabrina Ramet suggests, the primary consideration for the West should have been preventing Serbian aggression and war, not preventing the break-up of Yugoslavia.[35] Early provisional recognition of Slovenia and Croatia, or as Stevan K. Pavlowitch suggests, simultaneous conditional recognition of all republics when the war broke out in June 1991, along with discussions of military aid to the attacked republics, would have been a more promising approach to the crisis. This would have given the West leverage to extract from Croatia, in as much as was feasible, the actions necessary to ensure minority rights for the Serbs.[36] It would also have given the Croats assistance in meeting the Serb invasion.

What might have been done to prevent the fighting in Bosnia is a closer call. A republic with a decisive three-way ethnic split (43.7 per cent Moslem, 32.4 per cent Serb, 17.3 per cent Croat plus 5.5 per cent Yugoslav), Bosnia was recognized as a key republic in the choice between war and peace in Yugoslavia. Several attempts had been made to get an agreement to prevent the breakup of Bosnia–Herzegovina. In late 1991, for instance, a moderate Muslim organization had sponsored an accord between the Muslims and the Bosnian Serbs which was accepted by Karadzic, but rejected by Alija Izetbegovic as too favorable to the Serbs. And at a conference held in Lisbon in late February 1992, European negotiators succeeded in getting preliminary consensus on an agreement that was apparently more favorable to the Muslims than the Vance–Owen plan (negotiated in 1992–3), but this was also rejected by Izetbegovic because it involved an ethnic division of the republic.[37] Former Ambassador Zimmerman views Izetbegovic as 'somewhat over-his-head' politically. While he believed that the secession of Bosnia from Yugoslavia would lead to bloodshed, he was prompted to go for independence by the opportunity for quick recognition by the European Community. Zimmerman believes that taking more time to work out guarantees of Serb rights in

Bosnia might have prevented war. But Izetbegovic is a decent man who can be talked into unwise moves by more radical colleagues. In late March and early April, however, fighting was already going on in both Croatia and Bosnia, in some cases involving the Yugoslav army. It is unlikely escalating violence could have been avoided, whatever the policy on recognition. Lenard J. Cohen, a critic of the recognition decision, notes that Serb paranoia made it especially important that the Bosnian Serbs had guarantees of their rights. But that argument cuts both ways. Are a paranoid Serb people or government going to be appeased by constitutional guarantees from a Muslim dominated Bosnian government?[38]

While the rights of the Serbs throughout the former Yugoslavia were a realistic and valid concern, especially in Croatia where the chauvinistic attitude of the government toward the Serb regime was well known, it is doubtful that iron-clad guarantees for the preservation of those rights would have had an appreciable effect on the Serbian attitude and actions. The Milosevic and Karadzic regimes were driven by an authoritarian and expansionist logic that had little to do with human rights or any of the other attributes of democracy. The Bosnian Serbs had declared their own republic in March, 1992, and made numerous military preparations, unlike Izetbegovic's government.[39]

'Cautiously diplomatic' policies

By the summer of 1992, the situation in Bosnia was deteriorating badly. There was increasing polarization along ethnic lines as attempts to find an accommodation between Karadzic and Izetbegovic collapsed. In reaction to the vote for independence in February, which the Bosnian Serbs had boycotted, Serbian autonomous regions were being proclaimed, and by March, gangs of masked men were blocking routes into Sarajevo. By the end of the month Bosnia–Herzegovina was appealing to the UN for a peacekeeping force to stop sustained fighting between Bosnian Serbs on the one side, and Muslims and Croats on the other. In April, fighting intensified, now involving the JNA. In mid-April, Federal jet fighters were reported to have attacked Croatian militia positions in four Bosnian cities, with violent clashes occurring in a half dozen cities.[40]

During the conflict in Croatia the Europeans had played the dominant role, as the EC's special envoy, Lord Carrington, mediated truces. But as the focus of the conflict in the former Yugoslavia moved from Croatia to Bosnia, the US had to re-assess whether it could afford to continue to recognize the European lead, or, alternatively, should it take the lead to promote its version of policy? The US had resisted the European lead on recognition of Slovenia and Croatia, preferring to hold off in the hope that this would have a re-straining effect on the Serbs and allow a UN peacekeeping force be put into place (this was approved by the UN on 7 April). As the time for the Bosnian referendum on independence approached, US officials confronted the ques-tion of when and how to recognize Bosnia, since it was assumed that the results of the referendum would be for in-dependence. It was a foregone conclusion that Croatia and Slovenia would be recognized. Regarding Bosnia, there was fear that recognition might spark conflict, but there was also an argument that recognition could contribute to stability. Baker believed that Bosnia and Macedonia should be recog-nized at the same time as Croatia and Slovenia. Izetbegovic and Gligorov, the two most reasonable men in the Yugoslav conflict, had played by the rules. They had not, officials at State reasoned, pursued independence unilaterally or violated Helsinki principles, as had Croatia and Slovenia. To refuse to recognize Bosnia and Macedonia would appear to penalize the states that had done everything by the book. The Europeans agreed to recognition of Bosnia on 6 April at their next meeting, and the US followed one day later. But Macedonia, Bush realized, would have to wait. Greece ob-jected to recognition and the EC was reluctant to challenge its preferences. The US limited itself to a bland statement that positive consideration would be given to Macedonian recognition, even though the name 'Macedonia' could not be used because of Greek sensibilities.[41]

In early May, Barbara Crossette wrote in the *New York Times* that there seems to be no move to raise the response to the war beyond the 'cautiously diplomatic'. This was an apt des-cription of the US response, as it turned out, for the next three years. The US had recalled Ambassador Zimmermann from Belgrade, and the Council on Security and Cooperation in Europe (CSCE) had finally suspended Yugoslavia from membership, in spite of Russian opposition. But in a reversal soon after, it reduced the penalty for Yugoslavia only to suspension from discussions on Yugoslavia until the end of June. Imposing sanctions or a show of force had apparently been ruled out. And in contrast to the Gulf War, there had been no statement from a high official on the situation in Bosnia–Herzegovina. Crossette reported a pervasive sense of helplessness, even those who were most critical of the Bush policy found it difficult to recommend a course of action that would have a mitigating effect in Bosnia. The weak response from the West produced a corresponding reaction in Bosnia. As Kenneth Jensen of the US Peace Institute put it, when it became obvious that there was not going to be a Balkan version of Desert Storm or meaningful European intervention, then there 'was no reason to take/the UN Secretary-General's representative Cyrus Vance or any other mediator seriously in Belgrade'.[42]

By Baker's account, he continued to push for a harder line with the European allies through May. Everyone agreed that the situation was terrible, Baker states, but they could not agree on sanctions or the use of force as a means to deal with the problem. In late May at a conference on aid for the former Soviet Union in Lisbon, Baker, reviewing the deteriorating situation in the former Yugoslavia deplored 'European indifference, even inaction', and professed puzzlement. 'The only lever we have is to isolate Milosevic', he said, 'and I just can't understand how Europe can stand by and let this happen'. The Europeans were extremely leery of deeper involvement in the crisis in the former Yugoslavia. In Baker's words, Sarajevo was beginning to sound to Europeans like Saigon, or to John Major, like Northern Ireland. Baker attributed much of the European problem to the fact that the EC would not act without first achieving unanimous agreement on a course of action. What we are seeing once again, Baker informed the President from Lisbon, is that the Europeans 'want to be active but need a push from us to do so', even on any issues where they want to be active and we agree that they should be. According to Baker's account, his talks with the Europeans, including his observations at a press conference, left the Europeans 'squirming'.[43]

In late May, a slightly harder US line was visible, reflecting an effort by the US to take the lead after a period of inaction. Secretary of State Baker deplored the humanitarian situation in Bosnia, implicitly comparing Serbian actions to Nazi behavior. Anyone looking for reasons not to act in this kind of a situation, Baker warned, is on the wrong wavelength. Reflecting an impatience with the pace at which the Europeans were moving and a concern with public opinion, the US was increasing its diplomatic involvement in the Bosnian theatre. Reacting to US pressure, the UN Security Council voted 13–0 for a trade embargo on the former Yugoslavia, with passage of the measure made possible by the inclusion of language clarifying that the Serbs were not wholly responsible for the crisis in the Balkans. An economic embargo was now in effect, but enforcement was haphazard. The Serbian economy was in bad shape and sanctions continued to hurt it. The effect on Milosevic's behavior was debatable, but concern with sanctions was probably an important factor encouraging him to put pressure on the Bosnian Serbs to come to a settlement after the spring of 1993. But the ability of the Serbs to continue to live with sanctions proved to be considerable.[44]

A related question is the extent to which Milosevic was responsible for what was happening in Bosnia. The Bosnian Serbs forces and the Serbian paramilitaries often acted independently of Belgrade and, as events in 1993–5 were to demonstrate, were devoted to continuing the struggle even after Milosevic's support had declined. But Milosevic had been an important force in starting the insurgency in both Croatia and Bosnia, and the crucial involvement of the Yugoslav military in both conflicts was clear. On 27 April, a new Federal Republic of Yugoslavia was announced by Serbia and Montenegro, thus tacitly recognizing Bosnian independence by excluding it from the new federation. And on 5 May, the 'Yugoslav' government had ostentatiously renounced authority over army forces in Bosnia, claiming that any remaining troops were part of independent local forces. But most of the arsenal and 85 per cent of the army personnel stationed in Bosnia remained there under the new status of Bosnian Serb 'militia' and most non-Bosnian Serbs had earlier been replaced with Bosnians recruits in preparation of the war. Serbia continued to provide a steady flow of supplies and volunteers. In the view of Stephen Schwartz, the Krajine are mainly 'primitive hinterland' lacking economic infrastructure, and the Serb hold on major parts of Bosnia was tenuous and would be threatened by a cessation of Milosevic's support. This latter assertion was borne out in 1995.[45]

The slaughter in Bosnia continued into the summer and behind every proposed solution to deal with the crisis seemed to be an obstacle. Russian Foreign Minister Andrei Kozyrev traveled to Bosnia and returned very pessimistic after seeing how little influence he had with the Serbs. This was in sharp contrast to his attitude in Libson where he had been optimistic.[46] The international arms embargo was thwarted by a steady flow of arms from the outside. This added to those already in the area; the stockpiling of arms for decades made Yugoslavia 'one big arms warehouse', said a report in the *New York Times*. The embargo's main accomplishment, some believed, was to keep the break away republics from getting any, since the Serbs already had plenty.

Because of the shortage of food and medical supplies, President Bush and Secretary Baker were pushing for a UN resolution to support the use of force to get humanitarian aid delivered, but even this was more than the Western powers were anxious to bite off. One analysis predicted it would take 50 000 troops and an extensive air operation to secure Sarajevo airport and the two mile stretch of valley road from airport to town.[47] And the Vietnam model, on many a diplomat's mind, seemed to suggest that once you start down the path of military involvement, there is a strong likelihood of being caught up in an endless escalation. The EC's Lord Carrington continued with his quest to negotiate a lasting ceasefire, but the difficulties he faced were illustrated by the fate of one agreement he secured. When the fighting parties agreed to put their heavy weapons under UN supervision for a ceasefire, a plan already approved by the Security Council was rejected by Boutros Boutros-Ghali. While the Secretary-General argued that the UN did not have the resources to implement the plan, the fact that it was arrived at without his participation seemed to be an equally important factor in his rejection of the plan.[48]

Nothing exemplified better the frustrating mix of tragic events on the ground, stirring rhetoric by diplomats, and confused and inadequate attempts to deal with the tragedy than the London Conference, held in late August to try to find a way to deal with the war. According to one account, while the conference opened to 'rousing condemnation of the Serbs' from nearly two dozen nations, there were virtually no calls for action beyond tightening economic sanctions. Among the outside powers, only the foreign minister of Turkey suggested the serious use of force. The Bush administration proposed more international inspectors for the international embargo, and the stationing of human rights monitors in what could become the next targets: Kosovo, Sandzak, and Vojvodina. Epitomizing the gap between rhetoric and action that characterized the conference was the admonition of the German Foreign Minister, Klaus Kinkel, who declared to the Serbs that the international community would 'never accept the acquisition of territory through force and terror'. Through all this, Mr. Karadzic is alleged to have sat in 'stony silence'.

At the London Conference, the Serbs agreed to many actions, which they could certainly not be expected to take seriously. Among other things, they were to lift the siege of Sarajevo and other Bosnian cities, dismantle detention camps, turn heavy weapons over for stockpiling, honor the borders of the other republics and recognize their governments, and return captured territory. The Western powers did not assign to these promises a high degree of credibility. Immediately after the conference they were expressing scepticism, and the scepticism was well-placed. British Prime Minister John Major, after stressing the commitments which the Serbs had made before the world, admitted that pressure would need to be applied to them. And President Bush would complain in the coming months, that the Serbs had promised at the London Conference to cease combat flights over Bosnia, but that they had actually increased them.[49]

The debate on the war

As the diplomats dithered and debated, commentators kept up a passionate debate between those who opposed military actions and those who favored it. Appalled by the humanitarian tragedy, the impudence of the Serbs, and the weak American response, critics urged a tougher response. Opponents stressed the lack of an American interest and the pitfalls of charging off on foreign policy tangents which are of low priority, and threaten to involve the United States with an endless embroilment in a foreign crisis. Christopher Lane, a political scientist, argued that we have no interest in the former Yugoslavia; the crisis has no connection to the global power balance and Great Power security interests. The European states are the only ones whose interests are even remotely jeopardized, and they are reluctant to embark on a crusade that will suck them into a quagmire. Vietnam and Lebanon should have taught us the intractability of conflicts that stem from ancient, unresolved national and ethnic antagonisms. David Hendrickson, co-author of a book critical of the Gulf War, came down on the same side of the argument. The administration is committed to aims that can be achieved only through large-scale force, he argued. He was against defining the problem only as Serbian aggression when the big problem is that the minorities cannot live together. While it is dangerous to change borders, the legitimacy of doing so was conceded when we recognized Croatia and Slovenia. The US goal should be not to deny the Serbs the autonomous enclaves they want or a Greater Serbia, but to contract Serb borders so that Croats and Bosnian Muslims also have the basis of a viable state.

On the other side of the debate, Anthony Lewis, a regular columnist in *The Times* and a persistent critic of the administration's policy, argued that using the Gulf War as a precedent, President Bush could have mobilized public opinion to take effective action in Bosnia. He has been a veritable Neville Chamberlain in refusing to face the challenge of Yugoslavia, refusing to provide international leadership and to call for the military action that everyone knows is needed to stop Serb aggression. If Bush had had the courage to act, the horror in Yugoslavia would have ended long ago. When the Serbs began lobbing shells into Dubrovnik a year ago, a few air strikes would have stopped them and headed off the tragedy that followed.

Another regular columnist in *The Times*, Leslie Gelb, put forward a more nuanced argument for a strong response, but was very pessimistic that such a response would be forthcoming from the Bush administration. Writing in early August, Gelb said Western officials had told him that nothing they are likely to do will compel the Serbs to stop killing Bosnian Muslims. A successful fight for Muslim survival is thought to be beyond practical means. No official expects the Serbs to wilt under UN sanctions for months or years. British Prime Minister Major seems ready to put additional diplomatic pressure on the Bosnian Muslims later in August, and he will also lean on the Serbs. But the main British idea is to sell the idea of creating safe havens that would be transformed into ethnic cantons, each with considerable autonomy. Bush has a much narrower focus – strengthen relief efforts – convoys and protection. Doubtful about sending in troops, in Gelb's view, bombing made much more sense. It is still not good, but is better than stressing humanitarian aid. Bombing would threaten Serbian military might; bowing to Serb demands only whets their appetite.

Most specific in formulating a call for action was former British Prime Minister Margaret Thatcher. According to her, the West should have given an ultimatum to Serbia, requiring that they: cease economic support for the war – with monitoring by international observers; recognize Bosnia and its territorial integrity and renounce claims against it; guarantee access for humanitarian teams; agree to demilitarization of Bosnia within the context of the demilitarization of the whole area; and promise cooperation in return of refugees. If the demands were not met, Prime Minister Thatcher suggested, the West should bomb bridges on the Drina River (impeding supplies going from Serbia to Bosnia), bomb military convoys, bomb gun positions around Sarajevo and Gorazde, and bomb military stores. If necessary, military installations on the Serbian side could be hit as well. To do this, US leadership is essential, but Serbia will not 'listen until forced to listen'.[50]

For the West the summer of 1992 was the time for decision on the Bosnian War. It was the time when the West was in the best position to influence the outcome and stop the Serbian momentum. Serb and Bosnian Serb ambitions were by now clear. There should have been no more illusions that they could be bought off with a few concessions, that the path of diplomacy and negotiation alone would lead to a satisfactory solution to the problem. As Baker put it, there was an air of unreality about Bosnia, those locked in their positions had a false sense of reality, believing the worst won't happen. It is 'easier to deal with Shamir and Assad than it is to try to affect Milosevic and Tudjman,' he said.[51] A truce had been reached in Croatia, but this had not stopped Belgrade from taking on Bosnia. Suspending hostilities in Croatia allowed it to support the war effort in Bosnia, allowed it to open a second front.

The general outline of the situation on the ground was clear. The Serbs controlled at least two-thirds of Bosnia and their armament far exceeded that of the Bosnians. The humanitarian situation was a disaster. One account described Bosnia as 'a handful of desperate cities controlled by the government', with people increasingly accepting their cause as lost. Of the land not controlled by the Serbs, the Croats controlled much of the rest, and as the fall went on, they showed an increasing tendency to collaborate with the Serbs.[52] During the summer the extent to which rape, concentration camps, ethnic cleansing, and destruction of cities and cultural edifices were routine Serb policy had become clear. The flood of refugees from Bosnia was the largest in Europe since World War II. It was not only deterrence of the Serbian/Bosnian Serbs that was at stake now. As it became clear that the West was going to do nothing, the Croats and Bosnian Croats were increasingly encouraged to join in the dismemberment of Bosnia. Like the Serbs, the Croats were accurately reading the signals sent by the West, and adjusting their policies accordingly. If the Serbs could take military action and get away with it, what was to stop the Croats from joining in and getting a share of the spoils? Many critics of US policy worried about the effect of the Serbian example of being rewarded for military aggression, on extreme nationalists and tyrants in other countries. But the real effect was on the Croats in Bosnia. As 1992 ended, and especially after the spring of 1993, it was clear that the Croats had already absorbed the lesson provided by the appeasement of the Serbs and were starting their own war of aggrandizement in Bosnia.

Among the allies, a vigorous debate had taken place. After a slow start during 1991, Yugoslavia had finally captured the attention of both the foreign policy elite and broader public opinion. Our interests, possible strategies and the likely costs of involvement in the conflict were as clear as they were likely to become. Several more years of pretending that negotiating positions could be disconnected from the military situation would do nothing to clarify the alternative for the US and Europe. Negotiation and diplomatic and economic pressure had not worked, and they were not likely to work. The West was faced with a choice of using military measures or continuing to tolerate the same outrages with which it had already seen.

Since there was only a small contingent of UN personnel in Bosnia, they were not the obstacle to a firm response from the West that they became later. But most important was the fact that the Serbs were still in doubt about the intentions and resolve of the West. Decisive military strikes now would have caught them off guard and checked their momentum. It would have raised doubts about the long-term prospects for their cause. It would have provided a check to the 'air of unreality' Baker found so pervasive. Nationalist fanatics are not noted for their susceptibility to negotiation; they are sometimes influenced by military realities. A harsh dose of reality would have been much more effective while there was still considerable doubt about the restraint the West was exercising. And the realities of military power would not have been lost on the Croats any more than they would have been on the Serbs. The Bosnian government would have been the main beneficiary of a firmer policy.

The summer of 1992 was the time to say, in former President Richard Nixon's words, 'We'll do nothing, or something'. The alternative was to have the 'worst of both worlds'.[53] In Bosnia the desire for peace was clearly given precedence over the desire for justice. The alternative to Western military action should not have been an arms embargo on all parties, in effect aiding the Serbs, and to a lesser extent the Croats. If, as the opponents of military intervention maintained, the key factor in the conflict was the ethnic division and hatred, with all the nationalist movements being more or less equally responsible for the situation, the Western response should have been to let all three ethnic groups fight it out and reach a settlement based on the forces on the ground. But given the overwhelming Serb superiority in access to arms, the effect of the embargo was to bolster the strength of the most extreme side. But the main priority of the West was not to stop aggression or to foster a long-term solution to the problem. It was to dampen the violence enough so that intervention would not be necessary, and public unease over the violence and atrocities would be limited. By its failure to act, the West ended up with the worst of Nixon's two worlds. After years of fighting among the parties in Bosnia and continued low-level Western and UN involvement, the US still felt compelled to intervene with troops on the ground more than three years later to deal with a situation that was still as salient in US domestic politics as it had been in 1992.

But intervention in Bosnia in the summer or fall of 1992 would have required strong and decisive leadership on the part of the United States. Baker maintains that the Gulf mobilization served as a model for the US effort to get a UN resolution passed to ensure the delivery of humanitarian aid in Bosnia. But the goals of that effort were far short of our objectives in the Gulf, and far short of what was needed in Bosnia. In order to take military action in Bosnia, the President would have had to mobilize on three fronts, none of which would have been an easy task: the European allies, American public opinion, and the US military. The record of the European allies in the crisis so far was a reliable indicator of their intransigence (further discussed in Chapter 10); public opinion, as we have seen, could have been mobilized by a determined president, at least for a while. The US military was opposed to intervention in Bosnia.

In an interview with Colin Powell, Chairman of the Joint Chiefs of Staff, *The Times* reported that Powell is questioning 'even the most limited forms of military intervention' to protect the Muslims. Consistent with his view that the proper wielding of military power requires clear cut military goals, an all-out offensive to obtain them, and no leaving the field of battle until they are obtained, General Powell did not find Bosnia a congenial place for that kind of battle. Talk of a limited involvement in Bosnia reminded Powell of Vietnam. 'As soon as they tell me it's limited, it means they do not care whether you achieve a result or not. As soon as they tell me "surgical", I head for the bunker.' Reacting to an editorial critical of those who continued to 'dither' over Bosnia, Powell wrote an op-ed piece where he further outlined his views. Whenever the military had a clear set of objectives, he wrote, as in Panama, the Philippine coup and Desert Storm, the result had been success. Military force is best used to achieve a decisive victory. But when the nation's policy had been murky – the Bay of Pigs, Vietnam, Lebanon – the result had been disaster. In Bosnia, we are dealing with an ethnic tangle with roots reaching back a thousand years. Powell apparently viewed the situation in Bosnia as too complex to be susceptible to the kind of military approach he advocated. When administration officials prepared a diplomatic protest to the Serbs requesting they stop using military planes to shadow relief flights, military and civilian officials at the Pentagon softened the language to avoid the implicit threat of military action. Powell also questioned the need to establish an air exclusion zone over Bosnia. Powell suggested limited bombing would not stop the Serbs from doing what they had been doing. Arguing in opposition to that kind of action, he suggested that it is difficult to locate artillery (for bombing), intervention would mean Washington was taking sides and compromising its neutral status, and the warring parties might retaliate against UN relief efforts. It is clear from Powell's remarks and his writing that his thinking was deeply influenced by Vietnam and Lebanon. It was also reported that while Powell is the most prominent and articulate opponent, his philosophy on using force was widely shared by senior military officials, who recalled the Vietnam 'quagmire'.[54]

The President, the last hope of those who wanted to move toward the use of military force in Bosnia, showed no signs of doing so. While the campaign rhetoric for a stronger stance in Bosnia by Democratic Bill Clinton probably pushed Bush toward a tougher stand on the delivery of humanitarian aid than he otherwise would have taken, he showed no signs of seriously considering military actions that would have made a difference in the military situation. The President did support a ban on Serbian combat flights over Bosnia, an issue that was hotly debated in the administration, supported using NATO warships to enforce the economic blockade in the Adriatic, and supported sending UN peacekeepers to Macedonia to serve a 'trip wire' function and prevent Serbian intervention there. Approval for enforcement of the no-flight rules, however, did not come until the following spring.[55] Those favoring more forceful action in Bosnia had no choice but to hope that Bill Clinton, after his November victory, would try to implement some of his campaign promises on Bosnia. And going into the Balkan winter, the situation for Sarajevo and the government and people of Bosnia remained particularly grim.

CORE ASSUMPTIONS OF BUSH ADMINISTRATION POLICY

Serbia is the main culprit

As the war in Bosnia opened, the United States continued to blame Serbia and the armed forces (the Yugoslav People's Army [JNA] and the Bosnian Serb militias) it unleashed as the main culprit for the violence in Bosnia. While acknowledging the culpability of Croatian and Bosnian forces for some of the terror, the US made it clear that Serbia's aggressive actions were primarily to blame for the situation in Yugoslavia, and that the US was unalterably opposed to Serbian actions.[56] Edward J. Perkins, the US Permanent Representative to the UN, on 30 May 1992 deplored the aggression of the Serbian regime in Bosnia: it represents a clear threat to international peace and security, and Serbia must reverse its brutal aggression. The US will not have normal relations with Belgrade until it ends its occupation of neighboring states.[57] At a meeting of the Council on Security and Cooperation in Europe (CSCE) on May 6, the US condemned the perpetrators of violence in Bosnia and urged that Serbian representatives be excluded from all CSCE activities. Similarly, M.T. Niles, Assistant Secretary of State for European and Canadian Affairs, on 11 August told the Senate Armed Services Committee that the determination of President [Slobodan] Milosevic to create a 'Greater Serbia' posed an enormous challenge to the international community. Washington believed that without Serbian support from Belgrade to the Bosnian Serbs, the conflict in Bosnia would not persist. Radovan Karadzic can be a semi-independent actor, but he cannot be a completely independent actor. In line with the US position, on July 9, the CSCE condemned 'Serbian aggression' and called for an end to the violence.[58]

The US/world will not stand for these atrocities

If US spokesmen were unambiguous in placing the blame for the problems in Yugoslavia on Serb aggression, they were equally candid in speaking of the atrocities and war crimes that occurred, and in affirming that these actions would not go unpunished. Some did charge, however, that the administration was tardy in making known the extent of atrocities taking place. President Bush spoke of a 'vile policy' of ethnic cleansing, the deliberate murder of innocent civilians, a true 'humanitarian nightmare'. Administration spokesmen were eloquent in their denunciation of the Yugoslav events. Acting Secretary of State Lawrence Eagleburger said at the London Conference on Yugoslavia in August 1992 (co-chaired by the UN and the EC) that

> The civilized world simply cannot afford to allow this cancer in the heart of Europe to flourish, much less spread. We must wrest control of the future from those who would drag us back into the past, and demonstrate to the world – especially to the world's 1 billion Muslims – that the Western democracies will oppose aggression under all circumstances, not oppose it in one region and appease it in another.

Eagleburger's reference to a region where the West opposed aggression presumably applies to the conflict with Iraq, an appropriate and telling analogy. In the same speech, Eagleburger asserted that the people of the former Yugoslavia [Serbia] can still refuse to 'drink the lethal brew' which their leaders have put before them. They can make a choice between joining democratic and prosperous Europe, or joining their leaders in the present march of folly. In an interview, Eagleburger went even further in condemning Serbian territorial gains and stressing US opposition to them.

> We are not going to recognize any fruits of their aggression as far as Serbia is concerned or Croatia either, for that matter ... Our fundamental objective is the *status quo ante*.

He went on to say that he believes it is possible to restore Bosnia 'as a multi-ethnic state, with the right of minorities, with the ethnic communities of each respected,' and that there isn't anybody in Serbia who doesn't understand that the US will not accept a conclusion to this 'mess' that doesn't permit the Bosnian Muslims to go back to their homes.

John R. Bolton, Assistant Secretary for International Organization Affairs, made explicit references to the Nazi movement and implied comparisons to the Yugoslav situation. The international community, when it realized what had been committed by the Nazis in World War II, took a vow of 'never again.' He limited his promise of help, however, to the punishment of individuals who would be held accountable for violations of international law.[59]

Serbs have frequently broken agreements

US officials admitted, in the early stages of the conflict in Bosnia–Herzegovina, that the Serbs had a very bad record in keeping agreements, and did not adhere to the stipulations of UN Resolutions. Secretary Eagleburger said on the MacNeil–Lehrer News Hour, that there had been 'deal after deal after deal', and yet nothing happened. Karadzic agreed at the London Conference in August, where general principles against aggression and for Bosnian territorial integrity were adopted, that the Bosnian Serbs would collect their heavy arms and turn them over for temporary supervision by the UN within 96 hours, which never occurred. Following the London conference, President Bush stated in October that there had been an agreement on a ban on military flights over Bosnia – yet the bombing of defenseless population centers actually increased. A spokesman went on to say that this flagrant disregard for human life and the London agreement required a response. We would take steps to see that the ban was respected. Until February 1994, however, except for the protection of humanitarian operations, force was never used by the US, NATO, or the UN to enforce agreements, in spite of the continuing record of violations.[60]

Punitive measures enforced against Serbia, but the US pledges not to use force unilaterally

The United States had imposed diplomatic sanctions against Serbia (Serbia–Montenegro) in May 1992, including co-sponsoring a trade embargo legitimized by UN Security Council Resolution 757, and the freezing of assets. An earlier economic embargo against Serbia, imposed in December 1991, had been lifted when the UN-negotiated cease fire was agreed upon in Croatia in March. Earlier, the US had also recalled the US Ambassador in Belgrade to Washington, and had terminated landing rights for Yugoslav National Airlines. On June 23, Secretary Baker indicated that he would recommend to the President that he refuse ambassadorial recognition from Belgrade, close the Yugoslav consulate in Chicago, and support suspension of Serbia as participants in international organizations. At the London Conference, a decision was also made to place 'early warning' monitors in neighboring states and regions, including Albania, Macedonia, Romania, Bulgaria, and Hungary, and to convene negotiations in Geneva on Yugoslavia, co-chaired by Cyrus Vance representing the United Nations, and Lord Owen representing the EC.[61]

Nonetheless, in spite of the clear determination of Serbia's responsibility for aggression, the intense and moral US rhetoric about the need to take action, and the negligible effect the imposed punitive measures had on Serbia, the US did not move to respond in a more forceful way.

Defense Secretary Cheney did indicate that the US was prepared to provide air and naval escort protection for humanitarian relief convoys to Sarajevo, if explicitly authorized by the UN Security Council. But any more general commitment of force that might change the political situation was ruled out. Secretary Baker, before he left to run President Bush's campaign, announced that the US had initiated discussions at the UN on Chapter VII sanctions – 'Action with Respect to Threats to the Peace, Breaches of the Peace, and Acts of Aggression' – against Serbia, but ruled out the use of force until all available political, diplomatic, and economic remedies are exhausted. He stated that there would be no unilateral use of US force, that we are not and we cannot be the world's policeman. The President, and Baker's replacement as Secretary of State, Lawrence Eagleburger, also repudiated the use of force in such a complex situation as Bosnia. Eagleburger, typically blunt and colorful, proclaimed the use of force to try to bring about a peace settlement as 'just far too dangerous'. Those who write about using force should think about having the responsibility for the young Americans that might not come back from such involvement. On the MacNeil–Lehrer program, he was even more explicit.

> I'm not prepared to accept arguments that there must be something between the kind of involvement of Vietnam and doing nothing, that the *New York Times* and the *Washington Post* keep blabbing about, that there must be some form in the middle. That's, again, what got us into Vietnam – do a little bit, and it doesn't work. What do you do next?[62]

Clearly, Eagleburger found it hard to conceptualize a military response outside of the Vietnam context. The US and the UK did agree in December to sponsor a UN resolution to enforce compliance with the 'no-fly' zone for Bosnia. But that resolution bore fruit only when it was finally enforced on 28 February 1994, when US F-16s shot down 4 Serbian planes.

10 The Clinton
Administration I:
Strategies and Obstacles

Only when the war spread to Bosnia in the spring of 1992 did the critics' analysis of Bush administration policies begin to resonate, at least with that group of people who follow foreign policy. The growing scale of the war, the increasingly convincing evidence of widespread atrocities against civilians and the realization that there was a pattern to Serb behavior made the repugnance toward Serb actions and the resultant indignation more intense.

As the Bush administration repeated its intention not to get involved militarily in Bosnia, the critics, including president-elect Clinton who campaigned on a platform of military action in Bosnia, began to formulate strategies that would put military pressure on the Serbs. In this chapter, we examine several 'packages' of more militant options that were proposed, the strengths and weaknesses of each, and the restraints and limits on the administration's ability to implement them.

MILITARY STRATEGIES

UN peacekeeping and humanitarian operations

Discussion of options for the use of military force should start with the humanitarian operations option, in which the West was involved for much of the war. United Nations troops, consisting of British, French, Dutch, Canadian, and other troops from around the world, were deployed in both Bosnia and Croatia. The troops in Bosnia were instructed to use force 'where armed persons attempt by force to prevent United Nations troops from carrying out their mandate'. That mandate, initially limited to providing humanitarian supplies and securing Sarajevo airport, was later expanded to monitoring and enforcing a 'no-fly' zone and deterring attacks against six safe areas, the cities of Sarajevo, Tuzla, Srebrenica, Gorazde, Zepa and Bihac, and their surroundings.[1]

The Secretary General estimated that 40 000 peacekeepers were needed fully to protect humanitarian convoys and Bosnians in 'safe areas', and 17 000 were required minimally to carry out these mandates. In early 1994, however, only about 14 000 UNPROFOR troops were in Bosnia, and something over 30 000 in all of the former Yugoslavia. Moreover, some of these troops lacked the training or supplies to be deployed in Bosnia. And it was only in January 1994, 19 months after UNPROFOR was authorized in Bosnia, that a full-time Special Representative arrived in the former Yugoslavia to provide overall leadership and improve coordination and cooperation. UNPROFOR also coordinated with NATO. In August 1993 NATO agreed to provide UNPROFOR with close air support to defend UN troops anywhere in Bosnia and to carry out air strikes consistent with UN mandates. Before NATO could act, however, the call for strikes would have to originate with the UN, and it was only when the Special Representative arrived that those calls could originate in Bosnia.[2]

But the real problem with the UN peacekeeping operation was much more fundamental than problems with organizational arrangements. UNPROFOR's ultimate goal in Bosnia was not to promote a just and durable peace that would reflect the origins of the war and the culpability of the various parties. Their mission was rather to provide some humanitarian assistance, try to contain the fighting, and wait for the negotiating process led by the Co-Chairmen of the Steering Committee of the Conference on Yugoslavia to bring an end to the war. The crux of the matter was that the UN's primary mission was to get peace, making concerns with justice secondary. Moreover, it was assumed that establishing peace required treating all the warring parties the same. This approach was not unique to the UN since the underlying philosophy was shared by most of the NATO powers, but especially Britain and France. Since stopping the conflict was the priority, the UN had to be most concerned with dealing with the Serbs; they had the military capabilities and were usually on the offensive. As documented by David Rieff, this resulted in UNPROFOR avoiding actions that would antagonize the Serbs, striking deals favorable to the Serbs that would at least temporarily stop the fighting, and sharing relief goods with the Serbs in order to obtain permission to get convoys through. But the other side of the policy was complaining about US encouragement of the Bosnians. After criticizing the presence of Joint Chiefs of Staff Chairman John Shalikashvili and UN delegate Madeleine Albright at the opening of the American embassy in Sarajevo, the top UN official in Bosnia, Yasushi Akashi, said, 'If anything emboldens the Muslim government to fight on, it's things like this. They can point to that and say, 'See, the Americans are with us.' We can only hope that the failure of NATO to come to their aid around Gorazde will convince them that the US cavalry isn't around the corner.' This incident happened after Akashi himself had blocked airstrikes during the siege of Gorazde, suggesting something about his motivations for doing so. The logic of UNPROFOR's situation thus ensured that only timid action would be taken over the whole range of issues calling for a military response, from getting convoys through to retaliation for Serb violation

How the war was interpreted had a direct effect on the behavior of UNPROFOR. A UN official is quoted depicting the Bosnian army as fighting a defensive war, showing tremendous motivation, and a willingness to continue fighting rather than settle for a peace plan (European Action Plan) which they believed was unjust. But, the UN official complained, the Europeans, and we can add, most of the UN officials, treated the Bosnia army as 'just another warring faction on the march'.

Commenting on military action around Sarajevo, a Bosnian general raised a similar question of how the behavior of the Bosnian army should be evaluated. The general pointed out that the Serbs have to keep pounding the Sarajevo suburbs of Rajlovac, Ilijas, and Vogosca to prevent a breakout by the Bosnians, since these suburbs lie at the weakest points of the Serb siege line. But the Bosnian army does the same thing inside the city – carrying out operations against Serb lines. These operations have triggered heavy retaliatory bombardments and hundreds of civilian casualties. The UN had long criticized the Bosnian army's disregard of civilian lives. One British officer, for instance, complained that neither side in the war 'gives a damn' about civilian lives.

Interpretation of the war also had a direct impact on UNPROFOR behavior when deciding what to do with captured arms. Noting the Bosnian army's attempt to capture Vitez in central Bosnia along with the arms factory there, Bosnian officials were apprehensive that the UN troops would destroy the factory, just as they had destroyed weapons abandoned by a fleeing Croatian militia rather than let Bosnian troops acquire them.

Were the Bosnians fighting a justifiable defensive war where their actions should be treated different than Serbian actions? Should arms captured from the Serbs or Croats be destroyed or turned over to the Bosnians? Obviously, in any war actions are taken that disregard civilian losses if the action is considered sufficiently important. No nation is expected to renounce war as an instrument of policy because war sometimes kills civilians. But for most of the war in Bosnia, the philosophy underlying UNPROFOR's decisions on the kinds of issues discussed here was that all factions should be treated equally. The Bosnians were just another faction with the same moral standing as the Serbs or Croats.[3]

This indifference to who 'won' the war, as long as it stopped, was thus the explanation for seemingly puzzling statements by UN generals early in the conflict that the best thing the West could do to end the conflict was not to bomb, but to make it clear to the Bosnians that no help would be coming from the West. From the UN perspective, it was unfortunate that the Bosnian government refused to 'come to its senses and surrender'.[4] Once one accepts that the primary UNPROFOR objective was brokering a peace, the peacekeeping effort in Yugoslavia becomes intelligible. UN officials and UNPROFOR either refused to stand up to the Serbs, or in some cases refused to believe the Serbs were more prone to ruthless behavior than, for instance, the Bosnians. Relief convoys were often delayed for days or completely prevented from delivering supplies, on a Serb whim, and there was often very little UNPROFOR would do about it. In some places, the Serbs routinely got a share of the humanitarian deliveries, once they did go through, as their price. There is evidence that a more aggressive stance by the UN would have been respected by the Serbs, but UNPROFOR, bound by the logic that it could only carry out its mission if it avoided offending the Serbs, would not test the limits of what an aggressive approach might yield. Individual commanders did challenge the Serbs, often with good results. But these commanders also tended to be relieved of their duties by New York. US Major General Patrick Hughes, a director of intelligence on the joint staff, indicated the presence of UNPROFOR had often given Serbs a great advantage by stopping conflict and arranging for the passage of materials and supplies when it was in their interest.[5]

In one infamous incident in January 1993, Dr Hakija Turaljic, a highly respected member of the Bosnian cabinet, was returning to Sarajevo in a French armored personnel carrier. Stopped by Serb troops and armor, the French battalion commander, instead of calling for help from the UNPROFOR airport garrison, actually sent away three British fighting vehicles that had happened on the scene and had offered help. The French commander then allowed the rear hatch of the personnel carrier to be opened to demonstrate that no arms or unauthorized personnel were there. At this point, a Serb fighter pointed a machine pistol into the rear of the vehicle and cut Turaljic to bits. The Bosnian Serbs apologized for the incident, but it was indicative of the accommodating role the UN troops played.[6]

The congruence of UNPROFOR attitudes and objectives was also apparent from their talk and behavior. The Secretary-General's Special Representative, Yasushi Akashi, is quoted calling Radovan Karadzic a 'man of peace', and similar sentiments were expressed by others such as Co-Chairman David Owen. UN High Commission on Refugees (UNHCR) personnel who accompanied UNPROFOR officials to meetings with both the Bosnian Serbs and the Bosnian Presidency often commented on how much more at ease the UN commanders seemed at the Bosnian Serb headquarters in Pale than when meeting with Bosnian government personnel. At UNHCR, one senior UN official was routinely referred to as 'Mrs. Mladic'. According to Rieff, many UN officials held the view that the real villains of the Yugoslav breakup were not Karadzic or Milosevic, but Franjo Tudjman, Hans-Dietrich Genscher, and Alija Izetbegovic, in descending order of culpability. Senator William Cohen, after hearing stories of UN soldiers playing soccer and field hockey with Serbian soldiers and roasting a pig with them, suggested that the Stockholm syndrome was at work and that UN soldiers were a tool of Serb strategy.[7]

A substantial difference existed in the purpose and modus operandi of UNPROFOR and UNHCR personnel in Bosnia. UNHCR was focused on humanitarian relief to the victims and routinely took substantial risks to deliver it. They complained about the lethargy of UNPROFOR in assisting them and dealing with Serbian obstructionism, their devotion to not rocking the boat and their willingness to serve as a fig leaf for the great powers. UNPROFOR, on the other hand, saw UNHCR as irresponsible, not conforming to the UN mandate and compromising the UN mission to act as a mediator, not as an advocate. And in terms of the commitment to fulfilling the basic humanitarian mission, the Government Accounting Office (GAO) report suggests, rather delicately, a difference in commitment between the groups.

> Different priorities of the military and humanitarian operations underlay their mutual suspicion. UNPROFOR emphasized security and protection of the convoys and its own troops. For example, a spokesman for one contingent in central Bosnia said it had to be accountable for its own protection since it had suffered so many casualties. UNHCR staff, on the other hand, emphasized delivery of aid.[8]

The more conservative UNPROFOR strategy might have been justified if there had been better prospects of getting a genuine settlement, but as had become clear only months into the war, the Serb payback for UN efforts to treat them as serious negotiators was not a settlement, but continued conflict.

Epitomizing the dilemmas inherent in the 'peacekeeping' approach was the policy of protecting 'safe areas', approved by the UNSC in early June 1993. While the policy was aimed at preventing the destruction of Muslim cities and their populations, in fact the inhabitants sometimes ended up trapped in a small area and at the mercy of the attacking Serbs, since the

UN forces had neither the resources nor the will to put up an adequate defense or respond to aggressive actions by combatants.[9] The complete bankruptcy of the safe areas policy was clear to everyone in July 1995, when the Serbs overran Srebrenica with only farcical resistance from the UN, creating 40 000 refugees and casting doubt on the continued UN presence in the former Yugoslavia.

It has been argued that the international presence restrained Serb behavior and bought time that allowed Bosnia to develop its forces and augment its firepower. But it was also used by the French and British as a justification for not undertaking bombing or other major military actions, either because of the likelihood of UN troops being hit by friendly fire, or because of the fear that such action would spark retaliation against troops by the Serbs.[10] At a low cost to the providers, therefore, the troops supplied a modest amount of humanitarian and peacekeeping assistance, but with the consequence of preventing more aggressive action by the West that might have had a deterrent impact on Serb behavior.

Maintaining the UNPROFOR troops in Bosnia while continuing negotiations to end the violence was seen by the Europeans as a low-cost, low-risk approach to the Yugoslav problem, as well as the best way to bring about a solution. But there was a general expectation that if an end to the war could be negotiated, the US would then have to make a substantial contribution in troop strength to enforce the cease-fire. With the completion of the Dayton Agreement, American troops were deployed in a peacekeeping function. The level of violence and the cost to the peacekeeping forces was extremely low by the time of the elections in September, lower than many critics expected.

Air and naval strikes

Air strikes were the weapon of choice for many who favored a more aggressive stance for the West in Bosnia. Seen as relatively low-cost in terms of casualties and potential for tying the West down in Bosnia, they also promised to be moderately effective in slowing down the Serbs (see Table 10.1). Jeanne Kirkpatrick, US representative to the UN under Reagan, favored the UN moving from a stance of neutrality to taking

Table 10.1 Military options

	Advantages	Disadvantages	Effectiveness	Cost/Risk to West
Peacekeeping	Appearance of neutrality	Politically ineffective	Humanitarian; limits violence?	Low
Air strikes	Minimal commitment	Hard to control effects	Limited, unpredictable	Limited
Lift and strike	Combines ground and air power; morally appealing	Could spread war; complications in supplying arms	Moderate	Limited
Ground invasion	High degree of control	Costly, long-term commitment	High	High

an active military role, delivering humanitarian aid by force, if necessary, enforcing a 'no-fly' zone, securing the release of those held in Bosnian and Croatian camps, and demanding the right of those who had been 'ethnically cleansed' to re-enter their home areas. Believing that Milosevic was a leader who 'responds to force and only to force; who acts with force as the preferred method of operation and who is very respons-ive to force,' Kirkpatrick and others argued that air power could be used to destroy Serb forces and artillery, to target command and control centers in Serbia, and to take out key bridges on the Drina River over which supplies were flowing to the Bosnian Serbs. Using naval bombardment and the destruc-tion of naval bases was also advocated by some proponents of air power.[11] The strategy of bombing in Serbia itself was attractive only in the early months of the war. As the economic sanctions on Serbia started to bite, Milosevic moved toward advocating a settlement that would allow him to negotiate relief from the sanctions. From that point on, especially after spring 1993, bombing would have to have been limited to Bosnian Serb targets. It is interesting to note that the UN negotiator, David Owen, not normally associated with military solutions, advocated the use of various mixes of bombing and lifting of the embargo at three different times, the summer of 1992, to implement the Vance–Owen plan in the spring of 1993, and to implement the Contact Group plan in 1994.[12]

Others doubted the efficacy of air strikes. Heavily wooded areas would make it easy to hide weapons, the fog and precipi-tation would hinder visibility and make it difficult to find targets, especially in bad weather conditions, and the Europeans were worried about the risk to their troops if air power was used on Serbian troops. Many in the Pentagon were opposed to the use of air power in the Yugoslav terrain. In their own words they do not 'do forests', but they do 'do deserts', a reference to the strategy followed in the successfully concluded Gulf War. Reportedly, the military could also 'do bridges'. In any case, managing air strikes properly would require putting in spotters and reconnaissance teams to call in the strikes, something that NATO had practiced on the NATO–Warsaw Pact central front for over 40 years.[13] Nonetheless, having to rely on personnel on the ground increased the chance of

NATO casualties, a thought that was alarming to many in the West even if the numbers were small.

Those opposed to the use of air power tended to believe both that air power alone entailed considerable risk for the West, given the nature of the terrain and the weather conditions, and that it ultimately would be ineffective. Only by having troops on the ground could one be effective in really controlling Serbian aggression and holding gains once they were made. Perhaps the most frequently asked question of air-power proponents was: what is the next step if air strikes do not achieve the desired results? Clearly, the assumptions behind this question were the assumptions that had been key during the Vietnam conflict. Once action is taken, if necessary, there would need to be an escalation of the use of force until the objective of the intervention was accomplished.

Prior to Secretary of State Warren Christopher's trip to Europe in the spring of 1993, the intelligence assessment in the US of the likely effect of bombing was not optimistic. The policy-makers were told that while Serbia itself contained numerous targets of strategic value which could be bombed, it was doubtful that attacking Milosevic would be successful in getting the Bosnian Serbs to the conference table, since they were not judged to be heavily dependent on Serbia for supplies. Bosnian Serb artillery, on the other hand, could be easily hidden in the wooded mountainous terrain and there was often cloud cover, making it even harder to hit. Added to these difficulties was the fact that the Bosnian Serbs would likely put howitzers and mortars next to schools or churches, thus possibly raising the political cost for the West of attacking them. The assessment was that bombing might have a deterrent effect, but the only thing that would be really effective would be to put in troops. In addition, some policy-makers worried that any solution that did not entail a massive use of force would be a partial solution that would in effect legitimize ethnic cleansing.[14] Admiral David Jeremiah, Vice-Chairman of the Joint Chiefs of Staff, told reporters in late April that air strikes could lead to a difficult drawn out commitment that would include civilian deaths and damage to civilian areas. He warned that bombing raids will not be a 'painless action' and that there would be damage to civilian areas. 'You cannot allow somebody to go forward and assume you're going to get in and out with a "quickie."'

On the other side, General Merrill A. McPeak, Air Force Chief of Staff, said that bombing Serb gun positions would be completely effective and pose 'virtually no risk' to attacking American warplanes. He admitted the terrain and weather are difficult, but said that Serbian anti-aircraft guns and surface-to-air missiles were relatively unsophisticated and presented little threat to American fighters. 'Give us time,' he said, and Western air forces will order strikes on 'everyone of those artillery positions and put it out of business.' McPeak also presented his views at the White House, where Colin Powell acted as honest broker among the disagreeing chiefs, but in a later press conference put a damper on the rosy predictions of McPeak.[15] Another Air Force general testified that you can take out artillery, but after the first time they will camouflage them. Without the threat of follow-up with ground forces, the Serbs would just 'ride out' a bombing attack. The consensus in the military and intelligence community about what could be done with air power in 1993 was very cautious. Almost two years later, military intelligence officials with the Joint Chiefs of Staff and civilian Defense department officials in hearings before Congress defended their information on targets and their ability to find targets, but were still pessimistic about their ability to apply air power to accomplish political ends.[16]

In August, General Shalikashvili, after the announcement of his appointment to be Powell's replacement as the Chairman of the Joint Chiefs of Staff, had a more up-beat assessment of what could be done in Bosnia. Previously critical of the West's delay in taking on the Bosnian problem, he said that

> We are not fighting a first-rate, fully combat-capable outfit like we have been preparing for I don't know how many years. Never underestimate the mess and the nastiness you get into, but I think we've had too much overestimating.

He went on to say that the crisis in Bosnia is 'a lesson to all of us' of the importance of America's leadership and the price we pay when it isn't there.[17] In light of the results of the summer 1995 bombing when we finally did get serious about using force, General Shalikashvili's assessment seems closer to the mark than that of many of the others from the military. The results of the allied bombing campaign in September of 1995 seem to confirm the general's view. The success of the combined bombing campaign and the simultaneous offensives by Bosnian government troops clearly indicated that the Serbian juggernaut, which had displayed its most arrogant attitude yet earlier in 1995, had been consistently overrated. The earlier rout of the Croatian Serbs no doubt contributed to the willingness to come to the table. But the actions in Bosnia itself must get the most credit.[18]

Others worried about the impact on the Russian attitude toward the conflict and actions they might take in response. Another possibility was that the Russians would not agree to a UN resolution authorizing the use of force. Leaving aside the fact that authority to enforce no-fly zones existed far in excess of its use, Kirkpatrick and others believed that sufficient legal basis existed for the use of force in Article 51 of the UN Charter, which provides for the 'inherent right of individual or collective self-defense' in the event of an attack against a member of the United Nations. They argued this authority allowed the US or the West to act without worrying about Russian agreement or formal UN resolutions. In any case, David Owen has argued that after the Serb shelling of Sarajevo in February 1994, Russia might have gone along with air strikes. As it turned out, the threat of strikes allowed the Russians to move troops into Sarajevo and put pressure on the Serbs to observe a heavy weapons exclusion zone and the Russians continued to cooperate with the allies even after the massive bombing campaign of September 1995.[19]

Lift and strike

'Lift and strike', ultimately Clinton's preferred policy, which Secretary of State Christopher carried to the Europeans in the spring of 1993, combined the use of air strikes with lifting the embargo on arms going into Bosnia. It had the morally-appealing virtue of allowing the Bosnians the arms necessary to defend themselves, thus permitting them to meet the Serbs on something closer to even ground. Many thought the embargo should never have applied to Bosnia in the first place, since it made no distinction between aggressor and victim, and it froze into place an overwhelming Serb advantage derived from having the use of the Yugoslav army. The Serbs thus possessed, without imports, a considerable supply of artillery, tanks, and aircraft. The Bosnians, however, had voluntarily given up some weapons before the war began in the interest of keeping the peace, and they had mostly rifles and light infantry, although this changed as enforcement of the embargo grew less stringent and they received some anti-tank weapons from Iran and other mid-Eastern countries (with US acquiescence). In some areas, the Bosnians and Croats gained weapons by taking control of police forces, confiscating arms from the territorial defense forces, or overrunning the arsenals of the Yugoslav Army. The Croats found arms supplies in Europe, and the Serbs had no trouble importing when necessary.[20]

While the embargo had leaks, lifting the embargo would have allowed the Bosnians to defend themselves, whereas retaining the embargo rewarded the Serb advantage especially in the early part of the war. Proponents of lift and strike could counter the arguments of those who maintained that only troops on the ground from outside could do the job, for, as Anthony Lewis answered, we have [Bosnian] troops on the ground, we just have to give them arms. The Bosnian troops were motivated, they represented a legitimate government, and even given the weapon imbalance between the two sides, they were making a respectable showing. For the advocates of lift and strike, therefore, this option had the advantage of limiting the risk and cost of intervention to the West, but in coordination with Bosnian ground efforts, it showed promise for redressing the balance on the ground.[21]

To opponents, however, particularly many Europeans, lift and strike was seen as the most alarming option. Even the British were willing to concede the potential effectiveness of air strikes, but they feared the introduction of more arms would only escalate the capabilities on all sides, raising the level of violence and threatening the expansion of the war to other parts of Yugoslavia. It was said it would bring the Serbian army in to Bosnia in greater numbers, that it would be like throwing gasoline on a fire. Many believed lifting the embargo would and the negotiations, lead to the withdrawal of UNPROFOR, and increase the involvement of the US. Critics of this option also raised questions of how arms would be supplied to the Bosnians, since they would have to pass over Croat-controlled territory. The Croats would take some off the top, further spreading arms around the theater. Also, once the arms were received, the Bosnians would need training with the weaponry which would delay any increase in their effectiveness while allowing the Serbs a head start in acquiring additional arms. The opponents of 'lift-and-strike' preferred living with the status quo to risking a larger war.

The official position of the Bosnian government was that they would prefer to have the embargo lifted, even if that involved the withdrawal of the UN troops and the end of humanitarian aid. In a Senate armed services committee hearing held in mid-1994, Senator Nunn read an excerpt from a May 1993 letter from the Bosnian government requesting the withdrawal of UN troops to facilitate the lifting of the embargo and the defense of Bosnia, in order to counter testimony to the contrary from Jean Claude Mallet from the French Defense Ministry. Ejup Ganic, member of the Bosnian presidency and vice-president of the Federation of Bosnia and Herzogovina, testified repeatedly that the government favored the withdrawal of the UNPROFOR troops if that was necessary to get the arms embargo lifted. He cited the need for arms in order to force the Serbs to the table, stating that the Serbs say privately that they will not negotiate with someone who does not have a military capability comparable to theirs.[22]

The Clinton administration also professed to favor lifting the embargo, although opponents questioned their commitment to this issue and the administration's statements and behavior often suggested otherwise. Walter Slocomb, Undersecretary of Defense for policy, testified in January 1995 that it was administration policy to promote a multilateral lifting of the embargo, and Senator Levin took issue with his statement. At the same hearing, Peter Tarnoff, Undersecretary of State for Political Affairs stated that the administration had long favored a lifting of the embargo and that it had been a mistake to impose it in the first place.[23] But the administration vigorously resisted attempts by the Congress to force a unilateral lifting, although the administration did cease to enforce the embargo in the Adriatic in the fall of 1994. Since most of the arms getting through were coming from the Danube side, this action was primarily of symbolic importance. While congressional actions did not force the administration into an outright repudiation of the embargo, they undoubtedly influenced the administration's strategy and political calculus.

Some questioned the legality of the embargo, arguing that since Bosnia was not even a state when the embargo was imposed, the restrictions could not possibly apply to Bosnian arms imports. Even Senator McCain, an ardent foe of US intervention in Bosnia, subscribed to the view that the embargo violated Article 2 of the UN charter which states that the right to self-defense is a pre-eminent right of international law and may not be abridged by actions of the security council.[24] The case in favor of a unilateral lifting of the embargo was obviously strengthened by this argument.

Opinions in the US differed on the effect the lifting of the embargo would have on the conflict. General Hughes, of the Joint Staff, argued that while some materials were still going from Serbia to Bosnia (in December 1994), lifting the embargo would broaden the conflict and increase the flow across the border, and any attempt by UNPROFOR to withdraw would destabilize the situation. In such a situation, he believed, the Serbs would be able to take the Bihac area. Everyone was better off with UNPROFOR on the ground.[25] Others, such as General Wesley K. Clark of the Joint Staff, believed that a unilateral lifting of the embargo would lead to a UNPROFOR withdrawal, and sniping and harassment of UNPROFOR while the withdrawal was taking place, there would be a drop in humanitarian assistance, Croatia would be encouraged to re-enter the war, and the pressures for a larger US role in aiding the Bosnians would be great. But General Clark believed that a multilateral lifting of the embargo would obviate many of the problems presented by a unilateral action. Representative Lee Hamilton, chair of the House Foreign Affairs Committee, believed that a unilateral lifting would threaten the peace talks, signal that the US was entering the war on the side of the Bosnians and make it responsible for their fate, and would encourage others to violate sanctions elsewhere.[26] It was generally agreed that a unilateral lifting of the embargo would involve the US more deeply in the conflict, especially in arming and training Bosnian troops, if not in carrying out bombing or injecting its own troops.[27] And while Senator Sam Nunn argued that lifting the embargo would likely lead Russia to lift the embargo against Serbia, former Defense official Richard Perle believed that the Serbs had the arms they needed, and Russia would be unlikely to provide more arms to Serbia.[28]

The lifting of the embargo was the most thoroughly debated strategy open to the US in Bosnia. This option combined the moral appeal of reversing the imposition of what seemed to many to have been a misguided policy from the beginning, with a relatively cost-free way of doing something about the Bosnia problem. As many pointed out, however, lifting the embargo would have increased pressure for other American actions, although no one knew exactly what they would be. As it turned out, the leaks in the embargo that assisted both the Croats and the Bosnians in strengthening their forces, combined with the NATO bombing campaign, brought changes in Bosnia that made the question about lifting the embargo irrelevant.

Invasion

A minority of analysts advocated a ground invasion of Yugoslavia, on the assumption that nothing else could deal with Serb aggression and provide the basis for a solution to the war. Lt General William E. Odom (retired) laid out a comprehensive plan for using troops to meet his objectives of reducing the violence, preventing the conflict from spreading beyond Yugoslavia, maintaining a context in which negotiations could take place, stopping ethnic cleansing and denying the retention of territories acquired through aggression.

General Odom believed that the US had a substantial security interest in influencing the development of events in Yugoslavia. That interest lay in maintaining stability in Europe and preventing the spread of the war to other countries. He believed that there was a good possibility of major destabilization if action was not taken. He therefore felt justified in proposing to send 300–400 000 troops to the former Yugoslavia, most of which would be European. But the Europeans would not act unless the US took the lead, and to those who insisted public opinion would not support sending troops, he replied that the public had to be prepared by having the

President explain the US national interest in Yugoslavia and the measures necessary to defend it.

Air strikes, according to Odom, risked bringing in the Russians and a heavier Serbian involvement, and would probably not have been effective in any case. He favored using the military to silence the Serbian tanks and artillery, then establishing well fortified holding bases in all parts of Yugoslavia. After major weapons had been dealt with, fighting would become sporadic and would cause only insignificant damage to the occupying forces. Dealing with insurgent actions would be the job of local authorities and the police, not the NATO forces. In order to make the action effective, however, it would be necessary to have troops in place 10–20 years. According to Odom, this was not an unreasonable time considering that the US has had troops in both Europe and Asia for more than that period of time.[29]

The invasion option, or escalating to the top from the start, had the obvious advantage of providing better control on the ground. Whether the control would be as complete and cost-free as General Odom predicted was an open question. As he freely admitted, the high level of commitment embodied in this plan made sense only if a significant American security interest was present in Bosnia. Obviously, many believed that was not the case. It was also very clear that most Americans were not ready to make the kind of commitment for which he was calling.

FOREIGN AND DOMESTIC OBSTACLES

The European allies faced a domestic mood similar to that in the United States. With their economies in the doldrums, experiencing high unemployment and the easing of the psychological pressures that were part of the Cold War, the horrible scenes and news from Bosnia were enough to evoke sympathy for the plight of Bosnia, but not enough to provide strong support for any politician brave enough to suggest more involvement.

Being closer to the Balkans and historically more involved, the Europeans tended to bring their own preconceptions to the conflict, and their positions on the war reflected assumptions about the actions of other countries in Europe as much or more than a weighing of the issues in the Balkans. These facts first became obvious with German pressure on the EC to recognize Slovenia and Croatia, and the later recriminations leveled against Germany that recognition helped touch off the Bosnian War.[30] These incidents and the historical alliance during World War II between Germany and Croatia kept alive suspicions that British or French support for Croatia would play into German hands, and tended to support French and British sympathy for Serbia.[31]

But the debate in Europe over the war nonetheless in many ways resembled the debate in the US. Just as in the US, those most strongly in favor of military intervention tended to be politicians out of power, editorial writers or commentators. But while the most hawkish sentiment regarding military intervention tended to be Dutch or German, no politician came to power advocating direct intervention, as did Clinton. Chancellor Kohl, although he rejected a military strike against Serbia by the West in the summer of 1992, by early 1993 did, along with Clinton, favor relaxation of the arms embargo for Bosnia. In the original draft of the resolution imposing the arms embargo, adopted 25 September 1992, the French proposed the establishment of an emergency intervention force to impose a cease-fire or at least take advantage of a cease-fire. The proposal had the support of near-neighbors to Yugoslavia like Austria, but generated little other support and was dropped. The French occasionally adopted more militant rhetoric especially after President Chirac came to power, the Bosnian Serbs took UN hostages, and the 'safe areas' of Srebrenica, Tuzla and Zepa fell in the spring and summer of 1995. There were other occasional flirtations with the idea of military action. But until the serious air campaign began in late August 1995 the European Union was never able to agree on meaningful military action.

Among journals, the *Economist* in London asked 'how the West can live with the moral absurdity that in the faraway Falklands and in Kuwait aggression was followed by severe punishment, while in the middle of Europe the conquerors can rage on undisturbed?', and the Munich-based *Süddeutsche Zeitung* opined that while the effect of air strikes might be limited, they might have a 'sobering effect' on the Serbs, lead to a stalemate and meaningful negotiations, and inhibit the Serbs from going into Kosovo or Macedonia.[32]

But the British, despite what the *Daily Telegraph* called 'deep divisions' in the country, consistently argued against a lifting of the arms embargo on the grounds that this would enlarge and spread the war. In the words of Britain's Foreign Minister Douglas Hurd, lifting the arms embargo on Bosnia, instead of leveling the playing field, would 'level the killing fields'. In early May 1993 while Christopher was arguing the case for a more forceful policy, in the House of Commons Hurd said, 'We believe we should be in the business of trying to stop the war, not equipping the parties to fight it out'. Lifting the embargo would allow more weapons to flow to the Serbs and the Croats, leading to an escalation in the fighting and a wider war, but Hurd occasionally conceded that air strikes might help. The Prime Minister, in a rare Question Time intervention, issued a 'sombre warning' against the dangers of being dragged down stage by stage into a European war over Bosnia or of being pushed by Washington into the conflict.[33] Interestingly, the Europeans were as obsessed as the Americans with avoiding a Vietnam-type disaster, and the analogy came up repeatedly as relevant to decisions on Bosnia. The Europeans also frequently reminded the Americans that they were the ones with the troops on the ground, and consequently it was easy for the Americans to suggest escalating the war when they were in no danger of having their troops hit by accident or retaliation.

Another factor in the reluctance of the Europeans to assist the Bosnians against the Serbs was the latent (and sometimes not so latent) pro-Serbian sentiment existent in Europe. The Serbs fought with the allies in World War II, and this has not been forgotten. Moreover, there is some anti-Muslim sentiment in Europe, including a fear that a Muslim state there might present a militant Islamic threat to Europe. Roger Cohen reports that France was traumatized by its recent experience with Islamic fundamentalism in Algeria. French and British officials speak privately of their concern over the emergence of and sort of Muslim state in Europe and note the close relations between Iran and Bosnia. Some Europeans have expressed the view that Serbian interests are European interests, and that a Muslim state in Southeast Europe might become an inspiration for ethnic or communal strife elsewhere. Ivo Banac listened with fascination as a British Member of Parliament referred to the Serbs as 'our allies' while arguing against any intervention against Serbia.[34]

Lord Owen, indefatigable in his efforts in fashioning and refashioning peace plans to end the conflict, often represented an important segment of British and French opinion. The Europeans generally presented an unbounded faith in what could be accomplished through negotiation and peacekeeping operations, all the while deploring the reluctance of the US to put troops on the ground and displaying a willingness to compromise on the multiethnicity of the Bosnian state in the hope of forging a Balkan peace. While punctuating his negotiating activities with occasional calls for the use of force, Lord Owen's entreaties for a firmer stand and the imposition of peace plans by force fell on deaf ears, as far as the Europeans were concerned.

UN pronouncements and resolutions constantly reassured the Bosnians that foreign governments would never recognize Serbian gains, and aggression would not be rewarded. They seemed as equally unable as US officials to grasp how unbelievable and transparent these promises appeared. In sum, what Sabrina Ramet says of the West applied especially to many Europeans. They wanted above all not to get involved, not to have life complicated by Bosnia.[35] In short, they produced the expected rhetoric, they remained involved at a low level, but in the end they refused to put forth the effort to deal with the problem in an effective way. They just wanted the Bosnian problem to go away.

But perhaps the most important factor in the European position was the failure by the US to promote a strong alternative. The Europeans have not shown much willingness to exert strong leadership in the alliance since Suez in 1956. While the British energetically and unilaterally prosecuted the Falklands War, and the French have occasionally taken military action in former areas of interest or influence in Africa, most recently Rwanda, the Europeans have been less likely to lead in matters that are of concern to both the US and themselves. The US has usually provided the strategic view and the Europeans have reacted to it. In this case, however, when the US Secretary of State went to Europe to sell the Clinton 'lift-and-strike' plan in the spring of 1993, Christopher was reported to be listening as much as selling. Several observers were of the view that if the US had insisted on stronger military action, then the Europeans would have had no option but to go along. They would have been shamed into it.[36] That sort of firm leadership was not forthcoming.

It is interesting to speculate on how differently things might have turned out if Margaret Thatcher had been in power in Britain. Reportedly one of the motivating factors in George Bush's decision to move against Iraq, she was an outspoken critic of the West's inaction in Bosnia. In the absence of strong Presidential leadership in the United States, Britain, the most consistent opponent of military action against the Serbs among the three major European powers, became the decisive actor. If that government had been pro-intervention, things might have turned out very differently.[37]

Another concern inhibiting a strong policy in Yugoslavia was fear of the Russian reaction. The Russians, Orthodox in religion as are the Serbs, have traditionally been allied with them. Russia has been reluctant to take action against the Serbs, but the Yeltsin government has gone along with many Western initiatives, and has itself shown considerable exasperation with the Serbs. After the initial outbreak of hostilities in the spring of 1992, for instance, Russian Foreign Minister Kozyrev stated that the Serbs must not flout CSCE principles and that if they do not 'take concrete steps' to correct the situation, the Russians would be forced to talk to them in a different language. A sympathetic *Izvestiya* article, while expressing optimism that Milosevic would use his influence to reverse the course of events, nonetheless suggested that if that did not happen, the introduction of military force would be justified.[38] As the strength of the right grew in Russia, Yeltsin came under greater pressure to formulate a lenient policy toward Serbia. The Russians were particularly sensitive to the charge that they were simply following US policy on Bosnia rather than carving out an independent Russian policy that reflected their historically unique relationship with the Serbs.[39]

Through 1993, however, the Yeltsin government was basically cooperative on Bosnia. They voted for the initial sanctions against Serbia imposed in the spring of 1992, and abstained on the harsher version voted by the UNSC in April

1993. The allies had agreed to postpone this vote until after the referendum on Yeltsin's policies in Russia. Russia also voted for a UN resolution to send UN peacekeeping troops to Macedonia where they performed a trip wire function, supported the creation of a 'no-fly' zone over Bosnia, and supported the creation of a war crimes tribunal in the former Yugoslavia.

The February 1994 shelling attack on Sarajevo put Russia in a difficult spot. The allies decided to ignore Russia's objections to an ultimatum against the Serbs, leaving Russia looking ineffective and uninvolved. Instead, the Russians took a major initiative, telling the Serbs that if they withdrew their weaponry from the exclusion zone around Sarajevo as NATO asked, the Russians would deploy their troops under UN auspices between Serb forces and Bosnian troops. This appears to have been primarily a means of saving face for Russia rather than reflecting a strong commitment to the Serbs. Russia then continued its high profile involvement in Yugoslavia, especially through the initiatives of the Contact Group. At the same time, they sometimes suggested relaxing the sanctions against Serbia as a reward for good behavior, and imposing sanctions against Croatia in response to Croatian military initiatives. They continued to complain about the US ignoring the Serbs, but Balkan envoy Vitaly Churkin expressed acute dissatisfaction with Serb independence of Russian direction and lack of gratitude for Russian help.[40]

As it turned out, Russian intransigence over actions against the Serbs became a threat only when no military action was taken, the conflict dragged on, and the political right gained strength in Russia. In any case, they showed themselves as impotent in influencing their Serbian friends as everyone else. While it was certainly wise to ask questions about Russia's reactions to the West's initiatives in Bosnia, the Russians were a less important sector than some surmised.

On the one hand, it is necessary to adjust to the post-Cold-War reality that Russia is no longer a significant military power in local conflicts such as Bosnia. While they certainly would have protested strong military measures by the West, there would have been little they could have done about them, and some observers feel that Russia's pro-Serb activities stem more from domestic political necessities than any real concern about Serbia among the foreign-policy elite. It is unlikely they would have risked military confrontation. The West had an interest in assisting the democratic alternative in Russia, but the West can hardly tailor its foreign policy to suit the Russians. But the West was correct to explain its policies and attempt to include the Russians in policy discussions to avoid isolating them more than necessary.

The lack of a Russian alternative to basically going along with NATO's policies is reflected in arrangements for implementing the Dayton Agreement. Moscow originally demanded that the UN oversee the operation, but fell back to insisting on full participation with the North Atlantic Council, an arrangement that would have given Moscow a veto. Later a compromise was announced that would permit Russian combat troops to partici-pate in a Bosnian peace force while claiming to be independent of direct NATO command.[41] It is especially noteworthy that this cooperation followed the extensive NATO bombing campaign which Russia opposed.

But it was at home that the President faced his toughest challenges. With a strong political base of support he would have found it easier to persuade the Europeans to go along with a firmer strategy toward Bosnia. Public opinion, as we have already seen, was at best lukewarm in support of inter-vention, but opinion could have been shaped by a determined president. The Pentagon and the Congress are at least as difficult to persuade. Still obsessed, as are many foreign policy institutions in Washington, with the 'lessons' of Vietnam, the Pentagon in the post-Cold-War period has come to have a very restrictive view of the kinds of war in which we should get involved. As the end of the Cold War has decreased the urgency of defending security interests, the ease of winning a war seems increasingly to be the criteria by which we choose the wars we will fight, especially in the Defense Department.[42] This tendency is encouraged by the fact that it is difficult to 'win' the kind of wars in which we are likely to get involved. The gist of the conventional approach is that wars in which we participate should use the force necessary to bring a decisive victory that will then allow withdrawal. Since the alternative to withdrawal is the further escalation necessary to accomplish the original objective, there is a strong incentive to avoid involvement.

The more flexible 'limited objectives' school advocated a more adaptable approach.[43] In the case of Bosnia, this would have allowed NATO to use a relatively low-cost strategy, for instance air strikes, do as much as could be done without great cost, and then withdraw or pursue other methods for attaining the original goals.

But the conventional approach had more support than the limited objectives approach. One instance is a poignant illustration of the pervasiveness of the conventional approach to thinking about foreign policy, and the hold it has on contemporary strategy. There was considerable support in the Congress for stronger military action in Bosnia, at least among the leadership. Both Robert Dole and George Mitchell, the Republican and Democratic leaders in the Senate, favored stronger action, as did Senator Biden and Senator Lugar, the Democratic chair and ranking minority leader respectively on the Senate Foreign Relations Committee. But at a meeting between some Congressmen and the President in late April to discuss strategies in Bosnia, Clinton is reported to have asked: if the chosen course of military action (chosen from the options being studied by the President) failed to stop Serb aggression, at what point should the government say it tried its best, it could do no more, and then get out. According to Senator John Warner (R–Virginia), a number of senators said quite bluntly that once we go in with our military, we could not accept failure. We would have to complete the job no matter what it took. It takes a very brave president indeed to attempt to turn around NATO policy on Bosnia when he must fashion a policy of limited commitment and limited cost in the face of that kind of opposition in the Congress and the military.[44]

Finally, a factor that tended to dampen any ardor to engage the West in the war was the often vicious fighting between Bosnian Croats and Bosnian government forces.

In May 1992, as the war in Bosnia escalated, Radovan Karadzic and Mate Boban of the Bosnian Croats met in Austria and signed an agreement to divide Bosnia between them, the 'implementation' of what Serbia's Milosevic and Croatia's Tudjman had agreed on a year earlier. The Croats oscillated between cooperation with the Bosnians against the Serbs, on one hand, and adjusting their battle strategy to divide up Bosnia with the Serbs. During the year from the spring of 1993 until the signing of the agreement creating the Croat–Muslim Federation in March 1994 the fighting was particularly heavy. Since the Bosnian Serbs and Croats both have adjoining 'homelands' made up of fellow ethnics, the Bosnian government is left in a constantly precarious position because of the threat of annexation. The Croat offensive against the Serbs in 1995 demonstrated that the Serbs are not the only potential threat to Bosnia. These activities bolstered the case of those who painted Yugoslavia as a complex mosaic of ethnic and religious groups in conflict with each other, capable of drawing the West into a quagmire if it were so foolish as to become involved militarily. While the difference between the systematic aggression and atrocities of the Serbs and the more sporadic and opportunistic forays of the Croats was substantial, the latter activities definitely complicated the situation. This was particularly true since discussion of lifting the arms embargo would have involved the transit of incoming arms over Croat-controlled territory, a difficult-enough operation under the best of circumstances.[45]

11 The Clinton Administration II: The Agony of Decision

The Bush administration policy since the war had begun in Bosnia, whatever its limitations, had been consistent. They refrained from the use of force, made that policy quite clear, and avoided any statements or actions that would suggest that they might use force. 'We don't have a dog in that fight,' Secretary of State James Baker had said.[1] Clinton, on the other hand, had promised change in the Bosnia policy and had been quite critical of the Bush policy of inaction. He advocated bombing of the Serbs if necessary to ensure that relief supplies went through and to open up the camps. He also said that lifting the arms embargo should be considered. He condemned the Bush approach as immoral and out of step with American values. But the Clinton performance once in office reflected the President's lack of experience in foreign policy, and the bold statements during the campaign appeared in retrospect to reflect more the partisan needs of the moment than a well thought out policy. Once in office, the Bosnia problem was discovered to be both more complex and more difficult than it had appeared. Although the Clinton people did become active in searching for a solution and trying to influence the events in Bosnia, their reluctance to recognize that both force and diplomacy were needed if meaningful results were to be achieved condemned their policy to the same kind of futility that previous Western efforts had met. Clinton's indecisiveness and inconsistency confused the world, and his statements promised much that his policies could not deliver. Table 11.1 is an attempt to categorize the shifting emphasis of policy in the Clinton administration during 1993 and early 1994. This table is necessarily subjective, since both policy and policy changes were often unclear and confusing.

189

Table 11.1 Clinton administration policy positions

Date	Position	Rationale
1992 Campaign	Use bombing to gain access to camps and get aid through; consider lifting arms embargo	Only force will compel the Serbs to agree to a satisfactory settlement; need negotiation process, but also need US independent position
10 February 1993	Will actively engage in V–O diplomacy; US would contribute troops to peacekeeping force; will not impose plan on warring parties	Concern about bombing and lifting of embargo on European troops; unwillingness to take responsibility of American lead
1 May	Promote lift and strike with Europeans	After rejection of V–O by Serbs, force is required to get compliance
22 May	Protect UNPROFOR troops in Muslim 'safe areas' through Joint Action Plan	Need for agreement with allies; perception of doing something without significant cost; acceptance of Serb aggression. In mid-June, Clinton administration positive toward O–S plan for 3-way partition, but will not impose it on Muslims.
1 August	Use air power (unilaterally?) To protect Muslim civilians	Need to act to prevent total victory of Serbs; need to deliver aid. New relations with Europeans: 'Don't ask, tell.'
September	Acquiescence in O–S plan; EU Action Plan; little or no talk of lifting the embargo	Human tragedy about which little can be done by outsiders
February 1994	Ultimatum to Serbs to pull weapons back; failure to comply would result in bombing. Accept peace plan (partition); willing to put pressure on all parties	Cooperation with other powers to stop war

Moreover, many additional statements that added confusion and inconsistency are not reflected in the table.

STAGE IV   A MORE FORCEFUL POLICY?
FEBRUARY 1993–FEBRUARY 1994

The Vance–Owen plan

As soon as Clinton was in office, a government-wide review of policy was undertaken. It considered all options, from the status quo to the large-scale use of force. It was a review from the ground up, not one starting from the assumptions of the Bush policy. But the White House was caught by surprise when David Owen and Cyrus Vance, negotiators representing the EC and the UN respectively, moved to get the UN Security Council (UNSC) to approve the plan which they had been developing for months. The rhetoric of Clinton's campaign had been at odds with the assumptions of the Vance–Owen (V–O) plan, which was based on a degree of *de facto* partitioning of Bosnia–Herzegovina. Izetbegovic had appealed to Clinton to reject Vance–Owen, stating that it would be tantamount to endorsing ethnic cleansing and a huge tragedy if Clinton bowed to pressure from the EC and the UN and endorsed V–O. In spite of his anti-Serb campaign rhetoric, Clinton was careful to retain the appearance of impartiality and reluctant to become too closely identified with the Bosnian leader.[2]

The first of many peace plans to be negotiated, the Vance–Owen plan (see Table 11.2) divided Bosnia into provinces which were then allocated according to a dominant ethnic group. The Secretary-General's report on the activities of the Conference on the Former Yugoslavia stated that the 'European Community ... [reiterates its] full support for the sovereignty, territorial integrity, and multi-ethnic character of the Republic of Bosnia and Herzegovina', and stated that there would be no acceptance that land can be taken by force by the Bosnian Serbs, but many in the US felt Vance–Owen went too far in legitimizing Serb gains and ethnic partition.[3]

While setting up procedures for democratic government at all levels and progressive demilitarization, decreeing full freedom of travel and protection of human rights, the real

Table 11.2 Peace plans/agreements

Plan	Sponsors	Organizational principle	Agreement?	Implemented?	Degree of partitioning	Other
Vance–Owen	EC/UN	decentralized, multiethnic Bosnia–Herzegovina	Serbs dissented	no	moderate	least land for Serbs (43%)
Joint Action Program	EC/US/Russia	6 'safe areas'	outside powers only	no	high	no roll-back of Bosnian-Serbs
Owen–Stoltenberg	Serbs/Croats	3 republics	Bosnians dissented	no	high	provision for unification w/Serbia; Croatia
European Action Plan	EU	variation on O–S	Bosnians dissented	no	high	Serbian sanction relief
Washington Agreement	US	Croat–Muslim Federation	yes	moderately successful	Croat–Muslim unification	Bosnian-Serbs invited
Contact Group Plan	EU, US, Russia	Republika Srpska/Croat–Muslim Federation	Serbs dissented	no	moderate	Serbian sanction relief
Dayton Agreement	EU, US, Russia	Republika Srpska/Croat–Muslim Federation	yes	in process	moderate	outside powers imposed (Serbs get 49% of land)

meaning of Vance–Owen lay in the segregation of the population by ethnic groups in the provinces. While Bosnia remained a sovereign and unified state, with only the central government given authority to conduct foreign policy, it was to be a 'decentralized' state and the constitution recognized three 'constituent people'. Three provinces each were to have a government dominated by the group making up a plurality in that province, the Bosnian Serbs, the Bosnian Croats, or the Muslim-dominated Bosnian government. In addition, Sarajevo and its environs was to be neutral territory. A number of international monitoring devices were also part of the plan, to remain in effect until the three 'constituent people' agree to dispense with them. Most importantly, a separation of forces and demilitarization of the whole country was mandated. Clearly, the proposed enforcement of the plan by UN or NATO troops would have to be an important part of the package if the plan were to be successful.

What such a plan added up to was a kind of hybrid state where a weak central government maintained a facade of multi-ethnicity, but the provinces in effect segregated people according to ethnic group or religion. To this extent, Vance–Owen was a Serb victor, since they were the ones who had all along been demanding separatism along ethnic lines.[4] On the other hand, it fell far short of the goals the Serbs fought for. The idea of 'Greater Serbia' was not one that could be satisfied by setting up semi-autonomous provinces in a multiethnic state. It required, rather, the unification of all Serbs in a unified state. From the Bosnian Serb perspective, Vance–Owen might be a slight improvement from the prewar situation where they were simply a minority without autonomy, but the proposed organization of the state of Bosnia still fell well short of creating a greater Serbia. Milosevic had several motives in accepting V–O, not the least was avoiding the stiffer financial sanctions the Security Council was threatening to impose. He was also apparently convinced, as the Bosnian Serbs were not, that the Serbs had what amounted to a veto in the proposed collective presidency, and that the plan, even if accepted, would never really be implemented. In this view, Milosevic may not have been too far from some of the Europeans who favored the plan. They acknowledged its weaknesses and said that the chances it could last five years were slim at best. But they saw no alternative.[5] At the same

time, Bosnians who prided themselves on their tolerance, demo
cracy and the multi-ethnic character of their country, would find
it very hard to swallow a division along ethnic or religious
grounds, particularly when it was the result of Serbian aggression and ethnic cleansing. The plan provided neither punishment for the Serbs nor compensation for the Bosnians. Its
attraction was that it restored land which had been lost to the
Serbs.[6]

The ambitious nature of the plan was inadvertently conveyed
by its language. One version of the plan, referring to the
promise that the victims of ethnic cleansing should be allowed
to return to the areas they fled, stated that 'it is very likely to
take more than a year for the many refugees and displaced
persons to return to their homes'. Leaving aside the odds
against the plan being accepted, the fighting stopped, or the
fears of those considering returning home overcome, those
who did return would have a good chance of finding that their
homes, churches or mosques, and the accompanying infrastructure had been deliberately burned, dynamited, or otherwise destroyed by the Serbs.[7] The daunting task involved in
implementing and enforcing such a plan, given all the parties'
experiences of inter-group conflict over the last few years, and
everybody's dissatisfaction with the results of a Vance–Owen
solution, further added an air of unreality to the plan. As
William Pfaff pointed out, the plan to implement Vance–Owen,
including the American commitment of a sizable number of
ground troops, would have been far more daunting and open-
ended than a direct military intervention to halt the conflict in
its early stages. Following several revisions, the Vance–Owen
plan was accepted by the Bosnian government and the Bosnian
Croats, and was signed by Karadzic for the Bosnian Serbs, only
to be rejected by the self-styled Bosnian Serb parliament in
Pale in the spring of 1993.[8]

The Vance–Owen plan generated tremendous controversy.
Many, especially in the West, criticized it for sanctioning
ethnic cleansing and legitimizing *de facto* partitioning of
Bosnia along ethnic lines. Others admitted its weaknesses but
saw it as the best that could be obtained under the circumstances, and believed it better than the alternative of continued fighting. David Owen is particularly sensitive to the
criticism, arguing that Bosnia under Vance–Owen would have

retained its territorial and political integrity better than under subsequent proposed plans. There is merit in this argument in that later plans based on Owen–Stoltenberg, including the Dayton Agreement, come closer to legitimizing a clear division of Bosnia on ethnic lines, and the Owen–Stoltenberg plan in particular provided for secession of an ethnic constituency and potential unification with either Serbia or Croatia. Furthermore, Vance–Owen gave the Serbs only 43 per cent of the territory, while later plans including the Dayton Agreement, gave them 49 per cent.

Owen was particularly distressed when the Clinton administration, after providing only lukewarm support for Vance–Owen and complaining about its inadequacies, promoted a follow-on plan (the Contact Group plan) which required the Serbs to withdraw from even less territory than was required by Vance–Owen. Owen himself advocated the use of air power to force acceptance of his plan, but this idea drew little support from the Europeans. He argues that the US encouraged the Bosnians to hold out for more than Vance–Owen offered, and he quotes Vuk Draskovic, the main opposition figure in Belgrade, as saying that the Americans took the worst possible course. They refused to get serious about Vance–Owen, but they also declined to take military action.[9]

In a meeting prior to the 10 February announcement by the administration that it could not accept Vance–Owen, the President had said that the US had to take the lead, and that if it didn't nothing would happen. But in a statement noting the carnage in Bosnia and criticizing the Bush people for not taking action, Secretary of State Christopher stated that the US had an interest in preventing the violation of international borders, in avoiding the spread of the war, and in avoiding the river of refugees that was spreading over Europe. In the end, however, Christopher had nothing to offer that would do anything about these problems. The US position was that it would increase the amount of humanitarian aid getting through, it would actively engage in Vance–Owen diplomacy, and it would contribute troops to the enforcement of a settlement, but their would be no attempt to push a settlement on the warring parties. 'We have no prescribed solution.' Christopher said, 'The solution is mainly up to the parties.' The US would ask the UN for enforcement of the 'no-fly' zone and tightening of economic sanctions, and the President also appointed Reginald Bartholomew as a special US representative to the negotiations to support Bosnian interests. But contrary to moving toward the use of force to change the situation in Bosnia, the Clinton administration moved the other way as it sought to increase Moscow's involvement in the process, hoping to use them to influence the Serbs to settle. The US would not oppose the V–O process, in other words, but at the same time it would not promote it. Christopher, in a later statement, commenting on his negotiations with the Europeans, stated that the administration had found that if they insisted on lifting the arms embargo, the Europeans would abandon their humanitarian efforts. Another official said that the Europeans were even more 'dug in' in their position on military action than Colin Powell. Another added rather pathetically that 'It's all very complicated'. But the President caught the public mood very well. 'Clinton senses that voters want more moralism, but not an invasion', said Thomas L. Friedman. The public mood seems to be: 'Do what is right, but not with my boy or girl'. The substitution of humanitarian air drops, which the President initiated, for meaningful action, accurately reflected this attitude.[10]

Negotiations continued, as did formal planning for dispatch of NATO troops to enforce the V–O treaty if it was approved (Christopher said the US would contribute 5–10 thousand) and a debate over whether the troops should be under UN or NATO control. The Serbs continued to shell both Srebrenica and Sarajevo and as Serb pressure on Muslim towns continued, the UN negotiated to remove Muslims from Tuzla. The Bosnian Serb rejection of V–O confronted the Western powers with a decision on their next steps. Clinton was incensed that, given a chance, the Serbs did not sign on to V–O. He was disinclined to take unilateral military action then, but he ruled out nothing except the introduction of ground troops.

The initial retraction by the administration of their promise to use military measures in Bosnia could be at least partially justified by the hope of getting a settlement on the basis of the V–O peace plan, not a totally satisfactory peace, but at least peace. But with the Serbs pressing their military advantage, if the administration was going to salvage any credibility for its approach to Bosnia, now was the time for effective action. Unfortunately, the next few months were to prove all too typical of the disastrous decision-making on Bosnia that was to characterize the next few years.

Making a decision – the 'American option'

Clinton administration decisions on the war were made by a group of advisors divided on what should be done on Bosnia and by a President who could not make up his mind. The decision-making process was unstructured and undisciplined, even chaotic. One official said of Clinton that rather than shape the debate, the President preferred to wait until his aides agreed on a course of action.[11] The trouble with that approach was that he often had a long time to wait. Clinton had wanted to avoid the kind of internecine struggle over foreign policy that had characterized the Carter presidency. But the Bosnia crisis was conducive to exposing fissures among the foreign-policy elite, and it did so in Clinton's inner circle. Clinton's National Security Advisor, Anthony Lake, was generally for a firmer policy in Bosnia. He believed there were security interests at stake in Bosnia but he was also concerned about and deeply affected by the atrocities taking place there. Warren Christopher, Clinton's Secretary of State, was criticized for not having a strong set of beliefs or bringing strong leadership to the Department. Initially on the hawkish side of Bosnian policy, he soon became more cautious, and had a strong tendency to explain what was going on there in a way that fit most comfortably with the policy he was advocating at the time. He was also not above retouching the record from time-to-time to fit better with his most recent position. Les Aspin, the Secretary of Defense, was famous for his informal (some said disorderly) style and, according to Elizabeth Drew, was basically against taking action in Bosnia, even though he had developed a reputation for being on the hawkish side. Vice President Gore consistently promoted a stronger policy and was reported to regularly press the President on the issue. Gore's analyses in meetings often got Clinton worked up, especially regarding the actions of the Bosnian Serbs. The Principals Committee, where policies were largely made, was made up of these men plus Colin Powell, Chairman of the Joint Chiefs of Staff, CIA Director James Woolsey, and UN Representative Madeleine Albright, who normally favored a tougher policy. Sandy Berger, Lake's Deputy, and Leon Fuerth, Gore's representative on the NSC staff also attended.

Descriptions of the process by which decisions were made are not complimentary. Drew suggests that: 'The divisions within the foreign policy group contributed to a division in the mind of a President who had few strong instincts on foreign-policy questions.' Adding to the divisions within the administrations, of course, were the divisions within the Congress and the general opposition in the military to becoming involved in Bosnia.[12] Although Powell's instincts and positions were clear, he was credited by the other side, Gore, Albright and Lake, with asking good questions about the goals of the interventionists' suggestions, the strategies they would follow, and what the next step would be, precisely the kind of questions that were not asked about Vietnam. On the other hand, nothing the long drawn out meetings where little was decided, one official maintained that 'it wasn't policy-making. It was group therapy – an existential debate over what is the role of America, etc'.[13] Particularly distressing was the tendency of Clinton to base his decisions on emotional reactions. Particularly telling was the effect of the dedication of the Holocaust Museum and the pictures of Srebrenica on Clinton's thinking. While all these have a place among the reasons for taking a particular decision, Clinton's tendency to let television pictures, books and other events sway his short-term thinking was not encouraging.[14]

The administration had to make three basic decisions if they were to set up a framework which would serve them long term. Since the premises of the campaign had obviously been called into question by their early months in office when they had essentially continued with the Bush approach, the rejection of V–O by the Serbs once again raised the nettlesome questions of what their policy was and what comes next. First, they had to decide to what degree they would countenance partition of Bosnia, or would they stand firm on a roll-back of Serb conquered territory, the re-establishment of Bosnia as a multi-ethnic state, the return of refugees, and so on. The original position of the administration on V–O suggested that there would be little compromise on this issue, or at least that the prestige of the administration would not be put behind any plan that abridged these principles.

Now, however, even the compromised V–O plan did not gain Serb agreement. Clearly, if the administration was to maintain a firm position on these issues, the old campaign promises that the US would use military force would once again be very salient. The use of force, as the campaign had suggested, was really at the heart of the issue. In spite of the opposition of the Europeans and the Russians, the lack of enthusiasm of the public and the some of the Congress, and the resistance of the military, a strong President who was determined to mobilize for a foreign-policy action and took the necessary action to demonstrate his sense of purpose could likely succeed in mobilizing a coalition, both domestic and foreign, to carry out his policy. It would not be easy, and it would be more difficult than it would have been for the Bush people who had this crisis to deal with before the positions of the Europeans and various groups had hardened, before peacekeeping troops were in place in Bosnia, and when the shock value of the use of military force would have been more effective. Still, the power of the President is considerable, and a determined president who was willing to take responsibility for Bosnia policy might well have forged a coalition that could have surmounted the many obstacles and used force to get a satisfactory settlement. More than one European agreed with a diplomat who said that the President 'should stop asking them their opinion on what he plans to do and start telling them instead what he plans to go ahead with, preferably with their support.'[15] The President could not know whether or not the Europeans would follow his lead for stronger action. But it was certain that unless he acted as if he were going to take such action whether or not they followed, it would never happen. Once Clinton took such a step and the Europeans did not follow he would have been faced with the third dilemma: whether to take independent action without the Europeans. But this kind of hard-nosed and long-term decision-making was foreign to the style prevailing in the Clinton White House. Much later in the war, when Anthony Lake did persuade the President to sit back, minimize the concerns of day-to-day events and try to formulate a strategy for the long haul, others habitually kept returning to focus on more immediate concerns.[16]

Clinton, working toward a decision on his policy in late April, had determined that the US would not act unilaterally. He was reinforced in this decision by Stan Greenberg, his pollster. Greenberg generally believed that support for foreign-policy actions was built and shaped and could not be determined until an action was announced. He told Clinton that there was increasing support for action in Bosnia, but no support for unilateral action. Clinton was very frustrated by the constraints imposed by the allies reluctance to act. Many times Clinton expressed his understanding of the Bosnian desire to have the arms embargo lifted, and said that if we were not going to help those people, at least we should lift the embargo and let them help themselves. 'If there were other countries keeping us from defending ourselves, I'd be pissed as hell or goddamn resentful.'[17]

According to Drew, after lengthy meetings over the weekend of 17–18 April, the principals arrived at two major options. One was a combination of bombing and lifting the arms embargo, with the bombing intended to keep the Serbs from launching major actions until the arms build-up and training would affect Bosnian capabilities. The second option was a ceasefire and the protection of Muslim enclaves. Lake favored the bombing action, consistent with his earlier advocacy, and Christopher and Albright supported that option as well. A majority in the group believed that the agreement of Serbia was necessary for a settlement and were worried that bombing might alienate Serbia and prevent it from cooperating, but they also didn't want to explicitly rule out bombing. The President also met with Congressional leaders, who asked some tough questions about both the perils of acting and not acting. There was strong support for the view that once the US went into Bosnia, we could not leave until the job was done.[18]

On 29 April Clinton met with the Joint Chiefs of Staff and Christopher, Lake, Aspin, Stephanopoulos, Berger and Fuerth. At that meeting the Air Force Chief of Staff General Merrill McPeak gave a very optimistic estimate of what could be done with air power in response to Clinton's probing questions. Earlier, military opinion on the utility of bombing had been pessimistic. Admiral David Jeremiah, the Vice Chairman of the Joint Chiefs, had said that bombing might cause civilian casualties and it wouldn't cripple the Serbian threat. But as the objective became more limited, Powell became more comfortable and seemed willing to go along with the lift and strike option.[19]

At the last meeting before Christopher's 1 May trip to Europe to try to persuade the allies to take stronger action, every option other than sending troops (except to enforce a peace settlement) was considered. In the end the President decided to advocate a proposal to lift the embargo and then conduct air strikes, if the Serbs took advantage of the interval before the arms reached the Bosnians. The meeting lasted five hours, and within hours of the time it was over Christopher was on his way to Europe to plead the case to the Europeans.[20]

There was much debate over whether Christopher did a plausible job of cajoling the Europeans to go along with his policy, or whether he was too conciliatory, thus inviting dissension or watering-down of the policy. Elizabeth Drew has argued that 'critics who said that Christopher could have succeeded if he had been tougher with the Europeans were off base'. The British and French were not receptive to the proposal, for the same basic reasons that they consistently opposed bombing of the Serbs or lifting of the arms embargo. They believed that the best way to resolve the conflict was to maintain 'neutrality' and not to take positions that were anti-Bosnian Serb. They were also afraid bombing would be ineffective, that it would endanger their troops and that it might spread the war. They were especially uncomfortable with the lifting of the arms embargo because of the effect it would have on widening the war. Only the Germans, among the larger powers, were receptive to a lifting of the embargo during the time of Christopher's trip. Drew argues that there was no reason for the administration to believe that the trip would succeed, that they had set themselves up for failure.

One British diplomat said later, 'We told them [not to come to us with a fait accompli] until we were blue in the face. We said we can't do "lift and strike", especially lift. Our troops are on the ground. We felt that it would inflame the situation

and could cut off relief.' There was nothing Christopher
could have done to get a different outcome.

British officials were reported to have said that the overwhelming majority of the Parliament opposed lifting the
embargo and for the government to go along with that option
would be to threaten its survival. Furthermore, the Clinton
people themselves are reported to have known that the odds
of turning the Europeans around were against them, and that
Christopher was a diligent salesman.[21]

But there is also evidence to the contrary. Christopher is
reported to have said at one point that the American 'direction' was on the table, not only for discussions, but also for
amendment. The President also said that the Europeans
never flatly rejected his proposed policy, but rather said that
they could do better. Furthermore, as events Drew herself
outlined show (described in Chapter 7), the President, the
person who most needed to be committed to the policy if it
was to be successfully promoted with the Europeans, was ambivalent about the policy.[22] But it is undoubtedly true that it
would have been extremely difficult to turn the European
thinking around at this point. Short of confronting a
President or a Secretary of State that convinced them that
the Americans were set on the policy they were promoting
and would probably go ahead with it whether or not the
Europeans went along, or at the very least they would make
life miserable for the Europeans until they did accept it, it is
hard to image Christopher's trip being successful. Favorable
conditions for acceptance of the Clinton plan did not exist in
the spring of 1993. Not only had the Clinton adminstration
already shown itself to be unsettled and inconsistent about
what its policy actually was, but the President's advisers were
divided on the approach to the war, and the President
himself was unsure of himself and changed his position from
day to day. To bring the Europeans along would have required not only an administration which knew its own mind,
but one that was determined to implement the policy and to
do its ruthless best to make sure that the allies also participated. The next two years of Clinton administration policy
were to show that such a description of the administration
and its intentions was wildly off target.

After the European trip

The failed trip to Europe had a big impact on Christopher. He now understood what a 'loser' the lift-and-strike policy was and he tried to turn the Bosnia issue off. He was convinced that any serious US involvement in Bosnia would be politically disastrous for Clinton. Furthermore, he wanted to get the President to stop talking so much. Clinton frequently made remarks that promised to deliver more than policy did, thus compromising his credibility and complicating even further an already bad situation.[23]

The Vance–Owen peace plan was dead, but the Europeans continued to pretend it was still on the table.[24] In the absence of a plan for military action, the allies looked around for a fig leaf to cover the increasingly desperate plight of Bosnian cities which were being besieged by the Bosnian Serbs. In early May, the UNSC passed a resolution establishing 'safe areas' in six Bosnian cities, but there was no provision for enforcement except for Srebrenica where there were 220 Canadian UN-PROFOR troops attempting to maintain the status quo! The resolution contained a ludicrously inadequate provision calling on the Secretary-General to deploy 50 more military observers to protect civilians in the safe areas. In early June, the Security Council voted to authorize the allies to use air strikes against Serbian forces besieging the six safe areas.[25]

Prior to the adoption of this resolution, a 'bizarre' ceremony was staged at the State Department; the foreign ministers of France, Great Britain, Spain, Russia and the United States signed a document (the Joint Action Program) pledging to protect the six safe areas in Bosnia, by force if necessary. This program was primarily motivated by a desire to show some ares of agreement among the Western powers and Russia, and to deflect a Russian attempt to convene the Security Council following the demise of the V–O plan.[26] The Bosnians and many others believed the Joint Action Program sanctioned Serb conquests, and the complete lack of any serious provisions for enforcement led David Owen to call the UNSC enforcement resolution (UNSC 836) 'the most irresponsible decision taken during his time as Co-Chairman of the International Conference on the Former Yugoslavia'. Clinton later seemed anything but enthusiastic about the safe areas decision, even though the US was pledged only to use air power to protect the UNPROFOR troops protecting the cities, not the civilians themselves.[27] The debate on the 4 June resolution had been one of the most divisive the Council had experienced since the war began, with the Council's five non-aligned members portraying the action as evidence that the big powers remained unwilling to use force to drive the Serbs back out of conquered land and impose a comprehensive peace settlement in Bosnia. Madeleine Albright stated that the US voted for the resolution with no illusions, as 'an intermediate step – no more, no less'. If the Serbs did not respect the terms of the resolution, she said, the US would press again for the lifting of the embargo.[28]

But by mid-June the President said that while he preferred a multi-ethnic state, if 'the parties themselves agree ... the United States would have to look very seriously' at a three-way partition plan proposed by Karadzic and Tudjman, later to become know as the Owen–Stoltenberg plan. It would have partitioned Bosnia between the three 'constituent peoples' leaving only a loose federation as central authority, and providing for possible future reunification between the Bosnian Serbs and Serbia and the Bosnian Croats and Croatia. US officials acknowledged that such a partition was probably the only practical solution, since the allies were unwilling to use force and Bosnia could not do it alone. Lord Owen had advised Bosnia that it could not win back much of the land lost to the Serbs, and that they would be well advised to take a hard look at the Owen–Stoltenberg (O–S) plan.[29] After the defeat of V–O, this was the beginning of a new approach to finding a solution to the war. Having failed to persuade the Serbs to accept V–O and being unwilling to do anything about it, the European negotiators now set about trying to persuade Bosnia that they had lost the war and would have to make the appropriate adjustments in order to reach a settlement.[30]

But this retreat from the harder position proposed by Christopher on his trip to Europe was interrupted by another incident that suggests much about the Clinton decision-making style on Bosnia. In July the President was attending a G7 summit in Tokyo and was very upset by the intensified siege of Sarajevo which he saw on television. Presidents have more time to watch television when they are travelling.[31] The

President told Christopher he wanted the options studied on what could be done about Sarajevo. On the early leg of that trip, Clinton had indicated to his friend Strobe Talbott that he was very concerned about the situation in Bosnia. There were risks in doing something, and risks in not doing anything, but he believed the biggest risk was in doing nothing. He was concerned that the fighting wouldn't stop until the Muslims were obliterated.[32] When Christopher relayed the President's request to Lake and added that he agreed, Lake took it seriously because it was a new position for Christopher. The President later added that he wanted the use of ground troops included as an option in the study, a change in position which Christopher also endorsed. One official explained Christopher's turnabout as an attempt to stay close to the President's position. There was even consideration of an option, backed by Christopher, for acting alone rather than trying to sell the plan to the allies. An early plan to introduce American troops was shelved because Aspin, Lake and Christopher all agreed that the number of troops required to relieve Sarajevo (70 000) was too high to be acceptable to Congress. The troops would also have to be brought in by overland routes since the Sarajevo airport could not handle that many troops. A later revised plan which required only 25 000 troops was also rejected as politically unacceptable.

The plan that was agreed upon was to use air power, first to move the Serbs back from Sarajevo, and then to get agreement on a settlement, an attempt in Lake's words, to 'relate [power] directly to diplomacy'. There were even strong statements that suggested that if the Europeans didn't agree, then the US might go it alone. State Department spokesman Michael McCurry said the US would be willing to carry out an air campaign against the Serbs whether or not it received NATO approval. One official, using a pun derived from the new policy on homosexuals in the military, said the new policy on dealing with the allies over Bosnia was 'Don't ask, tell'. Lake went to Europe to talk to the allies. In a reversal of their usual roles, the British were favorable, but the French were sceptical. But on 2 August, after a marathon negotiating session, NATO agreed to prepare for 'stronger measures' if the 'strangulation' of Sarajevo and other areas continued.[33]

Notwithstanding the negotiations, preparations and brave statements, divisions in the administration were never really worked out. Powell and others in the military argued in inter-agency meetings that bombing would kill civilians, Serb artillery could be easily moved, and bombing might not be effective. Aspin meanwhile was giving background interviews suggesting the Serbs would have to do more than they had been doing before bombing would begin. In the end, the Serbs pulled back from their mountain strongholds, let more supplies through and went back to the peace talks. It was enough to rob the allies of their resolve and the situation was once again back to normal in Bosnia. As Drew puts it

> Thus the policymakers were back to where they had been before all the meetings, the diplomatic to-and-froing, the bold pronouncements accompanying the setting of the latest policy.[34]

The next step, after the mid-summer feint to use force, part of the seemingly endless oscillation of the West between reliance on negotiation and the threats to use force to resolve the Bosnia dilemma, was the promotion of the O–S plan. As we have seen, both the Europeans and the Clinton administration began to move toward this alternative as early as June. Now that the aggressive polemics of July and August had been exhausted, it was back to business as usual. When it was clear that Vance–Owen was going nowhere, Lord Owen, joined now by the Norwegian diplomat Thorvald Stoltenberg, Cyrus Vance's replacement as co-chair, had continued to negotiate on the basis of the plan offered by the Croats and Serbs. It had an even shorter life span than Vance–Owen, since it was decisively rejected by the Bosnian parliament in Sarajevo in September. The Owen–Stoltenberg plan incorporated many of the characteristics of the earlier plan. It based the commitment to human rights on no less than 12 human rights instruments incorporated into the treaty, but with little discussion of enforcement. The plan also incorporated changes that can only be interpreted as concessions to the Serbs, but that also reflected the greater acceptance of ethnic partition, even in Bosnia, as the war wore on. Instead of the previous ten provinces, Owen–Stoltenberg reduced the number to three republics, one for each 'constituent people'. Now, however, any 'constituent republic' may become a party to an international agreement provided this is not inconsistent with the interests of the Union of Republics of Bosnia, as Bosnia would be called. Moreover, if the central government negotiates an agreement that would involve commitments or responsibilities that are to be carried out by the constituent republics, approval from the republics must be secured in advance. In addition, citizens were allowed to have dual citizenship, in the constituent republic as well as the Union of the Republic of Bosnia and Herzegovina. While the plan states that no republic may withdraw from the Union without prior agreement of all of the republics, it also set up the conditions necessary for withdrawal.[35]

Owen–Stoltenberg clearly hints at an accommodation with a Greater Serbia sometime in the future, possibly aggregating Serb areas into one geographically convoluted piece of territory, and even setting up a mechanism for the dissolution of the Union. Somewhat surprisingly, the main reason the plan was ultimately rejected lay with the issue of acceptance of the map rather than the basic framework of partition. Izetbegovic even agreed that the Bosnian Muslims might not object to secession in a couple of years if they were satisfied with the territorial division.[36]

While Clinton maintained that he would not pressure the Bosnians to accept O–S, the EC and the UN, in line with their declared policy of treating all parties equally, were less reluctant to do so. A State Department cable reported that UN officials were threatening to withdraw their humanitarian mission unless the Bosnian government accepted the carve up. David Owen tried to use Fikret Abdic, a Muslim strongman in Bihac who openly cooperated with the Serbs, to undermine and punish the Sarajevo government for its reluctance to endorse O–S. And although the US generally opposed European efforts to force compromise from the Muslims over land and a settlement, in August Warren Christopher wrote to Izetbegovic urging him to accept O–S.[37]

When in late September, despite the pressure to approve the peace plan, the Bosnian parliament rejected it, the Europeans placed much of the blame on the Bosnians' belief, encouraged by the Americans, that they could get a better deal by continuing the war. But some deputies said that by accepting the peace pact now, Muslims might be dooming Bosnia as a country just as the tide in the war was beginning to shift. Many also doubted the Serbs willingness to abide by the agreement. Buoyed by a few recent military successes, harbingers of more to come, and with the Americans more willing to continue sanctions on Serbia and less willing to pressure the Bosnians, there certainly was an element of realpolitik in the Bosnian position. But it was not that simple either. John F. Burns interviewed Bosnian legislators after the vote and found that many of them spoke of the agonies of conscience involved in rejecting a chance for peace, all of them being very aware that the decision could mean life or death for thousands of people. Whatever the impact of previous encouragement by the US, there now seemed little doubt that there was any illusion about American help. Clinton had told Izetbegovic to make the best deal he could. Izetbegovic, calling the choice a 'personal tragedy for all of us', made no recommendations on the policy but rather listed reasons for and against acceptance. But 'Have no doubt about this', he said, 'There will be no American intervention. We are on our own'. But perhaps the most powerful reason for rejecting the pact, Burns wrote, was one many legislators spoke of on the floor: an unwillingness to be associated in history with an agreement that would bring an end to Bosnia's existence after 1000 years as a territory where different people, faiths and cultures had mixed freely. One Bosnian government minister said that people feel, 'If they're going to hang us, at least don't ask us to give our consent'.[38]

For the rest of 1993, however, the Bosnians would not get much help or encouragement from the West. The Europeans wanted to keep the negotiating process going, fearing that otherwise positions would 'harden'. In the fall the Europeans introduced the European Action Plan, as the follow-up to the failed O–S. With the military tide slowly turning in favor of the Bosnians, the Bosnian Croat forces in retreat, and Serbia isolated and suffering under the economic embargo, Klaus Kinkel and Alain Juppé, German and French Foreign Ministers respectively, put forward a plan for the gradual lifting of sanctions against Serbia in return for Serb territorial concessions to the Muslims and the Croats, and resolution of hostilities between the Krajina Serb minority and Zagreb. In linking the lifting of economic sanctions against Serbia with the concessions by the Bosnian Serbs, this plan was the forerunner of the Dayton Agreement which was adopted over a year and a half later. According to French Foreign Minister Juppé, this effort collapsed largely because the United States and Russia did not give it their wholehearted support, thus encouraging the parties on the ground to continue fighting. The Serbs expected the Russians, and the Bosnians the United States, to give them the support necessary to get a better deal than was being offered by the Europeans. But negotiations continued with Izetbegovic again apparently considering a partition agreement that would allow the Croat and Serb minorities in Bosnia to opt for secession from Bosnia.[39]

When talks broke down, differences over only 3.7 per cent of territory separated the Serbs and the Bosnians, 1.7 per cent in the Bihac area and 2 per cent in the east of Bosnia. Intelligence reports from the major powers indicated that the Bosnians were getting substantial numbers of weapons from abroad, but mostly small weapons. Iran and Syria were suspected as the sources.[40] But in one of the puzzles of the war, or absurdities, depending on your point of view, the growing ability of the Bosnian government to defend its interests and even take back territory from both the Croats and the Serbs did not engender international encouragement, but rather increased the pressure for the Bosnians to settle. The end of the year brought another statement from David Owen that the Europeans would likely pull out early in 1994 if the Bosnians did not make peace with the Croats. As the *New York Times* reported, nobody seemed to believe anymore in a single Bosnian state, and the Bosnians were trying to get the best deal possible, if as looked to be the case, they were going to have to settle for a truncated Muslim state. In an attempt to gain access to the sea and a viable swath of territory instead of just isolated territories, they were even considering the partitioning of Sarajevo. And the Americans, while concerned about the premature lifting of sanctions on Serbia, had ceased to talk about the lifting of the embargo or the use of force against the Serbs. Christopher continued to follow his 'hands off' policy and to talk of a tragedy which is occurring about which little can be done by outsiders.[41]

Meanwhile, the public debate reflected a public and a foreign-policy community that was as deeply divided on the war as ever. James Chace quoted Warren Christopher describing the

Bosnia conflict as 'a humanitarian crisis a long way from home, in the middle of another continent' echoing similar comments made by British Prime Minister Chamberlain in the 1938 crisis over Czechoslovakia. Chace cited the United States' failed Bosnian policy as an example of what another British Prime Minister, Lord Salisbury, had called the 'commonest error' in politics, 'sticking to the carcasses of dead policies'. And earlier in the year, Leslie Gelb had decried the continued attempt to reach agreement between the warring parties in Bosnia without facing the military realities on the ground.

> Diplomacy without force is farce, but that is the present Western–UN course. It is cynical farce, for all the realists and neo-isolationists who espouse it know they are winking at Serbian genocide and merely delaying their inevitable confrontation with Serbia, at unforgivable cost in Muslim lives.

On the other side, Fareed Zakaria expressed hope that the three warring sides would accept the O–S peace plan and he suggested that advocates of American intervention could best contribute by keeping quiet, since false hopes of American assistance had kept the Muslims from accepting peace terms in the past. But David Owen best summed up the situation after one year of Clinton administration foreign policy. 'What we were to discover', he said

> was that the US could neither advocate a settlement nor abdicate from a settlement. They could not forego the appearance of exerting power, but they were not ready or seemingly able to accept the compromises and the responsibility that go with the exercise of power.[42]

STAGE V   OPTING FOR PARTITION:
FEBRUARY 1994 – AUGUST 1995

The 'European option'

The new year brought about three significant changes in Bosnia and the Great Powers' policies there, but the changes turned out to be of limited significance. Europe, the US and Russia were starting to see the utility of working together for some kind of solution to the dilemma in Bosnia. The February massacre in Sarajevo where a shell (presumably Serbian) landing in the marketplace killed 68 people accelerated that trend. The result was the formation of the Contact Group and a unified position on a peace plan that all the powers supported. In the end though, the Great Powers were not able to sell their peace plan to the Bosnian Serbs, and they were, just as previously, unable to do anything about the Serbian rejection. Consequently, the powers frequently fell back into their old way of bickering among themselves about what the next step should be. But the Americans were inexorably moving toward a larger role, and they had their first big success when the Bosnian Croats and Muslims were prevailed upon to sign an agreement creating a Federation in March. But the net effect of the efforts of 1994 were inadequate, as the increasing boldness of the Bosnian Serbs in the face of Great Power weakness led to the taking of hostages among UNPROFOR troops, the fall of the 'safe areas' of Srebrenica, and Zepa, and the general deterioration of the UNPROFOR situation.

The year opened with the French, as usual prone to oscillating between calls for a firmer policy and the use of force, on the one hand, and caution about the dangers of escalation, on the other, leading a movement to get the US to use air power, logistics or ground forces to protect the 'safe areas' as Serb pressures increased.[43] A month later, the allies were still having nasty exchanges when the 5 February shelling caused the marketplace killings in Sarajevo and put more pressure on the allies to do something. This episode, being more accessible to television than other 'safe areas', meant there was likely to be a significant response. After the shelling, leaders spanning the continuum on Bosnia policy from Senator Richard Lugar to British Foreign Minister Douglas Hurd agreed that the US must take a larger role, that nobody else could bring about a solution of the Bosnia problem. The February marketplace shelling resulted in the Europeans, the US, and the Russians agreeing on the need for a tougher policy on the Serbs and a larger US role.[44]

After refusing for a year to take part in negotiations on the war, the US told the allies it would press the Bosnian government to accept a peace plan that partitioned the country along ethnic lines. The negotiating strategy that was emerging was to use force if necessary, but to be willing to impose a peace plan while rewarding a cooperative Milosevic with loosened sanctions. This new direction would produce the peace plan fashioned by the Contact Group. Although it would not achieve a settlement, it was the forerunner of the Dayton Agreement, which did. The crucial fact was that now each country had accepted the primary goal of the other: to work together to get a satisfactory plan that the warring groups would be pressured to accept. And for the first time, the Americans were to be an important party to such an effort.[45]

The immediate reaction to the shelling was to set a 10 day deadline in which the Serbs were to end the siege of Sarajevo and either pull their heavy weapons back 20 kilometers or to turn them over to UN authority. An initial failure to set a deadline reflected a split among the EU countries, with Germany, France and Belgium favoring a readiness to use air power now, and Spain, Greece and Britain opposing it. The British, by one account, preferred leaving the reaction to the UN. UNPROFOR General Rose, with British support, tried to work out a ceasefire that would have made the ultimatum unnecessary. David Owen was concerned about the Russian reaction to independent NATO action. He was also reported to have believed that an ultimatum to the Serbs would be like waving a red flag at a Serbian bull.[46] He was proven wrong, however, when Serbian compliance was facilitated by Russia sending UN troops to Pale, thus providing the Serbs with a face-saving reason for complying with the NATO ultimatum, and simultaneously allowing Russia to bolster its own role in obtaining a settlement.

The White House reaction to the shelling was reported initially to have been hesitant, with Clinton uncertain what to do. Lake, Christopher and Albright reportedly pushed for a strong response, as did White House advisor David Gergen. Some officials were reluctant to take a hard line since there had not been positive confirmation that the shell had been fired from Serb positions. Congressional pressure helped promote a strong response, with 51 Senators urging the President to lift the arms embargo. While the terms of the ultimatum were never fully complied with, enough weapons were turned over that NATO was satisfied. But two months after the Sarajevo incident, Secretary of Defense Perry made it clear that the US would not take action to prevent the fall of Gorazde, then under heavy siege. The mildness of this response was attributed to a split between State and Defense.[47]

Following closely on the heels of the agreement on action after the shelling in Sarajevo was the formulation of a plan for a federation of the Croat and Muslim territories of Bosnia, the Washington Federation Agreement. Warfare between the two parties had been very destructive since the spring of 1993. After six months of work, the United States finally formulated a plan that was accepted by the two parties, made possible in part by the ouster of Mate Boban, the head of the Bosnian Croats.[48] In Washington in March, the Bosnian Croats and the Bosnian government, under pressure from Washington, agreed to join in a common federation, the Federation of Bosnia and Herzegovina, an entity that would have the possibility of later confederating with Croatia. The new entity's territorial basis was what each group could claim on the basis of ethnic majority in 1991. By virtue of its links to Croatia, it sanctioned the principle of partition, but also furthered the goal of maintaining a multi-ethnic Bosnia. The ultimate goal was to be bringing the Bosnian Serbs into the same framework. An important goal of the merger was to stop Croat–Muslim fighting and improve the military balance against the Serbs, partly by allowing better access to arms for the Bosnians.[49] The union was built on what had been an on again, off again alliance during what in the last year had become a complex three-way pattern of conflict. If the union worked, it had the potential to defuse the persistent problem of a Serb–Croat condominium in Bosnia at the expense of the Muslims and to isolate the Bosnian Serbs as the only party not willing to accept the legitimate Bosnian government. But the previous year of Croat behavior raised substantial doubt whether Tudjman's change of policy was permanent or a tactical adjustment to domestic and international pressures.[50] The Federation had sufficient longevity to become one of two entities (along with Republika Srpka) comprising the Bosnia–Herzegovina of the Dayton Agreement.

The offer to lift the sanctions imposed on Serbia was a crucial part of the Contact Group plan, and would also be a major factor in the Dayton Agreement. This was a point on which the Americans and Europeans had long disagreed. The Americans believed Serbia had played a key role in initiating the movement for a greater Serbia and encouraging the mobilization of Serbs in Croatia and Bosnia. They also believed that men and supplies from Serbia had been a key factor in keeping the war going and contributing to Bosnian Serb gains. Most Europeans did not deny there was some truth in these assertions, but tended to see them as much less important than the Americans did. The degree to which the objectives of Milosevic, who wanted to get sanctions lifted and had grown disillusioned with Karadzic's leadership and his cause, diverged from those of the Bosnian Serbs, had become increasingly obvious. This made it easier for the Europeans and the Americans to agree to a plan that offered loosening of sanctions as a key motivator for getting Milosevic to go along with the plan. The objective was not only to cut off supplies from Serbia, something that had worked only to a modest degree after the Bosnian Serb rejection of V–O, but to get Milosevic to use his leverage to bring Karadzic to the table and get a settlement.

There was some question, however, as to just how useful such a carrot would be in getting results from Milosevic. In spite of the considerable leakage of the sanctions, not surprising considering the price it imposed on Serbia's neighbors who were closely tied to the Serbian and regional economies, there was no doubt that the embargo had been very costly for Serbia. After sanctions were imposed in May 1992, one estimate was that it had cost tens of billions of dollars and economic output had dropped by half. At one point the inflation rate was reported as 300 million per cent per month. But imaginative changes introduced in early 1994, including the introduction of a new currency, had virtually eliminated inflation by mid-1994, and the economy was reported to be experiencing a rebound. The sanctions and the economic hardship accompanying them also helped solidify support for Milosevic. In Serb culture, already burdened with a martyr complex stemming from its long history of oppression, especially by the Ottoman Empire, the imposition of sanctions was seen as just one more instance of oppression which Serbs could easily resist, and which tended to portray Milosevic as a hero for leading the resistance. As a botique owner was reported to have said, 'We resisted the Turks for 1 000 years; we can resist the Americans for another two or three'. For Milosevic the sanctions were both a blessing, in that they tended to solidify support among some, especially those sectors of society that benefited from the organizations and mechanisms that developed to circumvent them, but they were also a scourge in that they weakened Serbia economically and militarily, and probably weakened Milosevic politically in the long run. There was no doubt, moreover, that he wanted to get relief from them.[51]

In an address to the French National Assembly on 7 June, President Clinton symbolized the new US role of working directly to bring about a settlement and his accommodation with the European and Russian positions of putting pressure on all parties to accept a settlement that ratified Serb gains. When asked about this, special envoy Charles Redman said, 'We had to jump over the moral bridge in the interests of wider peace and keeping Bosnia together'.[52] But, unfortunately, this 'peace plan', for the first time reflecting a consensus among the powers of the Contact Group (United States, Russia, France, Germany and Britain) fared no better than previous ones, and for the same reasons.[53] The political arrangements reflected in the map accompanying this plan were probably more realistic than previously. The Bosnian Croats and the Muslims were now united in a more viable state which gave access to the sea coast, reducing the division of Bosnia–Herzegovina to two parts, one controlled by the Bosnian Serbs and one by the the Muslim–Croat Federation. The Bosnian Serbs would have land in Eastern Bosnia and another large area in the west, but connected together by a narrow strip of the Posavina corridor in the north that left them vulnerable if attacked there. In any case, the fiction was still perpetrated that the state of Bosnia was a united and sovereign state of the three ethnic groups, and this was still unacceptable to the Serbs. The Bosnian government, unhappy with the extent to which the Serbs were rewarded (they were to be given 49 per cent of Bosnia) accepted the plan, but assumed that the Serbs would bear the onus of rejecting it. Milosevic, hoping to get the painful economic sanctions lifted on Serbia, urged the Bosnian Serbs to accept the plan, but to no avail. In fact, Karadzic had rejected the plan before the negotiations were even completed.[54] In exchange for partial lifting of the sanctions, Milosevic then cut off at least some supplies, soldiers and so on, to the Bosnian Serbs and agreed to the posting of UN observers on the Serb-Bosnian border to verify that Serb supplies and personnel are not going across the border. Milosevic had promised to close the border in the spring of 1993 after Bosnian Serb rejection of the Vance–Owen plan and there was been plenty of evidence that this pledge was being violated as well. A recent report indicated the extent of Belgrade's involvement in the Croatian Serb and Bosnian Serb war effort. The radar that permitted the shooting down of Captain O'Grady, the first downed American in Bosnia, was apparently part of an air defense system headquartered in Belgrade. Among other evidence, it was also reported that Croatian forces even captured records of Croatian Serbs being paid by Belgrade.[55] At the same time that violations were being reported, however, the US was suggesting that Milosevic recognize Croatia and Bosnia diplomatically in exchange for lifting the sanctions entirely.

With the rejection by the Bosnian Serbs of the Contact Group plan, Clinton threatened a unilateral lifting of the arms embargo, and the US stopped enforcing compliance with the arms embargo in the Adriatic. With the Nunn–Mitchell amendment Congress had voted a 15 November cut off of funds for enforcement, if the Serbs did not accept the proposed peace plan. The US henceforth would not divert ships carrying arms to Bosnia or Croatia nor share embargo-related intelligence with the allies. The US also voted for a UN General Assembly resolution calling for a lifting of the arms embargo. It passed 94–0, with 61 abstentions. And, indicating the new allied cooperation in the Contact Group had not erased all bitterness among the allies, British Defense Secretary Malcolm Rifkind attacked Republican Congressman Bob Dole for blaming Britain for a weak response in Bosnia. He is 'behaving disgracefully', Rifkind said, since the US has no troops on the ground, and Britain has 3800.[56]

As 1994 ended, the continuing war was interrupted by a truce negotiated by former US President Jimmy Carter, but the decline in violence was also helped along by the onset of winter and difficult fighting conditions. As spring approached, the conflict was no closer to a solution than it was three years earlier. The Croats and Muslims had reached a new agreement to use international mediation to resolve problems in their alliance, but Croatia was also threatening to expel the UN troops in Croatia, an act that would likely reopen the fighting in Croatia. A low profile UN approach still prevailed in Bosnia, with planes from various parties regularly violating the 'no-fly' zones.[57] Some in the new Republican majority in the US Congress, such as Armed Services Committee member William S. Cohen, Senate majority leader Bob Dole and others from the other side of the aisle were advocating either a sustained strategy of moving militarily against the Serbs, in order to change the course of the conflict, or alternatively, the withdrawal of UNPROFOR troops, or both. But even a spectacular Bosnian Serbia hostage-taking incident, involving UNPROFOR troops, failed to alter the status quo. In any case, there seemed little likelihood that any major policy changes in the role of UNPROFOR troops would occur. A Rapid Reaction Force of NATO troops was being sent to bolster the UN and was to be in place by August, but that seem aimed primarily at bolstering the present troops rather that undertaking a new role.

Conclusion

Reading of the frequent crises, the ad hoc and inconsistent US responses and the continuous feuding with the allies over Bosnia policy during the Clinton years, one may detect a whiff of surrealism that seems more appropriate in a Kafka novel. But the chaos represented a President with little experience in foreign affairs who had not yet gotten his moorings in an extremely difficult foreign-policy case. In fact there was no policy toward Bosnia, or put differently, there was a different policy for every crisis. Each unexpected development required the ad hoc fashioning of a new response, a response often at odds with previous responses, and often including threats for which there was no follow through.

Hard choices needed to be made on Bosnia policy, but Clinton was not willing to choose. His instincts were to intervene and help stymie the Serb military actions in Bosnia, but there was a price to be paid for that and the President was not convinced that the intervention was worth the price. The decision was more difficult because the European allies had fundamentally misconstrued the war and what should be done about it. Limited intervention may help end a war if the intervenor takes sides and tilts the balance in a way that allows one side to win. Impartial intervention may end a war if the outside power takes complete control of the situation and imposes a peace settlement that all respect. The first type of intervention is limited but not impartial, the second is impartial but not limited. The Europeans tried to carry out both a limited and an impartial intervention, and it did not work.[58] If the West was to succeed in Bosnia, the US would have to decide which alternative to follow, and help the Europeans give up their fence-straddling policy.

There were many things wrong in the Clinton administration's formulation of Bosnia policy. There had been a campaign position on Bosnia, but even more than in most campaigns, this position seemed to be one the President had adopted more for domestic reasons than for the merits of the policy. Secretary Christopher said that he had inherited one of the most difficult foreign-policy problems that can be imagined, and was still 'gathering the data.' One commentator suggested it was as if Churchill, having ousted Chamberlain from office in May 1940, had declared that the German problem was more complex than he had thought.[59] The President's capacity to absorb information sometimes seemed to work against him. Absorbing all points of view, he seems unable to settle on one position which he can implement.[60] The decision-making processes were not structured, the President was neither skilled nor particularly interested in foreign affairs, and his advisers as well as the Congress were deeply divided on Bosnia. Add to this that public opinion was also divided and not in a mood for foreign-policy activism. Moreover, to the extent that the administration did have, if not a policy, at least a disposition toward events in Bosnia, this disposition was frequently at odds with the approach of the allies.

The allies had their own troubles. Often divided themselves, lacking a track record of providing direction for the alliance in foreign affairs, and still unsure whether their identity was primarily European or primarily national, they were not in a position to provide the leadership that the US would not. The British were consistent in avoiding anything that might require a military cost, 'carefully plotting the radiating consequences of every move, spying the countryside for that dreaded "military quagmire" where political credibility has been known to disappear without a trace'.[61]The French were erratic, often defying predictions on whether they would advocate a hard or soft line in a given crisis, and as Malcolm Rifkind pointed out, their words sometimes outrunning their deeds. The Germans, after their initial role in the recognition issue, were for the most part passive.[62] The Europeans did have a policy, or at least a general direction that they adhered to with some consistency. But it was not the policy to do the job. What was needed was a long-term, consistent policy to provide the military pressure to match the negotiating objectives. The deteriorating situation in 1995 forced the Clinton administration into a major reorientation of its approach.

12 The Clinton
Administration III:
Reassertion of American
Leadership

STAGE VI USING FORCE TO GET A SETTLEMENT: AUGUST 1995–

Pressures and provocations: the change in Western policy

After the passive Western stance that characterized so much of Western policy since the Bosnian War began in earnest in 1992, it came as a surprise to many when NATO began an intensive bombing campaign of Serbian weapons, air defenses, munitions stores, and communications infrastructure in Bosnia in late August 1995. Making good on pledges given at a conference in London in July that there would be 'disproportionate' military action against the Serbs if they did not stop attacks on Bosnian 'safe areas', the new allied response was much different from the reaction following the 1992 London conference. There the allies had also condemned Serbian actions, but no military response was forthcoming. What provoked the West to change its policy and carry on sustained bombing campaigns that changed the military equilibrium in the former Yugoslavia? The immediate provocation was another shell landing in downtown Sarajevo, causing 38 casualties, and creating a public reaction of shock and repulsion not unlike the similar incident in early 1994. But other factors were at least as important in forming the West's new reaction.

The West had dropped the demand that the Serbs either take-or-leave the Contact plan, and instead offered it as a basis for negotiations. In addition, the allies offered to lift the embargo against Serbia if Belgrade would recognize the borders of Bosnia and Herzegovina. Serbia refused and the

Bosnian Serbs intensified their bombardment of Sarajevo, in turn provoking more allied bombing. The Serbs then took between 300 and 400 UNPROFOR personnel hostage. This humiliating event forced the allies to cease bombing, and the hostages were released in mid-June after negotiations. UN officials later admitted their release was contingent on NATO undertaking no new bombing.[1]

The UN-designated safe areas of Srebrenica and Zepa, with large Muslim populations, had been overrun in July of 1995, in spite of the UN pledge to protect them and in spite of numerous warnings to the Serbs. The Serbs this time threw caution to the winds and departed from their skillful game of pushing the West just far enough to accomplish their military goals, but not far enough to provoke a significant reaction. The UNPROFOR position had become such that there was considerable talk about the withdrawal of the UN troops, because of their vulnerability and impotence under the operative rules of engagement in the face of Serb actions. Before the start of operation Deliberate Force, as the bombing campaign was code-named, the West was careful to make sure its troops were not in a position once again to become victims of hostage taking. Threats by the European countries to withdraw their contributions to UNPROFOR were also encouraged by a strong movement in the US Congress to force President Clinton unilaterally to lift the arms embargo against Bosnia, whether or not the UN went along.

The change in policy was also facilitated by a major shift in European sentiment, especially in the government of the newly elected President Chirac in France. The fall of Zepa and Srebrenica evoked harsh and rather startling criticism from the French, especially considering the former policies of France. Prime Minister Alain Juppé said after the fall of Srebrenica that the French were ready to take part in a military action to retake Srebrenica. Since their troops were already in place as part of the Rapid Reaction Force put in to bolster the European presence after the hostage taking, they were ready to advance.[2] At one point, French President Chirac likened British Prime Minister John Major to Neville Chamberlain. If once again there is no will to act against the Serbs, said Foreign Minister Juppé, France is ready to let the arms embargo be lifted, withdraw UNPROFOR and let the combatants fight. This is a solution of despair, he said but it would be even worse for French troops to watch passively while ethnic cleansing is taking place.[3]

British Foreign Secretary Malcolm Rifkind, however, suggested that the French utterances were long on rhetoric and short on substance, and added that despite the French charges, British and French policy were the same, and had been for the past couple of years.[4] While the French continued to oppose air strikes and professed to favor using the newly introduced European Rapid Reaction Force to retake Serb-conquered 'safe areas', nonetheless, the abrupt shift in French pronouncements provided support to President Clinton's desire to take a firmer stand against the Serbs, and tended to push the rest of the Europeans in that direction.[5]

Of greater importance, however, was the Croatian offensive to drive the Serbs from areas taken earlier by Croatian and Bosnian Serbs. Having patiently waited their turn while building and rearming their military forces after their defeat in 1991, the Croats in early August began an offensive that captured the Croatian Serb rebel stronghold of Knin, and soon recovered all of the Serb-held land in Croatia except Eastern Slavonia, right along the border with Serbia proper, as Serbian refugees fled the formerly Serb-held lands.

This rapid offensive had an effect that is hard to exaggerate. In addition to displaying Serb weakness and lack of will, a reaction that many had predicted once the Serbs were faced with real opposition, it provided an object lesson to the West. Mesmerized by the Serbian juggernaut and the 'lessons' of Vietnam, the Western allies had stood by helplessly as the Serbs intimidated their foes, committed atrocities with little but rhetorical resistance from the West, and met only symbolic military opposition. Now, the Croatian army cleared its territory of the Serbian military in a matter of days, and the world saw panic-stricken Serb civilians fleeing the territories in which they had lived along with the Bosnian Serb troops that were supposed to be protecting them. The psychological impact of this abrupt reversal of fortune could not help but be dramatic, and this lesson in military initiative undoubtedly helped lift a psychological barrier that had until then discouraged Western action. With the Serbs, shorn of their aura of invincibility, and given the ease with which the Croatian army had routed the Bosnian Serbs, the allies could now summon the courage to conduct their own offensive against them.

The US (unlike Britain) did not condemn the Croats' offensive, maintaining that it would open opportunities for peace.[6] Some maintained that the US had given active support to the Croatian offensive through private firms who were training the Croats.[7] In any case, from a US perspective, the strengthened Croatian hand helped to restore the balance of forces, and improved the prospects for peace in the former Yugoslavia, including Bosnia.

Another pressure Clinton confronted on Bosnia was from the domestic arena. Still playing a passive and ineffectual role in a war he had promised to do something about three years earlier, Clinton was facing an upcoming election in little more than a year, and pressure from the now Republican majority in Congress as well. Congress was threatening to pass, over Clinton's veto, a measure that would force the US government to lift unilaterally the arms embargo on Bosnia and allow the Bosnians better to arm themselves. Bills passing both Houses of Congress by potentially veto-proof margins would have required the US unilaterally to end participation in the arms embargo against Bosnia either after UNPROFOR was withdrawn, or within 12 weeks of a request by the Bosnian government for UNPROFOR's departure.[8] Faced with growing Bosnian Serb assertiveness and Western humiliation as safe areas fell and hostages were taken, changing attitudes in Europe, growing domestic opposition and encouragement from Croatian successes, the prospects of putting this problem behind him with a radical new approach was bound to be appealing to President Clinton. He finally persuaded the increasingly receptive Europeans to implement part of the original solution (air strikes) to the Bosnian problem that he had espoused in the 1992 campaign.

In early August Anthony Lake and Peter Tarnoff launched an American diplomatic offensive with a trip to European capitals. Later in August, serious bombing of Serb positions and forces was added to the US strategy.[9] This time the damage done to the Bosnian Serb war machine was more than symbolic. With the Serbs already smarting from the Croatian pounding and its repercussions in Bosnia, the NATO bombing campaign (with approximately two-thirds of the sorties flown by Americans) had a serious effect on the Serbs and allowed the Clinton administration to get all three warring Bosnian parties to the table at Wright Patterson Air Force Base in Fairborn (Dayton) Ohio. Meanwhile, a Croat-Muslim offensive was taking advantage of the bombing and Serb demoralization to make significant gains on the ground. The Clinton administration delayed the meeting to give the offensive time to progress before starting the Dayton talks. The Bosian Serbs lost 20 per cent of the land under their control.[10] It was a measure of the demoralization of the Bosnian Serbs, and also a potential weak link in any agreement, that they agreed to representation at Dayton by Milosevic instead of their own leaders.

The Clinton administration had affected a major change in US policy, and for the first time in the war had taken military action that had a decisive impact on the Serbs and their ability to fight the war. While the Clinton administration refused to go along with many who advocated arming the Bosnians, the seriousness with which the West carried out the bombing indicated a major change in the objectives and the means being used to reach them. The assumption that had governed US policy from the beginning of the war: that through negotiation a settlement of the war could be attained even though the military situation and incentives on the ground were at variance with the proposals on the table, was finally jettisoned. Taking specific action to halt the Serb advances and ensure their willingness to come to the table, and all this with European cooperation, was a break-through approach. The American assumption now was that in order for fruitful negotiations to take place, force must be applied. Serious bombing early in the conflict might have stopped the Serbs then, and arms and assistance to the Bosnians might have given them near parity with the Bosnian Serbs by 1995. But as it was, the Bosnians were still militarily inferior, and the West, in order to make a serious effort for peace, would have to follow the negotiations by dispatching more troops to enforce a settlement.

The settlement that would be reached showed that the Clinton administration still adhered to previous policy on other issues. Nonetheless, the West had finally abandoned the

European approach on the battlefield and partially taken up the 'American option'. But the settlement itself would reflect more the assumption of partition inherent in the European approach.

The Dayton Agreement

The Dayton Peace Agreement displays similarities to the previous efforts at working out a comprehensive peace in the former Yugoslavia. As in previous settlement plans, the negotiators had to deal with the thorny issue of trying to preserve an integrated Bosnia-Herzegovina while still placating the Bosnian Serb demand for independence, or at least autonomy. It is not clear that the Dayton Agreement is any more successful at this than previous plans. Bosnia-Herzegovina is to continue as a sovereign state within its present internationally recognized boundaries. The central federal government will have responsibility for foreign affairs, customs and immigration policy, monetary policy, law enforcement, communications, transportation, and air traffic control between the two separate parts of Bosnia. Within this framework, two entities, the Federation of Bosnia and Herzegovina (henceforth the 'Federation') and the Serb Republic (Republica Srpska) will coexist. Provisions are made for democratic government, and presidential and parliamentary elections were held in September. Human rights are to be enforced, first internationally, and now by either the central government or the governments of the entities. The requests and rulings of the War Crimes Tribunal are to be respected, but were only laxly enforced militarily by the NATO international implementation force (IFOR). All people have the right to move about freely, to return to their homes, or to obtain just compensation for losses through ethnic cleansing.

The territory of Bosnia has been split, 51 per cent for the Federation (Croats and Bosnians) and 49 per cent to the Bosnian Serbs. Sarajevo is governed as a single entity within the Federation of Bosnia and Herzegovina. Gorazde, a remaining 'safe area' primarily in Serb-held territory, retains a secure land corridor to the Federation-held areas, and the status of Brcko, in the narrow Posavina Corridor tying the two parts of the Serb Republic together, was to be determined by

2. Dayton Peace Agreement boundaries

Note: Based on preliminary data; representation of agreement line not necessarily authoritative.

Source: US Department of State.

arbitration within a year. While there is no discussion of or provision for the union of either of the entities with either of the 'home' countries, Croatia or Serbia, there are now only two entities, and it is clear that the pressures for a break up of Bosnia and, especially for the Bosnian Serbs, eventual union with the 'homeland', are great. This pressure was being felt only days after the agreement was signed, as Bosnian Serb leaders declared the agreement unworkable.

The agreement obligated the parties to withdraw their forces behind agreed-upon cease-fire lines, and provides for confidence-building measures to promote peace. The parties were obligated to negotiate on arms limits for heavy weapons, and they were also prohibited from importing arms for 90 days and heavy weapons for 180 days. At the same time, the international arms embargo and the economic embargo on Serbia have been lifted.

The peace agreement is being enforced by a NATO troop force of over 50 000 troops, which has wide latitude in compelling adherence to the agreement and defending itself. While the Russians have participated in enforcement of the agreement, they have done so under a NATO command, and are accorded less than a full partnership in decision making. While not happy with the arbitrary way in which the Western countries dominated the negotiation process and the enforcement of it – as has been the case for the last four years of Western efforts in stopping the Bosnian War – the Russians had little alternative but to go along if they wanted to remain a player in the Balkan drama.[11]

While this agreement, unlike those before it, has passed the hurdle of acceptance by all parties (with Milosevic signing for the Bosnian Serbs), the basic grievances and dissatisfactions remain. The Serbs are reluctant to live under Bosnian government authority, the Croats will be tempted to dominate the Federation at Muslim and possibly Serbian expense, and the Muslims, the weakest militarily and lacking the intensity of their earlier commitment to multi-ethnic democracy, will be tempted (if not forced) to consolidate a defensible and homogeneous Muslim state. But at the same time, this agreement has benefited from a serious enforcement attempt by NATO and the political pressures on the Balkan parties that come from acceptance by the Western powers.

Evaluating and implementing the agreement

The success in negotiating the Dayton Agreement was the product of several factors. The Croatian offensive against the Serbs, in turn made possible by several years of rearmament and a decision by Tudjman to move to a more cooperative stance toward the Bosnians,[12] in conjunction with Bosnian strength on the battlefield, humiliated the Bosnian Serbs and showed for the first time that they could be defeated. The NATO air strikes did in Bosnia what the Croat offensives had done in Croatia, show that the back of the Serbian offensive was decisively broken. Given the balance of forces, it was unlikely that the war could be won by either side, and the Bosnian Serbs, abandoned by Milosevic, routed from Croatia, and pummeled by the NATO air war in Bosnia, had little option but to seek a negotiated settlement. The Croats, having regained control over most of the land they had previously held (except for Eastern Slavonia), were ready to settle at least temporarily for 'peace', and the Bosnian government, having regained much lost land (a considerable portion during the bombing), were facing a long, hard war if they chose to try and conquer all of Bosnia. The third factor that made the agreement possible was the US willingness to send ground troops to Yugoslavia, meeting a long-standing European demand and assuring the Bosnians that they could count on a meaningful NATO enforcement of the agreement. In addition, of course, the US pressured all sides to reach a substantive settlement.

There are two obvious weaknesses inherent in the long-term effectiveness of the Dayton Agreement. The forces on the ground still lack symmetry. In spite of the offensives the Bosnians have taken starting in the last half of 1994, their superior numbers, and their gains in weaponry, they nonetheless lack the heavy weaponry and the training that for so long allowed the Bosnian Serbs to effectively deploy so much firepower.[13] It is these imbalances more than anything else that had doomed negotiations before the Agreement. Seemingly forgetting the admonitions of Clausewitz and many other writers on international relations, much of the prior negotiation seemed to assume that endless reshuffling and reshaping of the territories, in some pattern that amounted to *de facto* partition would eventually motivate all parties to accept an agreement. What exists now that was not present before is an incentive to the Serbs (especially) to stop fighting. While the agreement seeks to limit and even decrease the number of arms in the Bosnia theatre, none the less the Americans have pledged to ensure that the Bosnians are adequately armed and trained to protect themselves. The US promoted policy of

giving arms to the Muslim–Croat Federation has met considerable opposition from many Europeans who consider it folly to
introduce more arms into the Balkan theatre, and this issue
remains a point of contention within the alliance.[14]

Directly related to the problem of asymmetry is a second
problem: that, to a substantial extent, the agreement was
imposed from above. The negotiations came close to failing
and further meetings of the principals have been required to
iron out problems that arose in the first months of implementation. All sides have shown a reluctance to live up to the letter
of the agreement. The fact that the Americans have committed troops to Bosnia, along with the Europeans, gives this
agreement added authority. The American commitment itself
is an astounding development considering the previous unwillingness to be militarily involved.

By late October 1996, progress has been made in implementing the Agreement, but there is much to do to create the
kind of Bosnia for which it calls. Presidential and parliamentary elections were held in mid-September, and although the
Organization for Security and Cooperation (OSCD) in
Europe approved the results of the elections, they were far
from satisfactory. Substantial voter fraud was reported,[15] and
hard-liners dominated as the winners for all ethnic factions.
Because of the unwillingness of the Americans to turn
Karadzic and Mladic over for war crimes trials, their influence
was still considerable in Bosnian Serb politics and the elections, although they were formally prohibited from participat-
ing. Bosnian Serb officials made numerous statements about
their unwillingness to accept a unified Bosnia.[16] Outside
Muslim elements also continued to pose a problem, especially
hard line Muslims from Iran. Moreover, the elections took
place in an atmosphere of intimidation, threats and violence.
Pressure from all ethnic groups on those seeking to return to
their homes to live or to vote impeded freedom of movement.
Expulsion of Muslims from Serbian area by Serbs also continued. Violence and bullying tactics were reported used by
the followers of Izetbegovic against Haris Silajdzic and his
followers as they competed with one another in the elections,
and there were calls in the SDA for a Muslim state.[17] The
Croats and Muslims continued to feud over the administration
and control of Mostar, in spite of their formal unification in

the Federation. Municipal elections for all of Bosnia have twice been postponed because of widespread voter registration fraud. Some observers suggested that the elections that were held would do more to legitimate and encourage ethnic division than to promote the unification of Bosnia envisioned by the Agreement, and Senator Robert Dole, campaigning for the presidency in the US, had suggested that the presidential and parliamentary elections should also be postponed.[18]

The IFOR forces have kept order in Bosnia and done so with almost no casualties. All sides have pulled back their forces behind the separation lines, and returned troops and armaments to barracks. But the timidity of the IFOR forces in apprehending war criminals and their unwillingness to get involved in organizing and carrying out the unification and operation of the civilian infrastructure had left a large hole in the attempt to provide the foundation for a united country. This timidity was driven above all by the American determination to avoid involvement in building the civilian infrastructure, difficult operations of apprehending individuals or keeping order that would cost lives and recall similar actions in Somalia. This concern was all the more acute since the US elections are scheduled for November and the US troop presence in Bosnia is not popular with the US electorate. Some diplomats suggested that the occupation forces required some form of military rule that would allow integration of the economic and political infrastructure to include utilities, traffic control, transportation laws, postage and so on, thus laying the groundwork for a unified country.[19]

Examples of the remaining division and operation of Bosnia along ethnic lines were obvious in the economic realm as well. Promised funds for economic development were not being disbursed, partly because of discrimination by lenders in determining to whom the money should go. Banks were mostly controlled by ethnic groups, and money is distributed accordingly. Widespread corruption was also a problem. It is hard to overemphasize the importance of this factor. If economic factors played a major role in the demise of Yugoslavia, as Susan Woodward argues, they will certainly play a big role in the resuscitation of the area. It will not be easy to rebuild economies that have been devastated by years of war and with large parts of the population displaced and uprooted.

There were signs of progress, however, in addition to the relatively quiet and uneventful nature of the occupation. Bosnia and the Federal Republic of Yugoslavia (Serbia and Montenegro) have exchanged ambassadors, and Yugoslavia and Croatia also recognized one another. Sanctions against Serbia were lifted by the UN, although there was some disagreement on that course of action, a move with which the US went along with some reservation. In addition, the US, by threatening to withhold promised arms deliveries, was able to facilitate the establishment of a joint defense ministry between the Croats and the Muslims. There was widespread agreement that occupation troops were required beyond the December 1996 scheduled withdrawal date. Although the issue was being soft-pedaled in the US election campaign, new troops were going into Bosnia even as the withdrawal started. It appears that troops will remain in the former Yugoslavia for some time. Many believe they will be required for at least two more years, when the next general elections are scheduled.

A new Bosnia?

Aside from the crucial question of whether the peace can be kept, the Dayton settlement must also be evaluated according to the kind of Bosnia it will produce if it can be successfully implemented. The best description of the feasible long-term solution in Bosnia may have been by President Izetbegovic when he said that the arrangements laid out by the Dayton Agreement 'may not be a just peace, but it is more just than a continuation of war'.[20] While there remains some commitment to democracy and a multi-ethnic society in Bosnia, the more-than-three years of war has taken its toll, yielding an unfortunate mix of authoritarian tendencies and Muslim radicalism. Even as early as the summer of 1993, Izetbegovic indicated that for the present he had given up on a multi-ethnic Bosnia.[21] The early Serbian claims of just this kind of government in Sarajevo have been turned into a partially self-fulfilling prophecy by the very people who made the charges. The *de facto* partitioning of Bosnia by ethnic groups as called for in the agreement is probably the best that could be done at this stage in the war, but it is questionable if even the fiction of a united Bosnia can now be maintained.

The European attempt to avoid taking sides in the conflict, whatever its value as a tactic to encourage a settlement, never reflected accurately the origins of the war. It is one thing to allege that the Croats and even the Bosnians have some-times behaved aggressively, have not kept agreements, have engaged in ethnic cleansing, have staged episodes of violence that rebounded to their own benefit, and have used propa-ganda. But it is not possible to produce a case that the Serbs have not done all these things more purposely, more consist-ently, more effectively, and more malevolently than the other parties, but especially when compared to the Bosnian govern-ment.[22] However tempting the calls for complete justice, for righting of the wrongs that have been done by Serbian aggressiveness, and for fulfilling the early American and UN assurances that the rewards of aggression and ethnic cleans-ing would not stand, the war developed a dynamic of its own. While bombing and arming of the Bosnians earlier in the war might have led to a different, more just and less risky (for the US) outcome, we are now in a different environment. It is clear there is now no going back to the *status quo ante*, that a settlement must be found that is possible and enforceable. There will be no full restoration of the pre-war situation or compensation for the ethnic cleansing and the reworking of the Bosnian ethnic map, as the Bush people so extravagantly and flamboyantly promised in the early years of the war. Satisfactory compensation to the victims will not and probably cannot occur. Nor will the atmosphere and culture of toler-ance and ethnic diversity that existed in Bosnia be restored, at least not for many years.

Nevertheless diplomacy and international solutions should begin with the current situation and work forward from there. The reason for the prolonged and ultimate failure of the West's Bosnia policy for most of the war was that it refused to face up to the realities on the ground and to assess realistically what kind of solution was required. To that end, the Dayton settlement represents a modestly promising road forward that entails only moderate risks. But given the politi-cal pressures to withdraw US forces from Bosnia quickly, it is certainly right that ensuring the build-up of Bosnian military strength is a necessary condition for a long-term solution. It is not, however, a sufficient condition. The new American involvement is a welcome step in ending this long and tragic conflict, but the fact that it is three years too late means that the potential results are considerably less than they might have been, and that they may well be purchased at a higher price in democracy and ethnic tolerance than would have previously been necessary.

Part V

The New Ethos on Intervention

13 The Reluctant Superpower

THE BOSNIAN FAILURE

Values

Since a consensus existed among the American people that the security interests at stake in Bosnia could justify only limited American involvement, the case for military intervention could be strengthened if it could also be justified on humanitarian grounds. But it is not easy to justify a foreign policy on humanitarian grounds. Proponents of military intervention in Bosnia have sometimes used the slogan 'never again', referring to the Nazi experience in Europe, to shame opponents into action against the carnage taking place in the former Yugoslavia. The passive Western response to the Bosnian episode, along with the rest of the post-World-War-II record, provides sufficient evidence to discredit once and for all the idea that nations willingly march out to help their fellow non-nationals, especially if there is a cost involved. Even after the Dayton Agreement, when it became clear that US troops were going to Bosnia, public resistance continues to confirm a passive stance toward Bosnia. The tendency to assume that we learned a lesson in World War II and that in the future we would respond appropriately to prevent atrocities is naive. Even when many believed there was a substantial security interest involved in opposing the Nazis, moving the country to involvement in the war was a slow and arduous process, and Franklin Roosevelt might not have succeeded in accomplishing it at all without the attack on Pearl Harbor.[1] The more recent cases of Cambodia, Rwanda and Bosnia amply reinforce the conclusions derived from that period, that altruistic foreign policy has very definite limits.

The limits on foreign-policy activism must be accepted, but the picture is not entirely gloomy. The low level of US involvement in Bosnia and the former Yugoslavia did reflect an attempt to deal with the humanitarian aspect of the crisis and right the wrongs being perpetrated there. The efforts of the US and European Union in the former Yugoslavia raised at least two questions of humanitarian concern that went to the heart of the purpose and priorities of US policy. One question pertained to the choice between ethnic partition vs. democratic rights, and the second whether humanitarian aid was effective or counterproductive to the well-being of the Bosnian people because of its effect on the war effort.

US sympathies were with the ideal of a universal democracy that would allow Bosnia to exist as a state for all people regardless of their ethnic origins. Because of the unique American experience of a nation based on and continually absorbing immigrants from other cultures, we were particularly concerned with and sympathetic to the principle of multi-ethnicity in Bosnia. It became increasingly clear, however, that in the face of Serbian (and Croatian) use of force this ideal could only be sustained through a commitment of assistance, probably including force, to the Bosnian government. In the absence of such a commitment, the idea of a Bosnia that adhered to the procedures of universal democracy would have to be compromised. Thus, the US joined the Europeans in promoting various versions of plans that proposed to end the war by, to one degree or another, carving Bosnia into ethnic enclaves, some that preserved the form of a centralized state (Vance–Owen), others that virtually invited union of the various ethnic groups with the 'home' country (Owen–Stoltenberg), or simply were to be implemented after the process of division by ethnic group may be too far advanced to stop (Dayton Agreement). Given the length of the war, the declining commitment to multi-ethnicity in Bosnia and, until recently, the unwillingness of the West to influence the military situation on the ground, it appears increasingly unlikely that any settlement can be implemented so that it does not leave Bosnia divided more or less along ethnic lines. Alternative solutions would have been a successful effort to adjust borders or reach agreement on some form of ethnic partition prior to the outbreak of violence, such as the ill-fated Lisbon plan, or the early use of force when conditions were more favorable to the restoration of pre-war conditions. As it stands now, the triumph of narrow ethnic nationalism threatens both individual liberty and democracy.[2]

A second value conflict that faced the US in Bosnia was the priority that should be given to turning back Serb (or Croatian) aggression and preserving the territorial and democratic integrity of Bosnia, versus providing humanitarian relief and using the peacekeeping forces to attempt to dampen down and keep a lid on the fighting. Clearly the emphasis was on the provision of humanitarian aid, since the UN and NATO forces did little else except occasionally shoot down a plane or do a few minor bombing runs. The effect was to allow the Serbs and the Croats to do all the damage they could while the West's humanitarian aid allowed survival from hunger as long as individuals did not become war casualties – and as long as the relief convoys could get through. The 'well-fed dead', Sarajevans took to calling themselves. After the fall of Srebrenica and the alleged massacre of thousands of Bosnian men, David Rieff asked, if the Bosnians are going to die like this, why not at least provide them with the arms to die while fighting back?[3]

Since it was clear the West was not a major military factor in the war (except for the impact of the arms embargo), the crucial question became: did the presence of UNPROFOR and UNHCR do more harm or good? The allies frequently used the presence of troops on the ground as an excuse for not bombing or taking action against Serbian provocations. Once hostage taking and the fall of the 'safe areas' to the Serbs revealed for all the world to see the hollowness of the military effort, the extent to which the West had manacled itself was clear.

There is no doubt that the humanitarian deliveries saved many lives and played an important role in keeping many Bosnians alive. Given the West's lack of will to counter the military offensives, it could be argued the UN presence, or at least the UNHCR (UN High Commissioner on Refugees), played a positive role. But if the West had been serious about taking an active role in the war, the UNPROFOR troops would either have had to change their mission or be completely withdrawn.[4] As became apparent in the summer of 1995, the attempt of the UN troops (as proxy for the West) to play the 'neutral' arbiter and purveyor of humanitarian aid proved to be unsustainable. The countries providing UNPROFOR troops were faced with the alternatives of getting serious about military action, or a withdrawal of troops who could no longer protect themselves from hostage taking, much less protect anyone else. The question of priorities and Western direction was finally resolved in favor of using military force to bring the warring parties to the table for serious negotiations.

Strategies

There were alternatives to the policies that were followed in Bosnia. The alternatives were inadequate and risky, but they promised a reasonable chance of success, and could hardly have been less successful than the ones the US followed. There is a strong consensus that no political leader could have justified the early dispatch of troops to Bosnia for a long period of time. The perception of American interests in Yugoslavia in a post-Cold-War setting simply did not justify the long-term placement of troops in the field. There were, however, less costly but still workable strategies of coercion. A well-crafted package of credible threats, which the US was willing to enforce if its demands were not met, might well have made a big difference in the war.[5]

In the summer of 1992, when Belgrade's role was prominent and obvious, bombing of supply depots, artillery, key bridges across the Drina River, and other strategic assets in Bosnian-Serb areas, Serbia and even in Belgrade itself if necessary, would have had a big impact on the war. At that time, Serbian momentum was not yet established, expectations of Western (and especially US) reactions were unformed, and UN troops were not in place. Sudden and substantial bombing would have been a shock to the Serbs, and combined with a serious effort to supply the Bosnians with arms and train them, would have probably had a profound effect on the whole conflict. Certainly it would have slowed the Serb momentum and allowed the Muslims to buy some time. Such action would also have put the Croats on notice that they could not treat Western preferences with impunity, but most importantly it would have raised grave doubts about the possibility of a Serb victory in the war. This would have led the

Croats to think twice about assisting the Serbs against the Bosnians, since they would not want to end up on the losing side of a confrontation. This awareness could have been crucial, since the Croatian choice of sides has been a significant factor in determining the outcome of the war. Given the opportunistic, as opposed to committed, nature of Tudjman's involvement in the conflict, it is hard to exaggerate the importance of this factor.

Because of the need to convince the public of the advisability of intervention, intervention prior to the summer of 1992 was not politically feasible. But that summer was the most appropriate time for the kind of offensive described above. By the time the Clinton administration came to power in early 1993, there were UN troops in place, the Serbs and the Bosnian Serbs had established momentum toward their objectives and would have been harder to influence, and the near completion of the Vance–Owen peace plan was strengthening opposition to military action for fear that it might jeopardize the negotiations. Moreover, it would have been less humiliating for an aggressive power such as Serbia to be stopped in the early stages of action rather than later. At the earlier time, it can always be claimed that there was no intention to take further aggressive action at all.[6]

Thus, if the West was to intervene effectively after the war had begun, it was important to move to stop Serb advances early rather than to attempt to roll back their gains later. As the war went on, the Bosnian Serbs formed an increasingly more complete view of US will and intentions, and it took stronger threats to get their attention as they constantly validated their assumption that the US was not willing to intervene. Opportunities for the use of force existed during the Clinton administration, but had to take account of the danger to UN troops, and to overcome the momentum of business as usual. Decisive action might have included, for instance, David Owen's recommended strategy of first withdrawing UNPROFOR, then lifting the embargo and bombing.[7]

The use of force, if implemented later in the conflict, needed to be directed primarily at the Bosnian Serbs alone, as Milosevic began increasing cooperation with the West in an effort to curb the Bosnian Serbs and get relief from the sanctions. Europeans and Americans disagreed over the extent of that cooperation, but any policy needed to be calibrated to maximize his contribution to curbing the radicals among the Bosnian Serbs. The Dayton Agreement did just that.

There were three basic arguments given for not intervening. The first one, used consistently by the Bush administration, was that if the US was not prepared to follow through with escalation if one tactic (air strikes, for instance) did not accomplish the objectives, then it should not begin the use of force. This argument we have dealt with in Chapter 8. It is hard to see how US credibility would have been damaged any more by at least trying something, even if not successful. The humiliation of the West as the war went on certainly came to equal any loss of credibility that would have resulted from leaving the field after failed bombing missions.

A second argument was that the use of air strikes, but particularly lifting of the arms embargo, would have spread the war. This argument, touched on in Chapter 5, is seldom spelled out in much detail, possibly because it is difficult to defend. The proponents of the view that lifting the embargo would have equalled spreading the conflict assumed that bringing more arms into the region would also have expanded it to more parties, eventually involving Kosovo, Macedonia, Albania, or possibly other states bordering the former Yugoslavia. But relying on the assumptions of the interventionist paradigm – on which so many US officials like Eagleburger and Vance learned their trade – would suggest that using force against the Serbs would contain the war rather than spread it, since it would deter them from expanding their operations. And when the Croats, after quietly preparing their operations, attacked the Serbs and in a matter of days had driven them from Croatia, the war may have technically been widened, but it was also quickly over. And once serious NATO bombing began in late summer 1995, there were no signs of an expanding war.

Inherent in the European view was the belief that if the intensity of the war was controlled by limiting the amount and sophistication of the arms coming into the area, a negotiated settlement could be worked out. There is very little evidence to substantiate that view. The ability of the Bosnian Serbs to import sophisiticated weapons more easily would have contributed, but probably not substantially, to their will to keep fighting and to their military capabilities and, if accompanied by a vigorous bombing campaign any effects favorable to the Serbs from lifting the embargo would have been offset. What was accomplished instead was to handicap the Bosnian government in the conflict and deprive the Serbs of an incentive to negotiate or to moderate their demands. After three years of war and failed negotiations in Bosnia, the threats either to lift the arms embargo (from the Congress) or to withdraw the UNPROFOR troops (from the Europeans) finally led the Clinton administration to the military option it had rejected for so long.

A third and related reason given for not intervening was the reluctance to 'take sides'. This argument was partially based on the assumption that the conflict was basically a civil war where all sides were at fault and to support one side at the expense of the other would only diminish the prospects for a negotiated settlement. The narrower and more credible version of this argument stated that regardless of who at fault for initiating the war, neutrality on the part of the West was necessary in order to serve as honest brokers to end the war. This argument was more prevalent in Europe than in the US, where the Serbs from the beginning tended to be blamed for the conflict. The flaw in this argument is the assumption that negotiations could succeed when the Serbs were winning and had reason to think they could make progress in obtaining their objectives. Third party mediation succeeds best when motivation and capabilities on both sides are similar, pushing both sides to settle. This certainly was not the case in the former Yugoslavia. The tendency for the US to talk tough but do nothing encouraged the Bosnian Serbs to believe they could make further gains, and paradoxically it encouraged the Bosnians to hope help was on the way.

Results

Until recently, Bosnian policy, for both the Bush and the Clinton administrations, had been a dismal failure. In mid-1995, after four years of war in Yugoslavia, of which three years were in Bosnia, large numbers of dead and wounded and large percentages of the population existing as refugees, we were roughly back to square one, with the war still in full swing, the main actors in the conflict still fielding effective fighting forces, and the West still debating whether to conduct air strikes and lift the arms embargo. The crux of the problem was the inability of both the leadership and the public to face up to the need for hard choices. The Bush administration from the beginning did not even try to reconcile the yawning gap between its talk and its action. What was lacking was the courage to tell the American people that there were only two ways to end the war. One was to allow the military action between the parties on the ground to play itself out until one party could no longer sustain the losses and was forced to sue for surrender, or until both had had enough and reached a stalemate that forced a settlement. The second solution was Western intervention that tilted the balance of forces until a stable solution could be sold to or imposed on the warring parties.

Instead, the leadership tried to have it both ways. For most of the Clinton administration the rhetoric has been out of line with the military policy, but that policy has resulted in numerous twists and turns that confused all observers in the short run, but developed a remarkable consistency in the long run. Both the Bush and Clinton administration's policy was to placate the public by reacting to crises and showing concern, but refusing to do anything to change the situation in Bosnia, since that would involve costs and risks they were not willing to take. Thus, after years of war, in mid-1995 we were still dealing with some of the same decisions that dogged the leadership in the summer of 1992 – only this time, it was clear that the policy of the status quo could not continue.

One of the most puzzling aspects of the Bosnian involvement was the willingness of the US leadership to play a passive role in the war, to countenance aggression and atrocities on the ground, literally in the presence of UN troops, to put up with (either directly or through the Western representative on the ground, UNPROFOR) incredible humiliation as the Serbs defied the West again and again, breached diplomatic protocol, and generally made fools of both Western military and diplomatic personnel. This can be partially but not entirely explained by the post-Cold-War changes in the international system and the resistance of public opinion to engage in a costly involvement. But this behaviour is doubly puzzling considering that a considerable number of the Western leadership were veterans of the Cold War who had been involved in going 'eyeball to eyeball' with the Russians and were willing to take the risk of doing so, seemingly with little reservation. These same leaders now could countenance three years of lies, deception and atrocities from the Serbs and still expect that any day, with no significant military pressure, a negotiated solution would be found. People who had believed in promoting a balance of power, avoiding power vacuums, arming rebel forces and promoting arms sales all over the world during the Cold War were suddenly in favor of arms embargoes to keep the level of violence low by preventing the victimized from defending themselves. All the while it was argued it was necessary not to take sides in the conflict and to keep channels of communications open. Some of these leaders endorsed the censure of Serbian leaders for war crimes, while still refusing to treat the Serbian military organization significantly differently from the Bosnians on the ground.

Such behavior toward the enemy during the Cold War, when the enemy was well defined and our purpose was clear, would have resulted in loud outcries from the opposition and the public, removal of the offending officials from office at the next election, and much wailing and lamentation in the press about the failure of the national leadership to defend the nation's interests. As it happened, only the last followed from this behavior during the Bosnian conflict. Some commentators, editorialists, and opposition were outraged, but most of the public and much of the opposition appeared to be at most only mildly upset about the state of US policy in Bosnia. Clearly the environment in which foreign policy was made had changed drastically. Still, the equanimity with which the West accepted humiliation and contempt from the Serbs was disturbing and puzzling.

In spite of the obsessive focus on the Vietnam experience throughout the Bosnian War, therefore, the West ended up in a stalemated situation somewhat analogous to Vietnam. In mid-1995, as the Serbs became bolder, taking hostages and invading 'safe areas' while the West stood by appearing increasingly helpless and incompetent, the UNPROFOR soldiers began to look more and more like hostages to the war. A realization grew that the troops might need to be withdrawn, and that to accomplish that action would require the temporary insertion of US troops. But this was what US policy had aimed at preventing for over three years. Refusing either to commit the force that might have turned the situation around, or to admit Western helplessness and provide the Bosnians with the tools to do the job themselves, the West tried to have it both ways and ended up accomplishing little toward ending the conflict or resolving the issues at stake.

Prospects

Before the recent change in US policy, the war would have continued until a solution more or less satisfactory to the Serbs/Croats was achieved or, a somewhat less likely scenario, the Bosnians were strengthened sufficiently to stand up to the Serbs, or the Croats, or both, and force a stalemate. Before the Croat offensive and the NATO bombing in summer 1995, it was clear that the war would end only when the settlement reflected more closely the military situation and degree of determination of the parties involved. But the Croat and NATO offensives did bring about a closing of the gap between the military situation and the political negotiations and by the end of 1995 there was a cease fire in the former Yugoslavia. The prospects for long-term peace have already been discussed in the preceding chapter. President Clinton and the European leadership believe, undoubtedly with justification, that a strong NATO presence is necessary before an end to the war can be achieved. Assuming that peacekeeping effort is reasonably successful, the important questions are: how long will the NATO forces have to stay, and what will happen when they leave. If the peace process does not work, not only the peoples of the former Yugoslavia will suffer. NATO, making this effort after avoiding it for so long, has its credibility and morale on the line. If the will to see through the mission is not there, or if the process simply doesn't work, a resumption of the conflict will mean it will continue as long as it takes to achieve some kind of equilibrium among the military forces in the area. It is not a pleasant prospect.

LESSONS FOR POST-COLD-WAR POLICY

The one important lesson to be learned from Bosnia that will be applicable to future US foreign policy is the need to be flexible, to give up old preconceived notions that involvement inevitably proceeds from one stage of escalation to another in a linear path, and that taking one step toward intervention inevitably leads to the next one if the desired results are not attained. In the present world, the links between what happens in two distinct regions of the international system are not so obvious as during the Cold War period, and old notions about deterrence, credibility, escalation and victory may have to be adjusted to fit a world not nearly as tidy, predictable and manageable as we often imagined the Cold War world to be.

If the US follows the prescriptions of the 'all-or-nothing' school and eschews intervention unless it can set clearly defined goals that have strong public support, execute strategies to obtain the goals neatly and in order, achieve victory or stay to finish the job no matter how long it takes, then the US military will seldom see action. If the standards for intervention are too strict, the use of military force will have to be avoided and the substantial equipment and resources which the federal budget still supports will primarily provide a symbol that the US remains a superpower.

What is needed is the ability to fashion creative and suitable policies to fit the circumstances of the moment, not the ability to fight the last war over again. The post-Cold-War period promises as many failures as successes, and certainly many mid-course corrections and revaluations. The hardest part of guiding foreign policy is likely to be the job of selling complex and ambiguous foreign policies in a world where voters seem to crave simple policies that can be explained in a slogan and produce results without cost. And this precedes the sometimes equally difficult task of getting allies to buy into a policy. Both Bosnia and the Gulf Wars have shown that, in many cases, little will be done unless the US takes the lead. The recent non-performance of the French toward the disaster in Rwanda, in France's historical area of influence, is another bleak reminder of this fact.

In this sense, as we have seen earlier, foreign policy has come to resemble closely domestic policy. To the leadership falls the tough job of deciding what should be done, and devising a way to do it that can stand the test of democratic processes. The best policies will require both the admission that only limited ends are feasible and explanations of why the limits are necessary. In some cases, the politicians will be forced to choose between surrendering the goals or paying a substantial cost to attain them. It was these kinds of dilemmas and choices that were not faced squarely in Bosnia. The leadership tried to convince the public they were doing something, but in the end they did little. And in the end the US ended up with a riskier and more problematic mission than if action had been taken earlier.

If limited objectives are necessary, and hard choices must be made, then cost–benefit analysis is the means by which those decisions must be evaluated. Many pre-Vietnam conflicts seemed to be relatively easy decisions.[8] At some point, it seemed clear to many people that the national interest demanded intervention, and the decision to intervene was made. Vietnam was the first major conflict where the consensus fell apart, but the leadership continued to fight the war and was unwilling to exit, even as public division and bitterness worsened. Most wars in the post-Cold-War era are going to resemble the dilemmas of Vietnam and Bosnia, that is to say, the dilemmas of limited wars. Decisions will have to depend on a cost–benefit analysis that determines not whether the war can be 'won', but whether the probable limited benefits to the parties concerned are worth the likely costs. The use of the term cost–benefit does not suggest that those kinds of calculations have not been used in the past, but rather that a more careful calculation of those two variables, however approximately, will need to be done, and the results explained more explicitly to the public. A second decision must be: if we go in and things go wrong, how and at what point should we get out? A third question will be, not will the public overwhelmingly support this action, but can the public be persuaded to tolerate this policy until we can accomplish enough of our objectives to withdraw?

Such questions will not lend themselves well to stirring speeches in the Congress or on national TV, but they will be taken seriously by elected officials who are more interested in political survival than they are in political posturing. In this sense the post-Cold-War period may be one of increased foreign-policy sobriety, as the question of the US role in these complex and sometimes non-solvable foreign-policy questions dominates the foreign-policy agenda. The lack of consensus and the intractable nature of the problems may lower the decibel level as the leadership seeks more pragmatic solutions to problems that are not susceptible to ideological flourishes or displays of machismo. We can hope that the experience in Bosnia will contribute to a more thoughtful, and above all a more frank, environment for making foreign-policy decisions in the United States.

Notes and References

1. The United States and the Post-Cold-War International System

1. Morton Kaplan initially used the term 'tight bipolar system', but in a more specific sense than I am using the concept here. *System and Process in International Politics* (NY: Wiley, 1957).
2. Kenneth A. Oye, 'Beyond Postwar Order and New World Order: American Foreign Policy in Transition', in Oye *et al.*, eds, *Eagle in a New World: American Grand Strategy in the Post-Cold War Era* (NY: Harper Collins, 1992) p. 6.
3. John Gaddis, 'The Long Peace: Elements of Stability in the Postwar International System', *International Security*, Spring 1986, pp. 100, 142.
4. Susan L. Woodward reinforces the point that the integrating function of the bipolar system affected both interbloc and intrabloc integration. Disintegration in Europe after 1989 occurred first in the Soviet bloc, then Yugoslavia, the Soviet Union and finally, Czechoslovakia. *Balkan Tragedy: Chaos and Dissolution After the Cold War* (Washington, DC: Brookings Institution, 1995), p. 349. She states that 'The viability of the Yugoslav regime, in fact, depended on its former position and a policy of national independence and nonalignment tied to the organization of the cold war world' (p. 16).
5. 'The Clash of Civilizations,' *Foreign Affairs*, Summer 1993.
6. Michael Lind, 'In Defense of Liberal Nationalism', *Foreign Affairs*, May/June 1994.
7. John Lewis Gaddis, 'Toward the Post-Cold-War World', *Foreign Affairs*, Spring 1991, pp. 105–8.
8. The phrase is Zbigniew Brzezinski's in *Out of Control: Global Turmoil on the Eve of the 21st Century* (NY: Collier Books, 1993) part I. James Goodby characterizes the new conflicts as driven by 'ethnic and nationalistic claims driven underground for decades by Communist repression ...', 'Commonwealth and Concert: Organizing Principles of Post-Containment Order in Europe', *The Washington Quarterly*, Summer 1991, p. 87.
9. Brzezinski, *Out of Control*, Part IV, and Max Singer and Aaron Wildavsky, *The Real World Order: Zones of Peace, Zones of Turmoil* (Chatham, NJ: Chatham House, 1993) p. 190.
10. Singer and Wildavsky, *The Real World Order*, p. 195.
11. Paul Kennedy, *The Rise and Fall of the Great Powers: Economic Change and Military Conflict from 1500 to 2000* (NY: Random House, 1987) especially pp. 514–40.

12.   Joseph S. Nye, *Bound to Lead: The Changing Nature of American Power* (NY: Basic Books, 1990). See especially the preface to the paperback edition (1991) p. xi.

13.   Atilio A. Boron, 'Toward a Post-Hegemonic Age? The End of Pax Americana', *Security Dialogue*, June 1994.

14.   As Nye puts it, 'America is rich but acts poor. In real terms, GNP is more than twice what it was in 1960, but Americans spend much less of their GNP on international leadership'. *Bound to Lead*, p. 159.

15.   Michael Mandelbaum, 'The Reluctance to Intervene', *Foreign Policy*, Summer 1994, pp. 14–16.

16.   Earl C. Ravenal has long argued the case for limited US defense and foreign policy commitments, and did so even as the Cold War continued. See a relatively recent article, 'The Case for Adjustment', *Foreign Policy*, Winter 1990–1. On the other side of the debate, Edward N. Luttwak deplores the timidity of US policy and strongly argues for a more assertive stance. 'Where are the Great Powers? At Home with the Kids', *Foreign Affairs*, July/August 1994.

17.   John E. Rielly, ed., *American Public Opinion and US Foreign Policy* (Chicago: Chicago Council on Foreign Relations, 1995) p. 6; and Arthur Schlesinger, Jr, 'Back to the Womb? Isolationism's Renewed Threat', *Foreign Affairs*, July/August 1995, p. 7.

18.   Alvin Z. Rubenstein, 'The New Moralists on a Road to Hell', *Orbis*, Spring 1996.

19.   Joseph S. Nye, Jr, 'What New World Order?', *Foreign Affairs*, Spring 1992, especially pp. 83–4.

20.   *Ibid.*, p. 84.

21.   Joshua Muravchik, *The Imperative of American Leadership: A Challenge to Neo-Isolationism* (Washington, DC: AEI Press, 1996) p. 3.

22.   Reprinted in Richard N. Haass, *Intervention: The Use of American Force in the Post-Cold War World* (Washington, DC: The Carnegie Endowment for International Peace, 1994) Appendix H.

23.   David Rieff, *Slaughterhouse: Bosnia and the Failure of the West* (NY: Simon & Schuster, 1995). That the problem with the United Nations Protection Force (UNPROFOR) lay primarily with the national governments is suggested by the fact that critics have begun suggesting that the NATO implementation force, as did UNPROFOR, spends much of its time protecting itself. *Washington Post*, June 25, 1996, A1.

24.   Richard N. Haass, 'Paradigm Lost', *Foreign Affairs*, January/February 1995, pp. 50–2.

2.   What Should Policy Be? Guidelines for Intervention

1.   Richard N. Haass, *Intervention: The Use of American Force in the Post-Cold-War World* (Washington, DC: The Carnegie Endowment for International Peace, 1994) pp. 6–7.

2.   *Ibid.*, Appendix C.

3.   *Ibid.*, p. 192. The term 'limited war' gained currency after the Korean War. Louis J. Halle, *The Elements of International Strategy: A Primer for*

the Nuclear Age (Lanham, MD: University Press of America, 1984) pp. 68–9.

4. Both former Secretary of Defense Les Aspin and former Secretary of State George Shultz have stressed the need for flexibility on this complex question. See Halle *ibid.*, p. 184, for Aspin's remarks, and for Schultz, Fareed Zakaria, 'A Framework for Interventionism in the Post-Cold War Era', in Arnold Kanter and Linton F. Brooks, eds, *US Intervention Policy for the Post-Cold War World: New Challenges and New Responses* (NY: W.W. Norton, 1994) pp. 185–6.

5. William Safire column, *New York Times*, January 7, 1993, A23.

6. *New York Times*, April 28, 1993, A1.

7. Colin Powell, *My American Journey* (NY: Ballantine, 1995, 1996), pp. 643–5; *New York Times*, October 8, 1992, A35; and 'US Forces: Challenges Ahead', *Foreign Affairs*, Winter 1992/1993.

8. Secretary of Defense William J. Perry said that, 'In this post-Cold War era, we are even less likely to rely on all-out military force to give us overwhelming victory. We're more likely to use selective force to achieve limited objectives'. News Release, Office of the Assistant Secretary of Defense (Public Affairs), 15 June 1994.

9. Richard N. Haass, 'Paradigm Lost', *Foreign Affairs*, January/February 1995, p. 56.

10. Quoted in Charles F. Hermann, *Crisis in Foreign Policy: A Simulation Analysis* (NY: Bobbs-Merrill, 1969) p. 176.

3. The Development of the War in Yugoslavia

1. Dusko Doder, 'Yugoslavia: New War, Old Hatreds', *Foreign Policy*, Summer 1993, p. 5.

2. Alex N. Dragnich counts five empires that have wielded power in the Balkans, omitting only the Germans, whose influence grew during the twentieth century. *Serbs and Croats: The Struggle in Yugoslavia* (NY: Harcourt, Brace, Jovanovich, 1992) pp. xiii–xiv.

3. The quote is by Robert D. Kaplan. Rebecca West wrote 'I hate the corpses of empire; they stink like nothing else'. Both quotes are in Kaplan, *Balkan Ghosts: A Journey Through History* (NY: Vintage, 1993) pp. xiv, 57.

4. Robert J. Donia and John V.A. Fine, Jr., *Bosnia and Herzegovina: A Tradition Betrayed* (NY: Columbia University Press, 1994) p. 72.

5. Branka Magas, *The Destruction of Yugoslavia: Tracking the Break-up, 1980–92* (NY: Verso, 1993) p. 191.

6. Susan L. Woodward stresses the relationship between reform and disintegration in *Balkan Tragedy: Chaos and Dissolution After the Cold War* (Washington, DC: Brookings Institution, 1995), chapters 3 and 4. While most observers have stressed the relationship between Serbia and Croatia as essential to the integrity of Yugoslavia, she sees the Serbian–Slovenian nexus as key. See also Magas, *The Destruction of Yugoslavia*, pp. xiii, 220.

7. Mihailo Crnobrnja, *The Yugoslav Drama* (Montreal: McGill-Queens University Press, 1994) pp. 148–51.

8. Woodward, *Balkan Tragedy*, pp. 89, 91, 110.

9. Albert Wohlstetter, *Wall Street Journal*, July 1, 1993, editorial page. The autonomy of Kosovo and Vojvodina within Serbia was also an irritating grievance for the Serbs, and one to which they had tried unsuccessfully to negotiate a solution. See Crnobrnja, *The Yugoslav Drama*, pp. 94–5.

10. Woodward, *Balkan Tragedy*, p. 96.

11. Magas, *The Destruction of Yugoslavia*, p. 191.

12. Dusko Doder, 'Yugoslavia: New War, Old Hatreds', *Foreign Policy*, Summer 1993, pp. 12–3. A move to further differentiate between the Serb and Croat languages from what is really a single language was one of the ironies, or absurdities, springing from the Croatian nationalist movement. See also Bogdan Denitch, *Ethnic Nationalism: The Tragic Death of Yugoslavia* (Minneapolis: University of Minnesota Press, 1994) p. 41.

13. Laura Silber and Allan Little, *Yugoslavia: Death of a Nation* (NY: TV Books, 1995, 1996) pp. 82–4.

14. Woodward, *Balkan Tragedy*, pp. 172 and 216.

15. Silber and Little, *Yugoslavia*, p. 209.

16. Cohen quotes Izetbegovic saying, 'Bosnia has lasted 1,000 years. I do not see any reason to break it up now. Bosnia is impossible to divide, because it is such a mixture of nationalities, just like the apartment bloc where I live.' Lenard J. Cohen, *Broken Bonds: The Disintegration of Yugoslavia*, first edition, (Boulder: Westview, 1993), p. 145. Speaking of the process by which an ethnic-based nation becomes independent, Susan L. Woodward points out that those governments which seize the initiative and succeed are 'far better prepared politically and economically than those for whom independence is a second-best choice or on whom independence is forced'. Unfortunately, given the way events unfolded in Yugoslavia, Bosnia falls more in the second category. *Balkan Tragedy*, p. 350. The Rieff quote is from David Rieff, *Slaughterhouse: Bosnia and the Failure of the West* (NY: Simon & Schuster, 1995) p. 131.

17. Lenard J. Cohen, *Broken Bonds: Yugoslavia's Disintegration and Balkan Politics in Transition*, second edition, (Boulder: Westview, 1995), p. 332.

18. Woodward, *Balkan Tragedy*, pp. 118–28; Silber and Little, *Yugoslavia*, p. 83.

19. Robert J. Donia and John V.A. Fine, Jr., *Bosnia and Hercegovina: A Tradition Betrayed* (NY: Columbia University Press, 1994) pp. 210–12, 237, 265, 279.

20. Cohen, *Broken Bonds*, pp. 128–35.

21. Donia and Fine, Jr., *Bosnia and Hercegovina*, 211–12. See also the revealing quotes on the various Yugoslav leaders in Cohen, *Broken Bonds*, first edition, pp. 199–200; and Crnobrnja, *The Yugoslav Drama*, p. 146. This assessment of the various leaders was also concurred with by US Secretary of State, James A. Baker, III. See his *The Politics of Diplomacy: Revolution, War and Peace, 1989–1992* (New York: G.P. Putnam's Sons, 1995), pp. 480–1.

22. Jeanne Kirkpatrick has argued this. Silber and Little argue that after the March meeting between Milosevic and Tudjman at Karadjordjevo where both leaders agreed that Yugoslavia was finished and concentrated on how to divide it up, Milosevic was already resigned to let Slovenia go. *Yugoslavia*, p. 144.

23. On US support for UNSC Resolution 713, see *US Department of State Dispatch* (hereafter *DSD*), September 30, 1991, p. 723.

24. Doder, 'New War, Old Hatreds', pp. 18–19; and Magas, *The Destruction of Yugoslavia*, p. 347.

25. Crnobrnja, *The Yugoslav Drama*, pp. 178–81; Silber and Little, *Yugoslavia*, pp. 218, 231.

26. Robert A. Levine, 'If It's Worth Doing At All, is it Worth Doing Wrong? Yugoslavia and the Next Time', RAND Issue Paper, Santa Monica, August 1993, p. 3.

27. In a parallel with the Cold War debates on Soviet goals and strategies, Yugoslav specialists cannot agree on whether Milosevic was pursuing a Greater Serbia.

28. Warren Zimmermann, 'Nationalism in Bosnia', *The Woodrow Wilson Center Report*, November 1994, p. 6.

29. Woodward, *Balkan Tragedy*. '[The focus on aggression] ignores the conditions that make such leaders [Slobodan Milosevic] possible and popular and therefore also ignores the policies necessary to end their rule'. See especially the introduction and pp. 13–17.

30. Silber and Little, *Yugoslavia*, p. 99.

31. V.P. Gagnon, Jr., 'Ethnic Nationalism and International conflict: The Case of Serbia', *International Security*, Winter 1994, p. 132.

32. *Ibid.*, pp. 140, 150, 133, 132, 158.

33. Lenard J. Cohen, *Broken Bonds: Yugoslavia's Disintegration and Balkan Politics in Transition*, second edition (Boulder: Westview, 1995) pp. 247, 329–33, 366–7 (n6).

34. Crnobrnja, *The Yugoslav Drama*, p. 154, 164. Alex N. Dragnich, a Yugoslav specialist, has argued that the government of Yugoslavia, not just Serbia, opposed the secession of the republics. But he conveniently forgets that the Serbs were instrumental in blocking numerous actions that might have contributed to a resolution of the crisis, including the economic and democratic reforms of Prime Minister Ante Markovic. *Washington Post*, September 25, 1994, C6.

35. The question raised by A.M. Rosenthal, *NYT*, December 23, 1994, A 35; and Sylvia Poggioli, 'Weekend Edition', National Public Radio, December 10, 1994. Raising the ante on those who support a democratic and multi-ethnic Bosnia, Flora Lewis suggests it may not be too late to apply the same formula to Yugoslavia as a whole and to reconstitute it as a state. 'Reassembling Yugoslavia,' *Foreign Policy*, Spring 1995.

36. A consistent and early critic of the propensity of American analysts to make Serbia the main culprit in Bosnian has been Alex N. Dragnich. The main flaw in his argument is that he fails to distinguish between the relatively democratic and flexible nature of the other republics and the authoritarian and expansionist nature of Serbian politics and

nationalism. All sides have had grievances, but the nature of the Serbian response was singular. See his 'The West's Mismanagement of the Yugoslav Crisis', *World Affairs*, Fall 1993.

37. Robert J. Donia and John V.A. Fine, Jr., *Bosnia and Hercegovina: A Tradition Betrayed* (NY: Columbia University Press, 1994 pp. 266–8); Cohen, *Broken Bonds*, second edition, pp. 279–81; *Washington Post*, February 6, 1995, A13. But as Stephen Schwartz points out, it is the Bosnians who were the true heirs to the multi-cultural legacy of Yugoslavia. 'In Defense of the Bosnian Republic,' *World Affairs*, Fall 1993. In contrast to the serious and perhaps naive Bosnian efforts at maintaining tolerance in an environment of violence, Milosevic's claim to carry the mantle of Yugoslavia certainly cannot include the multiethnic tradition.

4.   The Nature of the War

1. *New York Times*, August 5, 1994, A1.
2. *New York Times*, November 28, 1994, A1.
3. The International Institute for Strategic Studies, *Strategic Survey: 1993–1994* (London: Brassey's, 1994) p. 100.
4. *Ibid.*
5. *New York Times*, April 5, 1993, A3.
6. The International Institute for Strategic Studies, *Strategic Survey: 1994–95* (London: Oxford University Press, 1995) p. 101.
7. *New York Times*, October 11, 1993, A1.
8. The International Institute for Strategic Studies, *Strategic Survey: 1995–1996* (London: Oxford University Press, 1996) p. 131.
9. *Ibid.*, pp. 131–2.
10. David Rieff, *Slaughterhouse: Bosnia and the Failure of the West* (NY: Simon & Schuster, 1995) pp. 130–3.
11. *New York Times*, August 1, 1993, L5.
12. Susan L. Woodward, *Balkan Tragedy: Chaos and Dissolution After the Cold War* (Washington, DC: Brookings Institutional, 1995) p. 270.
13. *New York Times*, January 23, 1994, L1; *Strategic Survey: 1994–95*, p. 96–7.
14. *Strategic Survey: 1995–1996*, p. 129.
15. *Strategic Survey: 1994–95*, p. 97.
16. This discussion of the use of the enemy in group dynamics is borrowed from David J. Finlay, Ole R. Holsti, and Richard R. Fagen, *Enemies in Politics* (Chicago: Rand McNally, 1967), especially chapter 1.
17. See for instance Charles G. Boyd, 'Peace Principles', *Foreign Affairs*, November/December 1995, p. 153. 'Centuries of perceived victimization and the resulting paranoia have produced a very real Serb demand for self-determination that any successful peace agreement must accommodate.'
18. The Serbian goals, values, rationalizations and behavior documented by Norman Cigar are reminiscent of those documented by earlier writers on terrorist and totalitarian movements. See Cigar's *Genocide in Bosnia: The Policy of 'Ethnic Cleansing'* (College Station, TX: Texas A&M

Press, 1995) Chapters 3–8. On the links between ethnic discrimination, aggression and terror, see Hannah Arendt, *The Origins of Totalitarianism* (NY: Meridian Books, 1958).

Serb responsibility for the worst of the mass killing is not limited to the early part of the war. After the fall of Srebrenica, a large number of Muslim men who escaped were found and massacred. One investigating reporter put the number at 2000–3000, the largest massacre of the war and the worst in Europe since WW II. David Rohde, Christian Science Monitor Radio, Public Radio International, 16 November 1995. See also *Washington Post*, 3 November 1995, A23; 26 October 1995, A1. Croat advances in the summer of 1995 resulted in widespread refugee movements (ethnic cleansing) and plenty of brutality. Nothing on the scale of Serb activities, however, was reported. In late 1994, officials of the UN War Crimes Tribunal said that the Bosnian government was cooperating fully with them, even when the subjects of their investigations were Bosnian military personnel. Other human rights organizations reported similar cooperation. Most human rights monitors observed, however, that Bosnian Serb authorities impeded the War Crimes Tribunal by blocking its passage to Serb-held areas. State Department, *Country Reports on Human Rights Practices for 1994*, Report Submitted to the Committee on Foreign Relations, US Senate, and the Committee on International Relations, US House of Representatives, February 1995, p. 762. Haris Hurem, a Sarajevo Muslim at one time a prisoner of the Serbs, recounted his views on the responsibility for the violence this way: 'Look, every side has its extremists. With the Serbs, it might be 40 per cent. With the Croats, maybe 15. With the Muslims, maybe 5. At least, that's how it looks to me. But those few extremists are enough to get things started, and before it's over everybody's involved.' William Finnegan, 'Salt City: Letter from Tuzla', *The New Yorker*, 12 February 1996, p. 52.

Of the 285 entries of atrocities reported to the UN by the State Department, 18 were perpetrated by Muslims. James K. Bishop, a top State Department human rights official, privately challenged Secretary of State Christopher's public assertion that all sides share responsibility, stating that the Serbs were responsible for the overwhelming majority of the incidents. *New York Times*, 25 June 1993, A3. This ratio is typical of reports by other sources. For a report on the use of ethnic cleansing by the Croats and Muslims, see the *New York Times*, 21 April 1993, A1; and *Bosnia-Hercegovina: Abuses by Bosnian Croat and Muslim Forces in Central and Southwestern Bosnia-Hercegovina* (NY: Human Rights Watch, September 1993). On the barbarous and treacherous attitudes of Slobodan Milosevic and Radovan Karadzic, see Warren Zimmermann, 'The Last Ambassador: A Memoir of the Collapse of Yugoslavia', *Foreign Affairs*, March/April 1995, especially pp. 4–5, 17–18.

19.   Andrew Bell-Fialkoff defines ethnic cleansing as 'the expulsion of an "undesirable" population from a given territory due to religious or ethnic discrimination, political, strategic or ideological considerations, or a combination of these'. 'A Brief History of Ethnic Cleansing', *Foreign Affairs*, Summer 1993, p. 110. Enlightening discussions of the authoritarian political culture in Belgrade and Zagreb and of extremist

attitudes and murderous behavior on the individual level can be found in Bogdan Denitch, *Ethnic Nationalism: The Tragic Death of Yugoslavia* (Minneapolis: University of Minnesota Press, 1994) especially pp. 72–5; T.D. Allman, 'Serbia's Blood War', in Rabia Ali and Lawrence Lifschultz, eds, *Why Bosnia?* (Stony Creek, CT: Pamphleteer's Press, 1993) pp. 62–5; and Misha Glenny, *The Fall of Yugoslavia: The Third Balkan War* (NY: Penguin, 1992) especially pp. 6–19.

20. David Rieff, *Slaughterhouse: Bosnia and the Failure of the West* (NY: Simon & Schuster, 1995) p. 187. The quoted phrase originally described Yugoslav military doctrine under Tito.

21. This account of the destruction of Vukovar relies heavily on Lenard J. Cohen, *Broken Bonds: The Disintegration of Yugoslavia* (Boulder: Westview Press, 1993), pp. 225–6. Later in the war, the State Department reported that 'Throughout 1994, the BSA [Bosnian Serb Army] continued to pound Bosnian populations [sic] centers with mortars and automatic weapons fire, causing the death of hundreds of civilians from January through October. The population centers most affected were Sarajevo, Gorazde, Mostar, Olovo, Tuzla, Visoko, Vares, and Breza. During the May offensive against Gorazde, Serbian shelling killed between 500 and 600 Bosnian civilians.' *Country Report on Human Rights Practices for 1994*, p. 760. On Croat use of indiscriminate shelling in Knin in their 1995 offensives, see *New York Times*, 6 August 1995, I1.

22. *New York Times*, 18 July 1992, A1.

23. Andrew Bell-Fialkoff, 'A Brief History of Ethnic Cleansing', pp. 117–8.

24. One Serbian rapist told his victim that 'We'll make you have Serbian babies who will be Christians'. *DSD*, 19 April 1993, p. 263. See also *New York Times*, 10 January 1993, 7 December 1994, A12; and Roy Gutman, *A Witness to Genocide* (NY: Macmillan, 1993).

25. *War Crimes in the Former Yugoslavia: Department Statement, US Report to the UN Security Council, DSD*, 28 September 1992, pp. 732–5. This and a subsequent seven reports were submitted to the UN in fulfillment of UNSC Resolution 771 calling on organizations to submit information from the former Yugoslavia. These were defined as incidents relating to 'mass forcible expulsion and deportation of civilians, imprisonment and abuse of civilians in detention centres, deliberate attacks on non-combatants, hospitals and ambulances, impeding the delivery of food and medical supplies to the civilian population, and wanton devastation and destruction of property'. For corroborating evidence see Roy Gutman, *A Witness to Genocide* (NY: Macmillan, 1993). See also *War Crimes in Bosnia–Hercegovina, Volumes I and II* (NY: Human Rights Watch, 1992, 1993).

26. Roy Gutman's book, *A Witness to Genocide*, may be the best account of the camps, containing many first-hand recitations of the conditions and practices in the camps. See also Bell-Fialkoff, 'A Brief History of Ethnic Cleansing', p. 119.

27. *New York Times*, 26 January 1994, A9.

28. Gutman, *A Witness to Genocide*, pp. 20–3.

29. On the assault on Muslim culture, see *ibid.*, especially pp. 77–83.

30. *Washington Post*, 23 August 1994, A13.

Part III   Introduction

1.   Stanley Hoffmann, 'In Defense of Mother Teresa: Morality in Foreign Policy', *Foreign Affairs*, March/April 1996, especially pp. 172–4. This article is Hoffmann's answer to Michael Mandelbaum's criticism of Clinton's foreign policy, 'Foreign Policy as Social Work', *Foreign Affairs*, January/February 1996.

2.   The Commission on America's National Interests, made up of distinguished foreign affairs specialists, concluded that 'values and interests are less dichotomous poles apart, and more alternative expression of valuation.' *America's National Interests*, The Commission on America's National Interest, July 1996.

3.   For examples see Robert W. McElroy, *Morality and American Foreign Policy* (Princeton: Princeton University Press, 1992). McElroy argues that there are three factors that motivate leaders to attend to humanitarian concerns: an individual leader's conscience toward norms of international morality, domestic political pressures to assuage public concern about humanitarian issues, and international pressures for a nation to conform to the understood international standards of behavior. See especially pp. 39–53. During the Bush administration, only the second of these three factors was important in encouraging intervention in Bosnia; Clinton may have been persuaded by the first two, and even helped to mobilize American opinion in favor of intervention, but was stopped by the lack of international cooperation.

5.   Security Interests and Other Interests

1.   Among them was Lt. Gen. William E. Odom. See his Statement in Hearing before the Subcommittee on European Affairs, Committee on Foreign Relations, United States Senate, 18 February 1993 (Washington, DC: Government Printing Office, 1993) pp. 69–77.

2.   These themes are developed in Bernard Gordon, *Toward Disengagement in Asia: A Strategy for American Foreign Policy* (Englewood Cliffs, NJ: Prentice-Hall, 1969).

3.   The International Institute for Strategic Studies, *Strategic Survey, 1993–1994* (London: Brassey's, 1994) p. 102.

4.   Bismarck is said to have remarked that the Balkans were not worth the healthy bones of a single Pomeranian grenadier. But at the same time, apropos the next section of this chapter on the danger of a spreading war, he also stated prior to WW I that, 'if there is ever another war in Europe, it will come out of some damned silly thing in the Balkans'. *The Oxford Dictionary of Quotations*, third edition (NY: Oxford University Press, 1979) p. 84.

5.   Susan L. Woodward was one of the most vocal proponents of the view that 'maintaining the alliance was [the US's] vital national interest'. She deplored the fact that the US focused on humanitarian justifications for its actions in Bosnia instead of explaining the security interests which should have underlain a more vigorous involvement in

the former Yugoslavia. *Balkan Tragedy: Chaos and Dissolution After the Cold War* (Washington, DC: Brookings Institution, 1995) pp. 11, 324–5, 398. See also Anthony Lewis, *New York Times*, 2 June 1995, A29. Regarding the post-Dayton-Agreement use of NATO, Jim Hoagland argues that enforcement of the agreement could be a means of transforming NATO into one where the Europeans play a more important role. *Washington Post*, 7 December 1995, A23.

6.   This is a concern raised by commentators with quite different perspectives on the international scene. See Zbigniew Brzezinski, 'NATO: Expand or Die?', *New York Times*, 28 December 1994, A15; Richard Perle, *Wall Street Journal*, 8 December 1994, A19; and William E. Odom, 'Invade, Don't Bomb', *Wall Street Journal*, 18 February 1994, A12.

7.   See Odom, 'Invade, Don't Bomb', and Richard M. Nixon, *Beyond Peace* (NY: Random House, 1994) pp. 153–5. In the later stages of the conflict, some evidence of the effect of Western policy on the Muslim world became available: Saudi Arabia, Iran and Turkey have given tens of millions of dollars in arms and support to Muslim fighters, according to Western diplomats. Furthermore, 'In a sense, the war in Bosnia has become the Muslim world's Spanish Civil War. Videocassettes with gruesome footage of the fighting are hawked on street corners in Cairo, Riyadh, Istanbul and Tehran. The plight of the Bosnian Muslims is decried in mosques across the Muslim world as another move by the Christian West to crush a resurgent Islam.' *New York Times*, 28 July 1995, A4.

8.   This judgement coincides with that of William Perry, Secretary of Defense under the Clinton administration, who stated on 3 November 1994 that there are 'three basic categories in which our military forces are being used and will be used. The first is those where vital national interests are at stake; the second is where national interests are at stake but are not vital; and the third is where we have humanitarian interests.' Bosnia (along with Haiti) 'falls in the second category ... a national interest but not a vital interest'. Quoted in Woodward, *Balkan Tragedy*, p. 519, n. 24. Secretary of State Christopher, on the other hand, has characterized the US interest in Bosnia as 'vital'. Alvin Z. Rublustein, 'The New Moralists on a Road to Hell', *Orbis*, Spring 1996, p. 293; and 'All Things Considered', Public Radio International, November 11, 1995.

9   For the arguments by Anthony Lake, see Elizabeth Drew, *On the Edge: The Clinton Presidency* (NY: Simon & Schuster, 1994) p. 144; for Peter Tarnoff, Hearings Before the Committee on Armed Services, United States Senate, 104th Congress, January 12, 1995, p. 5; for Margaret Thatcher, *New York Times*, May 4, 1994, A23; and for Charles Maynes, *New York Times*, July 27, 1994, A21.

10. This argument is based on Jack Donnelly, *International Human Rights* (Boulder: Westview, 1993), especially pp. 1–38. See also the range of arguments by scholars citing the increased shift toward concern with international human rights in Seyom Brown, *International Relations in a Changing Global System: Toward a Theory of World Polity* (Boulder: Westview, 1992) Chapter 6, especially pp. 113–15. Stanley Hoffmann

contends that we are increasingly experiencing 'the collision between man as a citizen of his national community and what could be called an incipient cosmopolitanism, or man as a world citizen'. See also Arthur M. Schlesinger, Jr., *The Cycles of American History* (Boston: Houghton-Mifflin, 1986) pp. 109–11. The framework for bringing peace to Bosnia recently signed in Dayton, Ohio, cites no less than 15 international conventions on human rights to be applied in Bosnia-Herzegovina. See 'Constitution of Bosnia and Herzegovina,' Annex I in *Proximity Peace Talks*, Wright-Patterson Air Force Base, Dayton, Ohio, 1–21 November 1995.

A War Crimes Tribunal has been set up in The Hague to prosecute individuals guilty of war crimes in the conflict in the former Yugoslavia. This tribunal is based on UN Security Council Resolution 827 which determined that the actions of such a tribunal would contribute to the restoration of peace and security. The organization Human Rights Watch had concluded by August 1992 that sufficient evidence existed against nine individuals to try them for war crimes, including Karadzic, Mladic and Milosevic. By December 1995, 56 individuals had been indicted by the Tribunal, but Milosevic was not among them.

Obvious contradictions exist between trying to negotiate a settlement to the war, while attempting to try the leaders who are doing the negotiating for war crimes. According a leader such as Milosevic legitimacy as a negotiator and head of state is obviously at cross purposes with trying, convicting and punishing him as a war criminal. As it has worked out so far, the tribunal has probably performed a useful service by starting a process that will attribute blame for the atrocities that have occurred in the former Yugoslavia to specific individuals and thus provide a sense of justice having been done. The legal proceeding and the charges against Karadzic and Mladic have also been useful in providing justification for removing them from the negotiations, thus ensuring progress on a settlement, and prohibiting Karadzic from having a formal role in the post election power arrangements. But he has continued to be influential since the countries that make up IFOR have refrained from arresting him. On the other hand, Milosevic's current role may give him a degree of immunity to the proceedings, or alternatively, if he were indicted, it would complicate the post-election arrangements. See also Christopher Greenwood, 'The International Tribunal for Former Yugoslavia', *International Affairs*, October 1993; Theodor Meron, 'The Case for War Crimes Trials in Yugoslavia', *Foreign Affairs*, Summer 1993; *Warcrimes in Bosnia-Hercegovina*, Volume I, Human Rights Watch, August 1992, pp. 5–6; *Washington Post*, 18 December 1995, A1.

11.   James E. Goodby, 'Peacekeeping in the New Europe', *The Washington Quarterly*, Spring 1992, p. 154; and David C. Hendrickson, 'The Recovery of Internationalism,' *Foreign Affairs*, September/October 1994, p. 32.

12.   The uses of the Uniting for Peace Resolution are discussed in A. LeRoy Bennett, *International Organizations: Principles and Issues*, fourth edition (Englewood Cliffs, NJ: Prentice Hall, 1988), pp. 142–3.

13. Philip Gourevitch, 'Letter from Rwanda: After the Genocide', *The New Yorker*, 18 December 1995, p. 78; *New York Times*, 17 May, A8 and 26 May 1994, A1.
14. *The World Bank Atlas, 1994* (Washington, DC: World Bank, 1993).
15. The operation in Panama is summarized in Richard N. Haass, *Intervention: The Use of American Military Force in the Post-Cold War World* (Washington, DC: Carnegie Endowment, 1994) pp. 30–1.
16. Philip Gourevitch, 'Letter from Rwanda: After the Genocide', pp. 91–2. Roger Winter, Director of the US Committee for Refugees, writes that if a 'fraction of the US troops who eventually joined the assistance effort had been deployed in a protection effort before the genocide began, or if the UN forces that were already there were authorized quickly to defend civilians instead of fleeing at the behest of the Security Council (led by the United States), much of the mass murder could have been prevented ... lacking was the will to take preventive action.' *Washington Post*, 23 June 1995, A22.

6. The Foreign Policy Mood in the United States

1. Gabriel A. Almond, *The American People and Foreign Policy* (NY: Praeger, 1950) Chapter 4, especially pp. 69, 71–2, 79.
2. Ole R. Holsti, 'Public Opinion and Foreign Policy: Challenge to the Almond–Lippmann Consensus', *International Studies Quarterly*, December 1992, pp. 439–41.
3. The term 'non-attitudes' was used by Phillip Converse to describe the lack of structure, consistency and coherence in foreign-policy opinion. Cited in *ibid.*, p. 443.
4. I have relied extensively on Holsti's excellent summary of the changes in the way public opinion's impact on foreign policy is evaluated. *Ibid.*
5. John Mueller, *War, Presidents, and Public Opinion* (NY: Wiley, 1973).
6. Holsti, 'Public Opinion and Foreign Policy', pp. 450–5.
7. Bert A. Rockman, 'Presidents, Opinion, and Institutional Leadership', in David A. Deese, ed., *The New Politics of American Foreign Policy* (NY: St Martin's Press, 1994) p. 73.
8. Francis Fukuyama, *The End of History and the Last Man* (NY: Avon, 1992) p. 283.
9. John E. Rielly, ed., *American Public Opinion and US Foreign Policy 1995* (Chicago: Chicago Council on Foreign Relations, 1995) p. 11; Jeremy D. Rosner, 'The Know-Nothings Know Something,' *Foreign Policy*, Winter 1995–6, p. 124.
10. 'Introduction: From Foreign Policy to "Politics as Usual"', in Deese, *The New Politics of American Foreign Policy*, p. xv.
11. *Ibid.*, p. xii. Evidence that the Gulf War was also that kind of war comes from E.J. Baumeister, Jr., managing editor of the *Trenton Times*: 'the American action in the Gulf did not generate long-lasting foreign-policy euphoria. Instead, nagging questions remain. "The legacy of the Gulf War is that my neighbors are trying to forget," says Randi Orlando, a barber who lives in the Trenton suburb of Hamilton

Township and who opposed the war. "It rarely comes up. But when it does, they wonder, since Saddam Hussein is still alive, whether we really won it"'. 'Looking Homeward: Regional Views of Foreign Policy', *Foreign Policy*, Fall 1992, p. 39.

12.   Bruce W. Jentleson, 'The Pretty Prudent Public: Post Post-Vietnam American Opinion on the Use of Military Force', *International Studies Quarterly*, March 1992, pp. 49–50.

13.   'Looking Homeward', pp. 46, 53. On regional variation in foreign-policy attitudes see also Peter Trubowitz, 'Sectionalism and American Foreign Policy: The Political Geography of Consensus and Conflict', *International Studies Quarterly*, June 1992.

14.   William Schneider, 'The Old Politics and the New World Order', in Kenneth Oye *et al.*, eds, *Eagle in a New World Order: American Grand Strategy in the Post-Cold War Era* (NY: Harper Collins, 1992) pp. 42–3, 63.

15.   See Godfrey Hodgson, 'The Establishment', *Foreign Policy*, Spring 1973.

16.   Robert W. Tucker and David C. Hendrickson, 'America and Bosnia', *The National Interest*, Fall 1993, p. 14. An early sample of Congressional debate on the war can be found in *Congressional Record*, 5 August 1992, pp. S11509–10, S11575–81; 6 August, pp. S11638–43; 7 August, pp. S11861, S11871–2; 10 August, pp. S11991–S12060. Ideology and party were no more useful for predicting positions on the war as it wore on. A mid-1995 article was titled, 'GOP Hopefuls Are All Over the Map on Bosnia', *Washington Post*, June 7, 1995, A29.

17.   Andrew Kohut and Robert C. Toth, 'Arms and the People', *Foreign Affairs*, November/December 1994, p. 54.

18.   George Gallup, Jr., *The Gallup Poll: Public Opinion 1992* (Wilmington, DE: Scholarly Resources, 1993) p. 139; George Gallup, *The Gallup Poll: Public Opinion 1993* (Wilmington, DE: Scholarly Resources, 1994) p. 42.

19.   George Gallup, Jr., *The Gallup Poll: Public Opinion 1993*, pp. 42, 41.

20.   Kohut and Toth, 'Arms and the People,' pp. 54–5.

21.   George Gallup, Jr., *The Gallup Poll: Public Opinion 1993*, p. 95.

22.   George Gallup, Jr., *The Gallup Poll: Public Opinion 1993*, pp. 42, 96; Kohut and Toth, 'Arms and the People,' p. 55.

23.   George Gallup, Jr., *The Gallup Poll: Public Opinion 1993*, pp. 43, 41, 96–7.

24.   *Ibid.*, pp. 41–4, 95–7.

25.   *The Gallup Poll Monthly*, February 1994, p. 13. On Somalia, see *New York Times*, October 6, 1993, A16; October 8, A34; and October 9, L1.

26.   Kohut and Toth, 'Arms and the People', p. 54.

27.   *Ibid.*

28.   George Gallup, Jr., *The Gallup Poll: Public Opinion 1993*, p. 42; *The Gallup Poll Monthly*, May 1993, pp. 11–13. The ambiguous and cautious attitude of the public was still evident in June 1995 when 34 per cent believed the US was too involved, 17 per cent not involved enough, and 43 per cent about right. *The Gallup Poll: Public Opinion 1995* (Wilmington, DE: Scholarly Resources, 1996) p. 91.

29.   A *Washington Post* poll, taken when the talks started, asked if citizens support sending '20 000 US troops to Bosnia as part of an international

peacekeeping force' and found 38 per cent in favor, and 56 per cent opposed. By almost identical numbers, 35 per cent believed that America's vital interests were at stake, while 56 per cent disagreed. *Washington Post*, 28 November 1995, A1. On peacekeeping versus peacemaking, see Kohut and Toth, 'Arms and the People', p. 47.

30. Stanley Greenberg, President Clinton's pollster, told the President that public opinion could be molded to fit the President's policy. Elizabeth Drew, *On the Edge: The Clinton Presidency* (NY: Simon & Schuster, 1994) p. 150.

7. American Perceptions: Civil War, Ethnic Hatred and Moral Responsibility

1. As a case in point, a prominent foreign policy scholar, William Hyland, referred to the war as a 'fight among gangsters'. See Rabia Ali and Lawrence Lifschultz, eds, *Why Bosnia? Writings on the Balkan War* (Stony Creek, CT: Pamphleteer's Press, 1993) p. xviii. Such confusion also existed among the highest officials. President Bush's National Security Advisor, Brent Scowcroft, reports that Bush would frequently react to news from Yugoslavia with the phrase: 'Tell me again what this is all about'. *Washington Post*, 3 December 1995, A34. It was also reported that one newly elected Congressman had trouble finding Bosnia on a map.

2. Zbigniew Brzezinski, 'Moscow's Accomplice', *Washington Post*, 8 January 1995, C 7.

3. A point made by Mihailo Crnobrnja, *The Yugoslav Drama* (Montreal: McGill-Queen's University Press, 1994) p. 187.

4. But the legal nuances, both domestic and international, continue to intrigue many scholars. Robert W. Tucker and David C. Hendrickson question the legality of secession and the consistency of the US position in international law. The use of the term 'aggression' both by the US government and in this book to describe Serb behavior has legal implications. Nonetheless, it is unfortunate but true that international law is not sufficiently well established in the international system to be a reliable guide to policy once full scale hostilities break out. 'America and Bosnia', *The National Interest*, Fall 1993.

5. David Rieff, *Slaughterhouse: Bosnia and the Failure of the West* (NY: Simon & Schuster, 1995) pp. 68–9. One indicator of the role played by religion is an incident that happened years before the war began, cited by the sociologist Bogdan Denitch. When Denitch was pretesting a survey questionnaire that included the question, 'What is your religion?', the first respondent replied, 'What is yours?'. Denitch replied, 'I am an atheist', to which the interviewee shot back, 'I know all you damn intellectuals are atheists, but are you a Catholic, Orthodox, or Muslim atheist? I want to know your nationality!' *Ethnic Nationalism: The Tragic Death of Yugoslavia* (Minneapolis: University of Minnesota Press, 1994) p. 29.

6. Andrew Bell-Fialkoff, 'A Brief History of Ethnic Cleansing', *Foreign Affairs*, Summer 1993, pp. 117–18.

7. Susan L. Woodward, *Balkan Tragedy: Chaos and Dissolution After the Cold War* (Washington, DC: Brookings Institution, 1995) p. 18.

8. See Noel Malcolm's review of Robert D. Kaplan's book in 'Seeing Ghosts', *The National Interest*, Summer 1993; and Ivo Banac, 'The Fearful Asymmetry of War: The Causes and Consequences of Yugoslavia's Demise', *Daedulus*, Spring 1992, p. 143.

9. The Congress of Berlin in 1878 followed the defeat of the Ottoman Empire in the Russo–Turkish War, ended the Ottoman occupation of Bosnia-Herzegovina, and began the administration of the territory by Austria-Hungary.

10. Malcolm, 'Seeing Ghosts', p. 85; Lenard J. Cohen, *Broken Bonds: The Disintegration of Yugoslavia*, second edition, (Boulder: Westview Press, 1995), pp. 327–33. Cohen's analysis complements Woodward's analysis, which emphasizes the contribution of the erosion of central government authority and individual security to the recent violence. *Balkan Tragedy*, see especially Chapters 1–3. The point on French and German violence is made by Flora Lewis, 'Reassembling Yugoslavia', *Foreign Policy*, Spring 1995, p. 135.

11. *US Department of State Dispatch Supplement (DSDS)*, September 1992, p. 14.

12. *New York Times*, 10 January 1993, IV, 4.

13. Robert D. Kaplan, *Balkan Ghosts: A Journey Through History* (NY: Vintage Books, 1993). See comments from Noel Malcolm, 'Seeing Ghosts', and Fouad Ajami, 'In Europe's Shadows', *The New Republic*, 21 November 1994, especially p. 37.

14. As reported by Elizabeth Drew, Defense Secretary Aspin and the Head of the Joint Chiefs of Staff, Colin Powell, were with the President as he related his impressions of the book. As he heard the President talk, Aspin thought, 'Holy shit! He's going south on "lift and strike"'. Aspin later told other high officials, 'We have a serious problem here. We're out there pushing a policy that the President's not comfortable with. He's not on board.' *On the Edge: The Clinton Presidency* (NY: Simon & Schuster, 1994) p. 157. A more cynical interpretation of Clinton's attempt to persuade the Europeans to adopt a firmer stance is Robert W. Tucker and David C. Hendrickson's view that the president may have been following Eisenhower's tactic of using the search for a consensus among allies and the Congress as a means of killing a plan for military action, a course allegedly followed by Eisenhower when pressed to intervene in 1954 in Indochina. 'America and Bosnia', p. 21.

15. *Washington Post*, 3 December 1995, A34.

16. *New York Times*, April 8, 1993, A1; May 8, L4; 19 May, A10; and 25 June A3.

17. See Chapter 4, note 18.

8. Vietnam and the Debate on Intervention in Bosnia

1. Useful sources on Vietnam include F.M. Kail, *What Washington Said: Administration Rhetoric and the Vietnam War: 1949–1969* (NY: Harper

and Row, 1973); George McTurnan Kahin and John W. Lewis, *The United States and Vietnam* (NY: Delta, 1969); Theodore Draper, *Abuse of Power* (NY: Viking, 1967); and Donald S. Zagoria, *Vietnam Triangle: Moscow, Peking, Hanoi* (NY: Pegasus, 1967).

2. One measure of sympathy for Bosnia was a vote by the UN General Assembly on 18 December 1992, by an overwhelming majority, to lift the arms embargo against Bosnia, to ask the Security Council to revoke Resolution 713, and to authorize 'all means possible' to preserve Bosnia's territorial integrity. Rabia Ali and Lawrence Lifschultz, eds, *Why Bosnia? Writings on the Balkan War* (Stony Creek, CT: The Pamphleteer's Press, 1993) p. xxviii.

3. Alex Roberto Hybel, *How Leaders Reason: US Intervention in the Caribbean Basin and Latin America* (Cambridge, MA: Basil Blackwell, 1990) especially pp. 5–8.

4. Robert Jervis, *Perception and Misperception in International Politics* (Princeton: Princeton University Press, 1976) pp. 217, 220; Yuen Foong Khong, *Analogies at War: Korea, Munich, Dien Bien Phu, and the Vietnam Decisions of 1965* (Princeton: Princeton University Press, 1992) p. 3.

5. Khong, *Analogies at War*, p. 256.

6. Michael Roskin, 'From Pearl Harbor to Vietnam: Shifting Generational Paradigms and Foreign Policy', *Political Science Quarterly*, Fall 1974. The term paradigm was originally popularized by Thomas S. Kuhn in *The Structure of Scientific Revolutions* (Chicago: University of Chicago Press, 1962). Arthur M. Schlesinger, Jr. also speaks of cycles in American foreign policy, but he sees policy oscillating between realism and idealism: *The Cycles of American History* (Boston: Houghton-Mifflin, 1986).

7. Khong, *Analogies at War*, pp. 258–9.

8. Roskin, 'From Pearl Harbor to Vietnam', pp. 568–9. In a close parallel with another war's end, 'Appeasement in the 1930s grew out of the belief that World War I could have been avoided by intelligent and conciliatory diplomacy'. Moreover, it is argued that the currently widely held perception, based on the experience of World War II, that Hitler could have been deterred by a strong stand by the Allies in the 1930s, is wrong, since 'Hitler preferred war to being contained'. Jervis, *Perception and Misperception*, pp. 267, 223.

9. Roskin, 'From Pearl Harbor to Vietnam', pp. 575–6, 581.

10. David Rieff argues that the difficulty the Germans had in Yugoslavia during WW II was much exaggerated in the debate on intervention in Bosnia. *Slaughterhouse: Bosnia and the Failure of the West* (NY: Simon & Schuster, 1995) p. 154.

11. Jervis quotes Glenn Snyder and Paul Diesing who find 'no examples … of historical analogies producing a correct interpretation of a message'. Quoted in *Perception and Misperception*, p. 228.

12. John McCain, *Wall Street Journal*, 15 April 1994, editorial page.

13. Since the argument was made earlier that there was no vital US security interest at stake in Bosnia, it may be argued that this lessens the need to stop aggression and explains why decision-makers did not give stopping aggression a priority. But many also argued that there was no vital US

security interest at stake in Vietnam. But in that case, under the influence of a different paradigm, intervention still took place.

14. *DSDS*, September 1992, p. 13. The full quote is in Chapter 9, p. 163.

15. *Public Papers of the President: George Bush*, 7 August 1992, p. 1320; and 11 October 1992, p. 1799. The Vietnam analogy was so pervasive that it was even used by UN Secretary-General Boutros Boutros-Ghali. He indicated that he would do as much as possible to contain UN intervention in Yugoslavia, since otherwise 'it would become a kind of Vietnam for the United Nations'. Quoted in Lenard J. Cohen, *Broken Bonds: The Disintegration of Yugoslavia* (Boulder, Co: Westview, 1993) p. 242.

16. Fareed Zakaria, 'A Framework for Interventionism in the Post-Cold War Era', in Kanter and Brooks, eds, *US Intervention Policy for the Post-Cold War World: New Challenges and New Responses* (NY: W.W. Norton, 1994) p. 192; and Richard Ned Lebow, 'Deterrence: A Political and Psychological Critique,' and other chapters and the conclusion in Paul C. Stern, *et al.*, eds., *Perspectives on Deterrence* (NY: Oxford University Press, 1989). See also Alexander L. George and Richard Smoke, *Deterrence in American Foreign Policy: Theory and Practice* (NY: Columbia University Press, 1974) especially pp. 33–4, and Chapter 21. Zakaria's position is the opposite of the sentiments expressed by George Bush when asked if the intervention in the Persian Gulf war would lead to US involvement in other conflicts. 'No, I think because of what's happened we won't have to use US forces around the world. I think when we say something that is objectively correct – like don't take over a neighbor or you're going to bear some responsibility – people are going to listen. Because I think out of all this will be a new-found – let's put it this way: a reestablished credibility for the United States of America.' Robert W. Tucker and David C. Hendrickson, *The Imperial Temptation: The New World Order and America's Purpose* (NY: Council on Foreign Relations, 1992) p. 153.

17. *New York Times*, 25 July 1993, IV 1. Burns maintains that it was a Serb belief in the likelihood of escalation that brought the Serbs to the table at the London Conference in the summer of 1992, and to the table in Athens in April 1993. When they decided that the threat would not materialize, they resumed their offensive. For a discussion of Serb responsiveness to the assertiveness of individual UN commanders taking convoys through, see David Rieff, *Slaughterhouse*, especially pp. 168–9.

18. *Public Papers of the President: George Bush*, 8 July 1992, pp. 1101–2; 10 July 1992, p. 1106; and 7 August 1992, p. 1320.

19. ABC NEWS Shows #ABC–51, Peter Jennings Reporting, 'While Americans Watched: The Bosnian Tragedy', 17 March 1994, p. 4.

20. The obsession with credibility on both sides of the debate over Bosnia is remarkable. As the Clinton administration seemed to be preparing for more assertive military steps, Secretary of State Warren Christopher began to talk about the need to preserve American credibility, thus contradicting the Bush people who seemed to believe that the best way to maintain credibility was to do nothing. This consistent focus on credibility by both officials and commentators suggests a widespread belief that it is easier to defend a policy if you can assert

the long-term effect on credibility, rather than simply talking about the job that needs to be done at the present.

21. Serbian behavior during the siege of Gorazde supports the point. In spite of previously repeated NATO/US threats that were shown to be bluffs, when the NATO will stiffened as a result of the shelling of Gorazde, the threat of intervention was sufficiently credible to induce a Serbian retreat.

22. Quoted in David Halberstam, *The Best and the Brightest* (NY: Random House, 1972) p. 175.

23. *Washington Post*, 22 April 1994, p. 1.

9. The Bush Administration: From Status Quo to Immobility

1. Sabrina Petra Ramet, 'The Yugoslav Crisis and the West: Avoiding "Vietnam" and Blundering into "Abyssinia"', *East European Politics and Society*, Winter 1994, pp. 196–8.

2. A CIA report completed in November 1990 predicted the break-up of Yugoslavia.

3. David Gompert, 'How to Defeat Serbia', *Foreign Affairs*, July/August, 1994, p. 35.

4. Susan L. Woodward, *Balkan Tragedy: Chaos and Dissolution After the Cold War* (Washington, DC: Brookings Institution, 1995), pp. 142–6; *New York Times*, March 18, 1996, A3. It was unclear, because of the conflicting responses to the questions, whether the Croats were in favor of being part of a reconstituted federation or confederation.

5. Woodward, *Balkan Tragedy*, p. 157; and Mihailo Crnobrnja, *The Yugoslav Drama* (Montreal: McGill-Queen's University Press, 1994), p. 157. See also the comments on the rigidity and authoritarian nature and negotiating style of Milosevic and Tudjman, as described by Bosnian president Izetbegovic and Macedonian President Gligorov. Izetbegovic's and Gligorov's assessments of each other and Slovenian president Kucan's flexible approach and democratic values contrast favorably to their assessments of Milosevic and Tudjman. Cohen, *Broken Bonds*, first edition, pp. 199–200.

6. Richard Schifter, Assistant Secretary of State for Human Rights and Humanitarian Affairs, *Department of State Dispatch (DSD)* 4 March 1991, pp. 152–3.

7. *Public Papers of the President: George Bush*, p. 483; Margaret Tutwiler, *DSD*, 3 June 1991, p. 395. Referring to Serbian blocking of federal constitutional amendments to further democratic reforms, Prime Minister Ante Markovic alleged the Yugoslav military, supporting the Serbs, acted in disregard of the civilian authorities. *DSD*, 1 July 1991, p 469.

8. *New York Times*, May 19, 1991, L10 and May 25, L5.

9. Sabrina Petra Ramet, 'The Yugoslav Crisis and the West', p. 199.

10. *DSD*, 1 July 1991, p. 468. Baker stated that, 'We want to see this problem resolved through negotiation and through dialogue and not through preemptive unilateral actions.' *DSD*, 1 July 1991, p. 468.

Baker's role during his visit to Belgrade has been seen as unclear and controversial. It was not clear whether an ambiguous message from Baker actually contributed to the decision of the army to intervene militarily, whether his advice not to intervene under any circumstances was simply ignored, or whether the leadership 'was given the nod by Baker behind the scenes to use force, but only if it became absolutely necessary'. See Lenard J. Cohen's account of the events surrounding Baker's visit, *Broken Bonds: The Disintegration of Yugoslavia*, second edition (Boulder, Co: Westview, 1995) pp. 217–22. For Baker's own account, see his *The Politics of Diplomacy: Revolution, War and Peace, 1989–1992* (NY: G.P. Putnam's Sons, 1995) pp. 478–83. But Ambassador Zimmermann argues convincingly that Baker did all it was possible to do to rein in the Serbs, short of actually threatening to use force. Warren Zimmermann, 'The Last Ambassador; a Memoir of the Collapse of Yugoslavia,' *Foreign Affairs*, March–April, 1995, pp. 11–12.

11. Marc Weller, 'The International Response to the Dissolution of the Socialist Federal Republic of Yugoslavia', *American Journal of International Law*, July 1992, p. 589; and Ramet, 'The Yugoslav Crisis', pp. 197, 202. For the German defense of their decision to recognize, see 'Recognition of the Yugoslav Successor States', Position Paper of the German Foreign Ministry, Bonn, 10 March 1993.

12. Ramet, 'The Yugoslav Crisis', pp. 199–200; and *New York Times*, 4 July 1991, p. 7. In a statement that preceded Baker's, Deputy Secretary of State Eagleburger on June 30 had said in an interview that the United States supported 'sovereign republics' and the idea of a Yugoslav confederation. Susan L, Woodward, *Balkan Tragedy: Chaos and Dissolution After the Cold War* (Washington, DC: Brookings Institution, 1995) p. 165. As David Owen points out, a serious effort to adjust the borders of the republics during the Croatia crisis might have helped prevent further war. *Balkan Odyssey*, (NY: Harcourt Brace, 1995) pp. 32–3.

13. Baker, *The Politics of Diplomacy: Revolution, War and Peace 1989–1992*, pp. 636–45; and Joshua Muravchik, *The Imperative of American Leadership: A Challenge to Neo-Isolationism* (Washington, DC: AEI Press, 1996), pp. 90–1. Owen is quoted on p. 91.

14. *New York Times*, July 6, 1991, L4.

15. Muravchik, *The Imperative of American Leadership*, p. 91.

16. Susan L. Woodward, *Balkan Tragedy: Chaos and Dissolution After the Cold War* (Washington, DC: Brookings Institution, 1995), p. 158–9; Lenard J. Cohen, *Broken Bonds: Yugoslavia's Disintegration and Balkan Politics in Transition*, second edition (Boulder, CO: Westview, 1995), p. 235.

17. *New York Times*, July 6, 1991, L4. Woodward, *Balkan Tragedy*, p. 168.

18. *New York Times*, July 7, 1991, L6.

19. *New York Times*, July 8, 1991, A13.

20. Muravchik, *The Imperative of American Leadership*, p. 92.

21. Woodward, *Balkan Tragedy*, p. 174.

22. *New York Times*, November 5, 1991, A3 and November 6, A16.

23. *New York Times*, August 30, 1991, A3.

24. Mihailo Crnobrnja, *The Yugoslav Drama* (Montreal: McGill-Queen's Press, 1994), pp. 160–1.

25. *New York Times*, September 20, 1991, A6.

26. Muravchik, *The Imperative of American Leadership*, pp. 96–7.

27. Woodward, *Balkan Tragedy*, pp. 165–9.

28. *New York Times*, January 16, 1991, A1; February 7, A3; February 22, L3; and James Bjork and Allan E. Goodman, *Yugoslavia, 1991–92: Could Diplomacy Have Prevented a Tragedy?* (Washington, DC: Institute for the Study of Diplomacy Georgetown University, 1993) p. 8.

29. See Paula Franklin Lytle, 'US Policy Toward the Demise of Yugoslavia: The Virus of Nationalism', *East European Politics and Society*, Fall 1992, p. 315; and Ramet, 'The Yugoslav Crisis', p. 200. For statements by Secretary of State Baker and Deputy Secretary of State Eagleburger on Serbian aggression and crimes, see *DSD*, 30 September 1991, p. 723; and *DSD*, 7 October 1991, p. 748.

30. Lytle, 'US Policy Toward the Demise of Yugoslavia', p. 313.

31. Bogdan Denitch, *Ethnic Nationalism: The Tragic Death of Yugoslavia* (Minneapolis: Univ. of Minnesota Press, 1994) pp. 51–3. This otherwise fine and superbly written book takes a dark view of German motives and actions, alleging that the language and imagery used by much of the German press describing Serbian culture and history is racist. On Izetbegovic's statement see Woodward, *Balkan Tragedy*, p. 261; on Carrington's see Cohen, *Broken Bonds*, first edition, p. 234.

32. Ramet, 'The Yugoslav Crisis', p. 202.

33. Analysts surveying the events in Bosnia in late 1991 and early 1992 come to quite different conclusions on which side should be blamed for the war in Bosnia. Compare Cohen, *Broken Bonds*, second edition, pp. 241–5; *Genocide in Bosnia: The Policy of 'Ethnic Cleansing'.* (College Station, TX: Texas A&M Press, 1995) Chapter 4; and Robert J. Donia and John V.A. Fine, Jr., *Bosnia and Hercegovina: A Tradition Betrayed* (NY: Columbia University Press, 1994) pp. 337–8.

34. *New York Times*, 16 January, p. A10. But there is also evidence that Milosevic's designs on Bosnia had little to do with democratic rights and much more to do with imperial designs. Cohen, *Broken Bonds*, second edition, p. 208.

35. Ramet, 'The Yugoslav Crisis', pp. 196–8.

36. Slovenia and Macedonia were commended in an EC study for their observance of human rights. Furthermore, as the Germans themselves point out, recognition of Croatia may have contributed to pressure on the Serbs to agree to a ceasefire in Croatia. 'Recognition of the Yugoslav Successor States', p. 4. See also Stevan K. Pavlowitch, 'Who is "Balkanizing" Whom? The Misunderstandings Between the Debris of Yugoslavia and an Unprepared West', *Daedalus*, Spring 1994, p. 213.

37. Cohen, *Broken Bonds*, second edition, pp. 241–5. Some controversy has developed over the failure of the Muslims to accept the Lisbon plan, in light of the conflict that followed. It has also been suggested that the US was at fault for indicating doubts about the plan, a contention that then US Ambassador to Yugoslavia, Warren Zimmerman, has denied. See *New York Times*, 29 August 1993, L10; and 30 September 1993, A24. Furthermore, the geographic questions and borders were not settled at Lisbon and it is questionable whether Karadzic was committed to

abiding by the Lisbon terms. See Paul Shoup, 'The Bosnian Crisis in 1992', in Sabrina Petra Ramet and Ljubisa S. Adamovich, eds, *Beyond Yugoslavia: Politics, Economics, and Culture in a Sheltered Community* (Boulder, Co: Westview, 1995) pp. 167–8, 171.

38. Cohen, *Broken Bonds*, second edition, pp. 242–4, 269.
39. Former Acting Secretary of State and former ambassador to Yugoslavia Lawrence Eagleburger had believed that Yugoslavia would not disintegrate and that Milosevic was someone with whom the West could do business. He later admitted that he had 'misjudged Milosevic', even though he had had a long-time acquaintance with him and a 'well-tested working relationship'. Lenard J. Cohen, *Broken Bonds: The Disintegration of Yugoslavia* (Boulder, Co: Westview, 1993). pp. 215–16, 221. Zimmerman maintains that Milosevic told him explicitly that 'you needn't worry about trouble in Bosnia. Serbs have no serious grievances in Bosnia; they're not being abused there. This is a big difference with Serbs in Croatia.' Warren Zimmermann, 'The Last Ambassador: A Memoir of the Collapse of Yugoslavia', *Foreign Affairs*, March–April 1995, pp. 17–19.
40. Silber and Little, *Yugoslavia*, pp. 212–7; *New York Times*, March 3, 1992, A9; March 28, L4; April 4, L3; April 6, A12; April 8, A10; and April 22, A10.
41. Baker, *The Politics of Diplomacy*, pp. 639–42.
42. *New York Times*, May 13, A10; May 15, A1.
43. Baker, *The Politics of Diplomacy*, pp. 645–8.
44. *New York Times*, May 25, 1992, L1 and May 31, A1.
45. Bjork and Goodman, *Yugoslavia, 1991–1992*, p. 11, and Stephen Schwartz, 'In Defense of the Bosnian Republic, *World Affairs*, Fall 1993, pp. 84–5. American officials in Yugoslavia estimated Milosevic could have stopped 80 per cent of Serbian actions in Bosnia if he had wanted to. Jenonne R. Walker, Hearing, Committee on Armed Services, US Senate, 102nd Congress, second session, August 11, 1992, p. 70. See also the discussion in Muravchik, *The Imperative of American Leadership*, pp. 156–7.
46. Baker, *The Politics of Diplomacy*, p. 648.
47. *New York Times*, July 5, 1992, L6; June 29, A6; and August 7, A1.
48. *New York Times*, July 18, 1992, L4.
49. *New York Times*, August 27, 1992, A1; August 28, A6.
50. The commentaries can be found in *New York Times*, May 29, 1992, A29; June 18, A27; August 3, A19; and August 6, A23.
51. Baker, *The Politics of Diplomacy*, p. 635.
52. *New York Times*, October 22, 1992, A1.
53. Monica Crowley, 'Nixon Unplugged', *The New Yorker*, July 29, 1996, p. 50.
54. *New York Times*, September 28, 1992, A1; October 8, A35; and Colin Powell, *My American Journey* (NY: Ballantine Books, 1995), pp. 543–5. In James Baker's view, the Pentagon, including Secretary of Defense Dick Cheney, was deeply opposed to any military involvement in Bosnia. *The Politics of Diplomacy*, pp. 648–50.
55. *New York Times*, October 2, 1992, A1; November 19, A1; and December 12, L7.

56. *US Department of State Dispatch Supplement (DSDS)*, September 1992, p. 22. See *Bosnia–Hercegovina: Abuses by Bosnian Croat and Muslim Forces in Central and Southwestern Bosnia-Hercegovina*, New York, Helsinki Watch, September 1993 for documentation of Croatian and Muslim atrocities. On Croat atrocities later in the war, see *Washington Post*, December 23, 1995, A12.

57. *DSDS*, September 1992, p. 22.

58. *Ibid.*, pp. 15, 26, 16.

59. *DSDS*, September 1992, pp. 1–3, 25; *New York Times*, 22 August 1992, L3; *DSDS*, September 1992, pp. 30–1; *DSDS*, September 1992, p. 14. At a later date, and more specifically, Eagleburger stated: 'We must make it unmistakably clear that we will settle for nothing less than the restoration of the independent state of Bosnia–Herzegovina with its territory undivided and intact, the return of all refugees to their homes and villages, ... and a day of reckoning for those found guilty of crimes against humanity'. *DSD*, 28 December 1992, p. 925.

60. *DSDS*, September 1992, pp. 12–13; *DSD*, 19 October 1992, p. 777. In fairness, one must note that the ceasefire agreement that ended the Croatian war has held, with occasional violations, until the summer of 1995. However, that came only after repeated failures. The *New York Times* reported that the ceasefire accord reached between Serbia and Croatia in January 1991 was the fifteenth ceasefire negotiated since the conflict began in July. *New York Times*, 3 January 1991, p. A1.

61. *DSDS*, September 1992, pp. 7, 15.
    Remarks by Lawrence Eagleburger suggest considerable faith in the power of sanctions and diplomatic penalties to force the Serbs to reverse course: 'The fact of the matter is that imperfect as the sanctions have been against the Serbs so far, it is clear they have made some real impact on the Serbian economy. The Serbs are looking at a winter that's going to be tough. If, in fact, those sanctions are really clamped down, there is ... substantial reason to believe that that's going to force real change in the attitudes of the Serbian Government and, hopefully, the Serbian people ...', *DSDS*, September 1992, p. 13.

62. *DSDS*, September 1992, pp. 13–16, 25.

10. The Clinton Administration I: Strategies and Obstacles

1. *Humanitarian Intervention: Effectiveness of UN Operations in Bosnia* (Washington, DC: United States General Accounting Office, April 1994) especially pp. 4 and 12.

2. *Ibid.*, pp. 3, 14.

3. David Rieff, in *Slaughterhouse: Bosnia and the Failure of the West* (NY: Simon & Schuster, 1995), gives an elegant explanation of UN policy and behavior; see especially Chapters 6 and 7. For an alternate viewpoint, see James A. Schear, *Washington Post*, 21 March 1995, A 17. The Akashi quote is from Joshua Muravchik, *The Imperative of American Leadership: A Challenge to Neo-Isolationism* (Washington, DC: AEI Press,

1996), p. 117. The other quotes and examples are from the *New York Times,* January 23, 1994, L1.

4. Rieff, *Slanghterhouse,* p. 175. As Rieff puts it, 'The Bosnian side ... had, as was once said of the Irish, the bad taste to be in earnest about the freedom of their country', p. 179.

5. *Ibid.,* p. 169; Hearing, Committee on Armed Services, US Senate, 103rd Congress, second session, December 1, 1994, p. 18.

6. Rieff, *Slaughterhouse,* p. 151; *New York Times,* 9 January 1993, L1.

7. Rieff, *Slaughterhouse,* pp. 166, 179 and 181; Hearing, Committee on Armed Services, US Congress, 104th Congress, first session, 12 January 1995, p. 18.

8. *Humanitarian Intervention,* pp. 37–8.

9. See Rieff on the extent to which the UN was doing the Serbs' work for them, in *Slaughterhouse,* Chapters 6 and 7; *New York Times,* 11 August 1993, A15. See also Alan F. Fogelquist, 'Turning Points in Bosnia and the Region', in Zalmay M. Khalilzad, ed., *Lessons From Bosnia,* Rand Corporation Conference Proceedings, 1993, pp. 12–13.

10. Illustrative of the limits the presence of the UN troops put on the likelihood of bombing is this comment, after the killing of 68 people in Sarajevo in February 1994, by British Foreign Secretary Douglas Hurd. Mr Hurd was discussing the possibility of bombing Serb forces in retaliation: 'We have to take into account consequences for the humanitarian effort and the food supplies of Sarajevo. We have to take into account the effect on the UN forces there, how they would be protected. That's not to rule out the use of air power. It's been clear since August in principle we are willing to use it'. MacNeil–Lehrer Newshour, 7 February 1994, transcript, page 9.

11. Hearing Before the Subcommittee on European Affairs of the Committee on Foreign Relations, US Senate, 18 February 1993 (Washington, DC: US Government Printing Office, 1993) pp. 7–21, 26–48; Sabrina Petra Ramet, 'The Yugoslav Crisis and the West: Avoiding "Vietnam" and Blundering into "Abyssinia"', *East European Politics and Societies,* Winter 1994, pp. 202–3.

12. David Owen, *Balkan Odyssey* (NY: Harcourt Brace, 1995), pp. 13, 102, 282, 297, and 304.

13. John Newhouse, 'No Exit, No Entrance', *The New Yorker,* 28 June 1993, pp. 46–8.

14. Elizabeth Drew, *On the Edge: The Clinton Presidency* (NY: Simon & Schuster, 1994), p. 149.

15. *New York Times,* April 29, 1993, A1; Drew, *On the Edge,* pp. 154–5.

16. Hearing, Committee on Armed Services, US Senate, 104th Congress, first session, 12 January 1995, pp. 19–20. In mid-September 1995, after a two-week bombing campaign, Secretary Perry indicated there had been problems finding the Serb guns. *New York Times,* 14 September, 1995, A1.

17. *New York Times,* 12 August, 1993, A22.

18. After one week of a large-scale offensive in western and central Bosnia by Bosnian forces on 11 September, the Bosnian Serbs, 'severely weakened .both psychologically and materially by the NATO air offensive,' were

forced out of 20 per cent of the territory under their control. *Strategic Survey: 1995–1996* (London: Oxford University Press, 1996) p. 134.

19.   Owen, *Balkan Odyssey*, pp. 257, 264–8.

20.   James Gow, remarks at the Woodrow Wilson Center, Washington, DC, 17 May 1994; Fogelquist, 'Turning Points in Bosnia and the Region', in Khalilzad, ed., *Lessons From Bosnia*, p. 11. Controversy erupted in Washington as it became publicized that the US had turned a blind eye to Iranian arms flows across Croatia to Bosnia during the Clinton administration in violation of the arms embargo. Republican criticism smacks of campaign hypocrisy, however, since (1) many Republicans, including then Senator Bob Dole, favored getting arms to Bosnia, and (2) it was widely rumored at the time that the US was involved in just such an operation and confirmation should come as no surprise to anyone who was paying attention. In preparation for upcomng hearings on his confirmation as the new CIA Director, however, former National Security Advisor Anthony Lake, who approved the policy, admitted that he should have informed the Congress about the policy. See *Washington Post*, 21 May 1996, A12; 2 June, A12 and 15 December, A18.

21.   In the summer of 1992, Lt. General Barry R. McCaffrey, Office of the Joint Chiefs of Staff, estimated the number of troops in Bosnia constituting the Bosnian Serb Army and Serb irregulars at 70 000, Bosnian Muslim Defense forces at 50 000, and Bosnian Croat forces and Croatian Defense Forces at 50 000. The Muslims were the least well armed. Hearing Before the Committee on Armed Services, US Senate, 102nd Congress, second & session, August 11, 1992, p. 26–7. A 1994 report from the International Institute for Strategic Studies gives these estimates on military troops: Bosnian Serbs, 80 000; Bosnians, 110 000 plus reserves; and Bosnian Croats, 50 000. The Bosnian Serbs were estimated to have 330 tanks, the Bosnians 20, and the Bosnian Croats 50. The Bosnians had few artillery pieces to the Bosnian Serbs' 800, and the Bosnian Croats' 500. *Washington Post*, 26 January 1996, A25.

22.   Hearing, Committee on Armed Services, US Senate, 103rd Congress, second session, 23 June 1994, pp. 29, 43, 58, 62.

23.   Hearing, Committee on Armed Services, US Senate, 104th Congress, first session, 12 January 1995, pp. 26–7, 10.

24.   Hearing, Committee on Armed Services, US Senate, 103rd Congress, second session, 23 June, 1994, pp. 48, 33.

25.   Hearing, Committee on Armed Services, US Senate, 103rd Congress, second session, 1 December, 1994, pp. 19–21.

26.   Hearing, Committee on Armed Services, US Senate, 104th Congress, first session, 12 January 1995, pp. 11–13; and *New York Times*, 5 May 1994, A27.

27.   See remarks by Warren Zimmermann, Hearing, Committee on Foreign Affairs, US House of Representatives, 103rd Congress, second session, 11 May 1994, pp. 22–3.

28.   Hearing, Committee on Armed Services, US Senate, 103rd Congress, second session, 23 June 1994, pp. 61, 65.

29.   Hearing Before the Subcommittee on European Affairs of the
      Committee on Foreign Relations, United States Senate, 103rd
      Congress, first session, 18 February 1993, pp. 67–77. Other people
      mentioned similar troop numbers: Senator Lugar, 300 000; and Cedric
      Thornberry, Civil Commander of UNPROFOR in Croatia, 250 000
      troops for five to ten years.
30.   See Chapter 9.
31.   Christopher Civiic argues that there were no grounds for British and
      French fears, fueled by German unification in October 1990, that
      'Yugoslavia's dissolution would open the way for Germany's entry into
      South-Eastern Europe as a dominant force and protector of a bloc of
      states ... made up of Austria, Croatia, Czechoslovakia, and Hungary'.
      According to Civiic, the reasons for German advocacy after July 1991
      for recognition of Slovenia and Croatia had to do with German do-
      mestic pressure to stop the slaughter in Croatia, a cause championed
      by *Die Welt* and the *Frankfurter Allgemeine Zeitung.* 'Who's To Blame for
      the War in Ex-Yugoslavia?', *World Affairs,* Fall 1993, p. 77. A similar
      opinion is reached by Beverly Crawford, 'Explaining Defection from
      International cooperation: Germany's Unilateral Recognition of
      Croatia,' *World Politics,* July 1996.
32.   On the intervention force, see James B. Steinberg, 'Turning Points in
      Bosnia and the West', in Khalilzad, ed., *Lessons From Bosnia,* p. 6. On
      Kohl's positions, see *Hamburg DPA,* 23 July 1992, *Foreign Broadcast
      Information Service, Daily Report–Western Europe (FBIS, DR–WE)* 24 July
      1992, p. 2; and *Berlin DDP,* 30 January 1993, in *(FBIS, DR–WE)*
      1 February 1993, p. 13. For the *Economist*'s statement, *Süddeutsche
      Zeitung,* 30 April, p. 4, in *FBIS, DR–WE* 3 May, pp. 16–17.
33.   The *Daily Telegraph,* 30 April 1993, pp. 10, 18, in *FBIS, DR–WE* 3 May
      1993, pp. 7–9.
34.   One Western official said Croatian President Tudjman was accurately
      reflecting the views of many Western governments when he said
      Europe would not tolerate an Islamic state in its midst, and therefore
      division of Bosnia into Serb, Croat, and Muslim communities was in-
      evitable. *New York Times,* 23 August 1992, A16, and 27 November 1994,
      IV:1; Ivo Banac, 'Separating History from Myth', in Ali and Lifschultz,
      ed., *Why Bosnia?,* p. 46. And a senior French diplomat said: 'Our inter-
      ests are closer to the Serbs' than you think'. We worry more about the
      Muslims than about the Serbs. Please don't arouse the Serb nation.
      You will go away and leave us with a bigger problem.' John Newhouse
      'No Exit, No Entrance', pp. 49–50.
35.   Ramet, 'The Yugoslav Crisis and the West', p. 202; a British official
      said, 'The familiarity with the conflict on the ground, valley by valley
      and politician by politician, has given us perspective. You've [the
      US] not been involved word by word and table thump by table
      thump. We know all sides are to blame'. *New York Times,* 4 February
      1993, A10.
36.   See Newhouse, 'No Exit, No Entrance', p. 49; and Leslie Gelb, *New
      York Times,* 31 January 1993, IV, 17. President Clinton himself said
      'The British and the French and the Russians never said to me flat

out they would never go along. They said they thought they could do better.' *Foreign Policy Bulletin: The Documentary Record of United States Foreign Policy*, July/August 1993, p. 18.

37. *New York Times*, 15 April 1993, A12. Lady Thatcher also suggested that the policy being followed in Bosnia could produce a world-wide Bosnian diaspora, with potential for terrorist activities.

38. *Izvestia*, 30 May 1992, p. 6 in *FBIS, DR – WE* 1 June 1992, p. 10.

39. On the opposition from the right, see *Sovetskaya Rossiya*, 17 December 1992, p. 3; *FBIS, Daily Report–Central Asia (DR–CA)* 6 January 1993, pp. 37–8; *Pravda*, 21 January 1993, p. 5, *FBIS, DR–CA* 3 February 1993, pp. 61–2; and *Kommerant-Daily*, 27 January 1993, p. 10, *FBIS, DR–CA* 3 February 1993, pp. 58–9. Yeltsin was constantly frustrated by pressure from the parliament on Bosnia; Woodward, *Balkan Tragedy*, p. 514, n. 67. The willingness of the Russian government to support the West to the extent it did on Bosnia may have been related to resentment that the Serbs gave their support to the 1991 coup against Gorbachev.

40. This analysis relies on Cohen, *Broken Bonds*, second edition, pp. 299–302, 307–10.

41. *Washington Post*, 29 November 1995, A27.

42. William Schneider, 'Introduction: From Foreign Policy to "Politics as Usual"' in David A. Deese, ed., *The New Politics of American Foreign Policy* (NY: St. Martin's Press, 1994).

43. A discussion of these approaches is in Chapter 2, pp. 18–20. For more on the views of two representatives of these approaches, see Les Aspin, *New York Times*, 1 May 1993, L6; and Colin Powell, in Newhouse, 'No Exit, No Entrance', pp. 46–8. Powell's aides are reported to have told the Congress that lifting the arms embargo would make little difference to the prosecution of the war, but would lead to more 'chaos'. Of course, the shades of opinion in the Defense Department and the military services were complex, sometimes following bureaucratic lines. It appears that in general the Air Force had a more favorable view of what could be accomplished with air power at relatively low cost, whereas the ground services had less faith in the results of a modern high-tech air war.

44. *New York Times*, 29 April 1993, A1.

45. On Croat military activity, see *New York Times*, 11 May 1993, A8; 2 July 1993, A4; and Lawrence Freedman, 'Why the West Failed', *Foreign Policy*, Winter 1994–95.

11. The Clinton Administration II: The Agony of Decision

1. Elizabeth Drew, *On the Edge: The Clinton Presidency* (NY: Simon & Schuster, 1994) p. 139.

2. *New York Times*, 28 January, 1993, A7; 31 January, L10; 3 February, A8; and 4 January, A3. At the news conference where Izetbegovic made his appeal to Clinton, it was suggested he might meet again with Karadzic. They had met in January for the first time since the war began.

Izetbegovic switched from Serbo-Croatian into English and said, 'They forced me to sit at a table with a man who inspired all those terrible crimes. Despicable is not too strong a word'.

3. UNSC Document, S/25221, 'Report of the Secretary-General on the Activities of the International Conference on the Former Yugoslavia,' 2 February 1993, pp. 5, 9; and David Owen, *Balkan Odyssey* (NY: Harcourt Brace, 1995) pp. 89–90.

4. Laura Silber and Allan Little, *Yugoslavia: Death of a Nation* (NY: TV Books, 1995, 1996) p. 276. The Serb rejection of arrangements where they would live as a minority with another ethnic group in power, while at the same time refusing to grant equal rights to other minorities is frequently remarked upon. See Lenard J. Cohen, *Broken Bonds: The Disintegration of Yugoslavia*, first edition (Boulder, CO: Westview, 1993) p. 125; Silber and Little, *Yugoslavia*, p. 192; and *New York Times*, 18 July 1992, A1 for a Western diplomat's statement that 'From the start it was clear that the operating principle for the Milosevic Government was that whatever happened, Serbs could not live under or with any other people, though other people would have to live under Serbs'.

5. Silber and Little, *Yugoslavia*, pp. 276–80, and *New York Times*, 4 February 1993, A10.

6. Many Bosnians resented the idea of having to live in an ethnically homogenous state, which was so contradictory to the premises underlying the Bosnian Government. *New York Times*, 7 March 1994, IV, 3. The Vance–Owen plan, setting up provinces based on ethnic composition, has the unfortunate effect of implying second class citizenship to those who don't identify with any ethnic group, notwithstanding the human rights guaranties. This presumably would include many of those with mixed marriages, those who identify themselves as Yugoslav, and members of minority groups other than Serb, Croat, or Muslim. As a young doctor in Sarajevo put it, 'We're neither Muslim, nor Croat, nor Serb. ... Imagine asking people who they are and the only thing they can come up with is 'I'm a Croat' or 'I'm a Serb' or whatever'. Quoted in Rabia Ali and Lawrence Lifschultz, eds., *Why Bosnia? Writings on the Balkan War* (Stony Creek, CT: Pamphleteer's Press, 1993) p. xxxiii.

7. UNSC Document, S/25403, p. 5; and Chapter 4, footnote 30.

8. 'Invitation to War', *Foreign Affairs*, Summer 1993, pp. 106–7. For a detailed analysis of all parties' reaction to the plan, see Cohen, *Broken Bonds*, first edition, pp. 247–8. The Bosnians finally accepted the plan partly because they (rightly) believed the Bosnian Serbs would reject it.

9. David Owen, *Balkan Odyssey* (New York: Harcourt Brace, 1995), pp. 121, 130, 105, 110 and 174.

10. *New York Times*, 11 February 1993, A1; 11 February, A12; 1 March, A6; 14 February, IV:13; 25 February, L19; and February 28, IV:1.

11. *New York Times*, 20 April 1993, A9.

12. Drew, *On the Edge*, p. 146. The foregoing analysis relies heavily on Chapter 10 of Drew's book.

13. Ibid., pp. 149–53; Colin Powell, *My American Journey* (NY: Ballantine, 1995) pp. 561, 560. Powell notes that 'the discussions [meandered]

like graduate student bull sessions or the think-tank seminars in which many of my new colleagues had spent the last twelve years while their party was out of power'.

14. Contrast the attitude of Senator John McCain, an opponent of intervention. 'When you're sitting there at the dedication of the Holocaust Museum, and Elie Weisel correctly points out that this tragedy is ensuing and we're doing nothing, that brings enormous pressure to bear ... The question is what is viable. We cannot confuse a desire to do good with viable military options.' *New York Times*, 5 May 1993, A16.

15. *New York Times*, 7 May 1993, A1.

16. Bob Woodward, *The Choice* (NY: Simon & Schuster, 1996) p. 261.

17. Drew, *On the Edge*, p. 150.

18. *Ibid.*, pp. 150–5; *New York Times*, 29 April 1993, A1.

19. Drew, *On the Edge*, pp. 154–5; *New York Times*, 29 April 1993, A1.

20. Drew, *On the Edge*, p. 155.

21. *Ibid.*, pp. 155–6.

22. *New York Times*, 7 May 1993, A1; *Foreign Policy Bulletin: The Documentary Record of US Foreign Policy*, July–August, 1993, p. 18.

23. Drew, *On the Edge*, pp. 159–63.

24. Owen, *Balkan Odyssey*, pp. 178–84.

25. *New York Times*, 7 May 1993, A11 and June 5, A1.

26. Drew, *On the Edge*, p. 162 and *New York Times*, 20 May 1993, A12.

27. Owen, *Balkan Odyssey*, p. 178 and *New York Times*, 22 May 1993, L4. According to testimony by Under secretary of Defense for Policy Walter Slocombe and General Wesley K. Clark, Gorazde, Srebrenica and Zepa were never considered defensible. Moreover, in mid-1993, heavy arms held by the Bosnian government at Zepa and Srebrenica were put into UN weapons storage sites in return for Serb agreement not to attack. When the Serbs moved on these 'safe areas' in 1995, these arms could not be used and UNPROFOR had nowhere near the firepower needed to repulse the Serbs. Hearing, Committee on Armed Services, US Senate, 104th Congress, first session, 13 July 1995, pp. 13–16.

28. *New York Times*, 5 June 1993, A1.

29. *New York Times*, 18 June 1993, A1 and 18 June, A8. As if US Bosnia policy were not confused enough, a controversy now developed over a letter Clinton sent to German Chancellor Helmut Kohl, encouraging him to support lifting of the embargo at the 21 June meeting with his colleagues. This seemed to contradict passive American behavior on the issue, and American officials ended up downplaying the significance of the letter. *New York Times*, 23 June 1996, A6.

30. *New York Times*, 31 July 1993, L1.

31. Drew, *On the Edge*, p. 273.

32. *Ibid.* The Muslims were estimated to control 15 per cent or less of the total area of Bosnia, the Serbs 70 per cent, and the Croats the balance.

33. The statements on relations with the allies are based on *The New York Times*, 2 August 1993, A3 and 3 August A1. The bulk of the analysis is based on Drew, *On the Edge*, pp. 274–9.

34. Drew, *On the Edge*, p. 279.
35. UNSC document, S/26337/Add.1, 23 August 1993, pp. 8–9, 5, 10. Earlier, Vance and Owen explained why, in the formulation of the Vance–Owen plan, they had rejected principles for creating a confederation of 'three territorially-distinct states based on ethnic or confessional principles. Any plan to do so would involve incorporating a very large number of members of the other ethnic/confessional group. Such a plan could achieve homogeneity and coherent boundaries only by a process of enforced population transfer ... Furthermore, a confederation formed of three such states would be inherently unstable, for at least two would surely forge immediate and stronger connections with neighbouring states of the former Yugoslavia than they would with the other two units of Bosnia and Herzegovina.' Quoted in Cohen, *Broken Bonds*, first edition, p. 259, n. 55.
36. Owen, *Balkan Odyssey*, p. 215.
37. These incidents are cited in Joshua Muravchik, *The Imperative of American Leadership: A Challenge to Neo-Isolationism* (Washington, DC: AEI Press, 1996) pp. 116–17.
38. *New York Times*, 3 October 1993, L10.
39. This account relies on Cohen, *Broken Bonds*, second edition, pp. 295–7. Regarding the easing of sanctions, David Owen argues that two mistakes were made in the handling of Milosevic. The first was in failing to press for drastic economic sanctions (an embargo) in the early part of the war, primarily a European failing, and the US was reluctant to grant Milosevic relief from sanctions in order to get a deal once he began to limit his support to the Bosnian Serbs, in the spring of 1993. *Balkan Odyssey*, pp. 134, 303, and 322.
40. *New York Times*, 21 November 1993, L7.
41. *New York Times*, 25 November 1993, A6; 3 December, A6; and 1 December, A8.
42. *New York Times*, 14 June 1993, A15; 28 February 1993, IV:15; 26 September, 1993, IV:15; and Owen, *Balkan Tragedy*, p. 232.
43. *New York Times*, 6 January 1994, A8.
44. *New York Times*, 5 February 1994, A4; 8 February, A1; and 14 February, A1.
45. *New York Times*, 11 February 1994, A1,
46. Silber and Little, *Yugoslavia*, pp. 312–13 and *New York Times*, February 8, 1994, A14.
47. *New York Times*, 11 February, 1994, A7; 14 February, A1; and April 8, A10.
48. Silber and Little, *Yugoslavia*, p. 321.
49. Susan L. Woodward, *Balkan Tragedy: Chaos and Dissolution After the Cold War* (Washington, DC: Brookings Institution, 1995) pp. 314–5.
50. See 'Framework Agreement Establishing a Federation in the Areas of the Republic of Bosnia and Herzegovina', and 'Outline of a Preliminary Agreement for a Confederation Between the Republic of Croatia and the Federation', Department of State, Washington, DC, 1 March 1994. Throughout the conflict, the one important obstacle to deterring the Serbs has been the on-again off-again nature of the

Croat–Muslim alliance. If it could be solidified, the Serb military advantage would suffer greatly. For more background on the Croat–Bosnian conflict and the pressures on Tudjman prior to signing the February agreement, see Cohen, *Broken Bonds*, second edition, pp. 275–81; 297–9.

51. *New York Times*, 30 May 1994, L3. Susan L. Woodward critiques the role of sanctions in ending the war in *Balkan Tragedy*, pp. 289–94.

52. *New York Times*, 8 June 1994, A16.

53. *Washington Post*, 6 July 1994, A6.

54. Silber and Little, *Yugoslavia*, p. 337.

55. *Washington Post*, 4 July 1995, A1. The evidence contradicts the opinion of some political and military leaders in Serbia that Milosevic sold out their cause by disowning the Bosnian Serbs. At most, the sellout was only partial. Cohen, *Broken Bonds*, second edition, p. 315

56. *New York Times*, 4 November 1994, A3 and 29 November, A16.

57. *Washington Post*, 21 February 1995, A1.

58. Richard K. Betts, 'The Delusion of Impartial Intervention,' *Foreign Affairs*, November/December 1994, p. 21.

59. Jonathan Clarke, 'Rhetoric Before Reality: Loose Lips Sink Ships,' *Foreign Affairs*, September/October 1995, p. 6.

60. Jason Deparle, 'The Man Inside Bill Clinton's Foreign Policy,' *New York Times*, 20 August 1995, VI:31.

61. *Strategic Survey, 1993–4* (London: Brassey's, 1994) p. 99.

62. Muravchik, *The Imperative of American Leadership*, pp. 119–20. Muravchik suggests French policy is fueled by little other than *amour propre* and has the primary objective of convincing Washington, Moscow and its European partners that France is a great power. By this standard, they certainly failed in Bosnia.

12. The Clinton Administration III: Reassertion of American Leadership

1. Joshua Muravchik, *The Imperative of American Leadership: A Challenge to Neo-Isolationism* (Washington, DC: AEI Press, 1996) p. 110.

2. *Agence Francaise Presse (AFP)*, 12 July 1995 in *FBIS, WE–DR*, 12 July 1995, p. 2.

3. *Press Association* (London) 15 July 1995 in *FBIS, WE–DR* 17 July 1995, pp. 4–7; Paris France-2 Television Network, 19 July 1995 in *FBIS, WE–DR*, 20 July 1995, pp. 1–2.

4. *Press Association* (London) 15 July 1995 in *FBIS, WE–DR*, 17 July 1995, pp. 4–5.

5. Yasushi Akashi, the top UN official in Bosnia, angered the US by assuring Radovan Karadzic and the Bosnian Serbs that the new 12 500-soldier-strong Rapid Reaction Force would not take sides or act differently than UNPROFOR previously had. *New York Times*, 22 June, A10 and 23 June, 1995, A7.

6. *Washington Post*, 8 August 1995, A15. This policy, combined with the ethnic cleansing of the new Croat areas as Serb refugees fled, naturally

led to criticism of Washington's acquiescense in the Croat offensive. A defense of the policy from an humanitarian perspective is that Croat atrocities against Serbs occurred, but not with the frequency that characterized many prior cases in the war. See *New York Times*, 5 October 1995, A15.

7. *Washington Post*, 11 August 1995, A1.

8. *Washington Post*, 27 July, A1 and 2 August 1995, A1.

9. Richard Holbrooke, 'The Road to Sarajevo', *The New Yorker*, 21 and 28 October 1996, pp. 88–9.

10. *Ibid.*, p. 99; *Strategic Survey, 1995–1996* (London: Oxford University Press, 1996) p. 134.

11. This summary relies on *Proximity Peace Talks*, Wright-Patterson Air Force Base, Ohio, Dayton, OH, 1–21 November 1995; and *Dayton Peace Agreement*, US Department of State, Bureau of Public Affairs, 24 November 1995. On the Russian role, see *Washington Post*, 29 November 1995, A27. The role the Russians are playing in this settlement parallels their roles in previous diplomacy. The West attempts to include them, primarily on Western terms, and the Russians have consented to cooperate.

12. Lenard J. Cohen, *Broken Bonds: Yugoslavia's Disintegration and Balkan Politics in Transition*, second edition (Boulder, Co: Westview, 1995), pp. 297–9. Silber and Little point out that the map that emerged from September's battles was remarkably similar to the divisions incorporated in the Dayton peace plan. Laura Silber and Allan Little, *Yugoslavia: Death of a Nation* (NY: TV Books, 1995, 1996) p. 363.

13. See Charles G. Boyd, 'Making Peace with the Guilty: The Truth About Bosnia', *Foreign Affairs*, September/October 1995, pp. 30–1; The International Institute for Strategic Studies, *Strategic Survey, 1994–1995* (London: Oxford University Press, 1995) pp. 97–8.

14. The promises of the administration on this point are reinforced by the Congressional Resolution, sponsored by senators Robert Dole and John McCain, pledging support for the peacekeeping operation provided that the Bosnians are given sufficient training and arms to survive after IFOR withdraws. Senate Joint Resolution 44, 29 December 1995, 104th Congress, First Session. Andrew Sullivan is wrong in suggesting that the arms limits for the region, set to go into effect if negotiated limits cannot be reached, preclude the arming of the Bosnians. The Bosnian government can never hope to match the combined military strength of Serbia and the Bosnian Serbs as Sullivan suggests. It would be a step forward if they could match the Bosnian Serbs alone, as specified in the agreement. *New Republic*, 25 December 1995, p. 6; *Proximity Peace Talks*, Annex 1-B, p. 4; *New York Times*, 3 September 1996, A10.

15. *Wall Street Journal*, 3 October 1996, A14.

16. Samantha Power, 'Pale Imitation', *The New Republic*, 14 October 1996, pp. 18–22.

17. *Washington Post*, 25 August 1996, A22; *Financial Times*, 13 September 1996, p. 3.

18. *Washington Post*, 30 August 1996; A subcommittee of the Organization for Security and Cooperation in Europe (OSCE) also recommended

postponement of the elections, but was overruled. National Public
Radio, 'All Things Considered', 1 October 1996; On the positive side,
there are new signs of Serb cooperation with The Hague in apprehending suspects indicted for war crimes. *Washington Post*,
25 October 1996, A29.

19. *International Herald Tribune*, 11 September 1996, p. 7.
20. *Initialing of the Dayton Peace Agreement*, US Department of State, Bureau
of Public Affairs, p. 4.
21. Silber and Little, *Yugoslavia*, pp. 303–4. The political logic of this
process, leaving aside the international pressures for a settlement, is
clarified by a *New York Times* account. Pre-war Sarajevo had a population of 450 000, with a dominant cosmopolitan culture that dis-
dained ethnic distinctions, and with many couples in ethnically
mixed marriages. The population in 1995 was estimated at 280 000,
with an estimated 100 000 of those refugees from villages suffering
under Serb ethnic cleansing and now moved into Sarajevo, bringing
a very different culture with them. One sixty-year-old Muslim carpen-
ter with two sons fighting on the front lines for the Bosnians, explained, 'We are not interested in these intellectuals who talk of
living together. They have all left Bosnia. It is the poor who remain
to fight. This country belongs to us now, not them.' *New York Times*,
28 July 1995, A4.
22. A position that Charles G. Boyd hints at in 'Making Peace with the
Guilty: The Truth About Bosnia'.

13. The Reluctant Superpower

1. Doris Kearns Goodwin, *No Ordinary Time: Franklin and Eleanor Roosevelt:
The Home Front in World War II* (NY: Simon & Schuster, 1994) especially Chapters 1–3.
2. Bogdan Denitch, *Ethnic Nationalism; The Tragic Death of Yugoslavia*
(Minneapolis: University of Minnesota Press, 1994) especially
pp. 141–7.
3. David Rieff, 'American and the World', National Public Radio, 31 July
1995.
4. David Owen asserts that by the summer of 1994 the UN troops were
inhibiting a settlement and were no longer needed for humanitarian
aid delivery. David Owen, *Balkan Odyssey* (NY: Harcourt Brace, 1995),
p. 366.
5. Owen repeatedly makes the point that such threats need to be tied to
specific demands, preferably implementation of a detailed blueprint
for peace that is a result of the negotiating process. Ibid., p. 166.
6. Alexander L. George and William E. Simons, *The Limits of Coercive
Diplomacy* (Boulder, Co: Westview, 1994) pp. 84, 275.
7. Owen, *Balkan Odyssey*, p. 289.
8. Contrast the agony and indecision over intervention in Bosnia with
David McCullough's account of a key decision during the Truman administration, intervention in 1950 in Korea:

[Nobody present had] the least doubt that what was happening in Korea was being directed from Moscow. But then this was also the prevailing view in the country and the press .... That everyone at the table was in fundamental agreement became quickly clear, Truman's own obvious resolution having stiffened them all .... Recalling the evening, Truman would write that what impressed him most was the 'complete, almost unspoken acceptance on the part of everyone that whatever had to be done to meet this aggression had to be done. There was no suggestion from anyone that either the United Nations or the United States should back away from it.' (*Truman* [NY: Simon & Schuster, 1992] pp. 778–9.)

Index

Index